URBAN TEENS in the LIBRARY
RESEARCH AND PRACTICE

EDITED BY DENISE E. AGOSTO
AND SANDRA HUGHES-HASSELL

AMERICAN LIBRARY ASSOCIATION
CHICAGO   2010

Denise E. Agosto, Ph.D., is an associate professor in the College of Information Science & Technology at Drexel University. Her research interests include public libraries, diversity issues in youth library services, youth information behavior, and gender and information behavior. Dr. Agosto has published more than sixty articles and book chapters in these areas, and she frequently speaks about her research at state and national conferences.

Sandra Hughes-Hassell, Ph.D., is an associate professor and director of the School Library Media Program in the School of Information and Library Science at the University of North Carolina at Chapel Hill. In her current research she focuses on social justice issues in youth library services and the role of school library media specialists in education reform. She teaches courses related to materials and services to children and youth and school library media programs.

The paper used in this publication meets the minimum requirements of American National Standard for Information Sciences—Permanence of Paper for Printed Library Materials, ANSI Z39.48-1992. ∞

Library of Congress Cataloging-in-Publication Data
Urban teens in the library : research and practice / edited by Denise E. Agosto and
    Sandra Hughes-Hassell.
      p.   cm.
    Includes bibliographical references and index.
    ISBN 978-0-8389-1015-3 (alk. paper)
    1. Young adults' libraries—United States. 2. Libraries and teenagers—United
States. 3. Libraries and metropolitan areas—United States. 4. Internet in young
adults' libraries—United States. 5. Urban youth—Books and reading—United
States. I. Agosto, Denise E. II. Hughes-Hassell, Sandra.
Z718.5.U73 2010
027.62'6—dc22

2009025147

ISBN-13: 978-0-8389-1015-3

Printed in the United States of America
14 13 12 11 10   5 4 3 2 1

CONTENTS

ACKNOWLEDGMENTS   vii

INTRODUCTION   ix

PART I   SETTING THE STAGE: WHO IS THE URBAN TEEN?

CHAPTER 1   WHO ARE URBAN TEENS, AND WHAT
DOES *URBAN* MEAN, ANYWAY?   3
Denise E. Agosto and Sandra Hughes-Hassell

CHAPTER 2   MOVING BEYOND THE STEREOTYPES: SEEING URBAN
TEENAGERS AS INDIVIDUALS   9
Sandra Hughes-Hassell, Lewis Hassell, and Denise E. Agosto

PART II   FOCUS ON RESEARCH: RESEARCH RELATING TO URBAN TEENS AND LIBRARIES

CHAPTER 3   REVAMPING LIBRARY SERVICES TO MEET URBAN TEENS'
EVERYDAY LIFE INFORMATION NEEDS AND PREFERENCES   23
Denise E. Agosto and Sandra Hughes-Hassell

CHAPTER 4   DEVELOPING A LEISURE READING PROGRAM THAT IS
RELEVANT AND RESPONSIVE TO THE LIVES OF URBAN
TEENAGERS: INSIGHTS FROM RESEARCH   41
Sandra Hughes-Hassell

CHAPTER 5   STREET LIT: BEFORE YOU CAN RECOMMEND IT,
YOU HAVE TO UNDERSTAND IT   53
Vanessa J. Irvin Morris, with Denise E. Agosto and
Sandra Hughes-Hassell

CHAPTER 6   URBAN TEENS, ONLINE SOCIAL NETWORKING,
AND LIBRARY SERVICES   67
June Abbas and Denise E. Agosto

CHAPTER 7   URBAN TEENS AND THEIR USE OF PUBLIC LIBRARIES   83
Denise E. Agosto

CHAPTER 8   PUBLIC LIBRARY WEBSITES AND URBAN
TEENAGERS' HEALTH INFORMATION NEEDS   101
Sandra Hughes-Hassell and Dana Hanson-Baldauf

CHAPTER 9   SPACING OUT WITH YOUNG ADULTS:
TRANSLATING YA SPACE CONCEPTS INTO PRACTICE   113
Anthony Bernier

**PART III   FOCUS ON BEST PRACTICE: MODEL
PROGRAMS FROM U.S. PUBLIC LIBRARIES**

CHAPTER 10   YOUTH DEVELOPMENT AND EVALUATION: LESSONS FROM
"PUBLIC LIBRARIES AS PARTNERS IN YOUTH DEVELOPMENT"   129
Elaine Meyers

CHAPTER 11   THE LOFT AT IMAGINON: A NEW-GENERATION
LIBRARY FOR URBAN TEENS   143
Michele Gorman, Amy Wyckoff, and Rebecca L. Buck

CHAPTER 12   BEFORE IT'S READING, IT'S WRITING: URBAN TEENS
AS AUTHORS IN THE PUBLIC LIBRARY   153
Autumn Winters and Elizabeth J. Gregg

CHAPTER 13   FOLLOWING AND LEADING TEENS ONLINE: USING DIGITAL
LIBRARY SERVICES TO REACH URBAN TEENS   169
Kara Reuter, Sarah Cofer, Ann Pechacek, and Mandy R. Simon

WORKS CITED   187
LIST OF CONTRIBUTORS   201
INDEX   203

ACKNOWLEDGMENTS

THE EDITORS EXPRESS THEIR appreciation to the contributors to this volume. Without their enthusiasm and dedication to the project, it would not have happened. We also thank the urban teenagers who inspire our work. To you we are indebted.

INTRODUCTION

AS LONG-TIME ADVOCATES for urban teenagers, we wrote this book to show how librarians can use current research about urban teens, their information habits and preferences, and their use of libraries to improve public and school library services. We also sought to showcase model library programs designed for—and by—urban teens, programs that have successfully incorporated lessons learned from research into program design and delivery. These model programs, which have improved the lives of many urban teenagers, can be modified and replicated to impact still more adolescents living in urban areas throughout the country. Reaching out to urban teens takes a lot of work, patience, and cooperation, but, as the many successful projects and programs in this book show, it is well worth the effort.

It is ironic that the two of us would find ourselves writing this book, considering our own teen lives. We spent them growing up in middle-class families in small-town Montana and rural Virginia, a far cry from inner-city urban life. So perhaps the best way to introduce this book is to explain how we each became interested in doing research with and for urban teens.

DENISE'S STORY

My role as an advocate for urban teens started with a simple observation when I was a young librarian in the early 1990s, fresh out of library school and traveling around the country to visit new libraries to apply for my first professional position. As an avid reader of YA literature, I sought out the YA departments in each of the libraries. In many—even most—of the libraries, I was surprised to find nowhere to sit down, nowhere to use the

YA materials, nowhere to just enjoy being in the teen section of the library. And certainly there was nowhere I could sit and chat with friends, had I been a teen myself.

After touring one particularly eye-catching YA department, newly renovated with expensive neon signage and flashy new bookstore shelving, I asked the library director why there was no seating anywhere in the department. "We want the kids to get their materials and leave," she explained. "We don't want a lot of teenagers hanging around the library and bothering people."

I was shocked—truly shocked—by this attitude. I vowed then and there to become an advocate on behalf of teens in libraries. And I have been one ever since.

Years later, after I had gotten a Ph.D. and had become a professor, I began collaborating on research projects with my colleague and coauthor of this book, Sandra Hughes-Hassell. Her observations that urban teens lacked a voice in the popular media and in the research literature led me to focus my advocacy interests on urban teens in particular, especially low-income minority teens living in inner cities. We have spent the past nine years researching and publishing together to give voice to this population and to study the ways in which public and school library services can help to improve urban teens' lives.

SANDRA'S STORY

In 1994 I moved from rural Virginia to Philadelphia to become the director of the Philadelphia Library Power project. Funded by the DeWitt Wallace–Reader's Digest Fund, Library Power developed a new, challenging vision for school librarianship by ensuring that all learners in schools—adults as well as children—had the resources and support they needed to become effective users of information and ideas. The Philadelphia Library Power project was one of many programs administered by the Philadelphia Education Fund—a not-for-profit organization dedicated to improving the quality of public education for underserved youth throughout the Philadelphia region. As director of the project I spent a great deal of time in Philadelphia public schools working with librarians, teachers, administrators, and students. My interactions, my observations, and the relationships I developed during the four years I led this project had a transformative impact on my life and on the focus of my work.

Through my work it became clear to me that public schools and public libraries are critical institutions for breaking the cycle of poverty and redressing social inequities. It also became clear to me that urban youth, and urban teenagers in particular, are stereotyped by the media. The children and teenagers I encountered in the schools were bright, focused, and eager learners. This was in sharp contrast to the images I saw on the evening news. The teachers (I consider school librarians to be teachers) too were passionate, innovative, and committed to reforming the educational system to make it "work" for all children—not just for those lucky enough to live in the more affluent neighborhoods in the city. My reaction to all

I saw and all I learned has been to focus, not only on supporting urban teenagers, urban teachers, and urban librarians, but also on telling their stories. I have been fortunate enough to find research partners, like Denise Agosto, who believe in urban youth, who are committed to social justice, and who share my desire to give "voice" to urban teenagers, who often go unheard.

OVERVIEW OF THE BOOK

This volume is divided into three sections. Part 1, "Setting the Stage," asks, Who is the urban teen? Part 2, "Focus on Research," presents the results of seven research studies involving urban teens. Each chapter includes recommendations for librarians serving urban teens to show how to transfer research results into effective library practices. Part 3, "Focus on Best Practice," presents four model programs from U.S. public libraries. Each of these four chapters focuses on lessons learned and includes ideas for implementing similar programs in other libraries serving urban teens.

Several common themes run through this volume. These include the importance of

- collaboration with other agencies serving the target population
- service design based on a clear understanding of youth development
- making culturally relevant resources available to urban teens
- including teens' voices and opinions in the design and delivery of library services
- serving as advocates for urban teens
- community outreach in both face-to-face and online modes
- understanding that social interaction and entertainment outlets help to advance adolescents' healthy mental and physical development
- the thoughtful design of library spaces for young adults
- the need to explore new media for library services and for interaction with urban teens
- basic information and literacy services as a key focus in library services to urban teens

Together these themes can serve as a useful framework for the thoughtful design of library services for urban teens.

Ultimately, this book shows how library and information science research can—and should—have a direct impact on public and school library services for this population. It also demonstrates that library services to urban teens are alive and flourishing, and that creativity and appreciation of adolescents are two of the most important elements in serving urban teens' information, social, entertainment, and other needs. Above all, the studies and programs profiled in this book show us that the best library and information services are based on an understanding of urban teens' needs, their development, their ideas and opinions, and their cultural and contextual backgrounds.

Finally, we must remember that it is not enough for librarians to assume that urban teens will use their services. Librarians must constantly update their services, advertise and promote them, and take them to places where urban teens choose to be. Only then will a larger percentage of urban teens turn to libraries to fulfill their wide-ranging developmental and informational needs.

PART I
SETTING THE STAGE: WHO IS THE URBAN TEEN?

CHAPTER 1
WHO ARE URBAN TEENS, AND WHAT DOES *URBAN* MEAN, ANYWAY?

DENISE E. AGOSTO AND SANDRA HUGHES-HASSELL

ONE OF THE GREATEST challenges in writing this book was answering the question, Who are urban teens? Are they teenagers who just happen to live in large cities, or do other demographic and social characteristics define this group? We examined many different definitions of *urban* and found it difficult to settle on just one. Our problem is a fairly common one, and pinning down a definition of *urban* can be tricky. According to the *Encyclopedia of Urban America*, "Widespread use of the term has been associated with widespread disagreement about its meaning and significance" (ABC-CLIO 1998).

In this chapter, we explore the multiple definitions of *urban*, with an emphasis on what these definitions suggest about urban teens. We also provide a brief overview of urban teens and their use of libraries.

DEFINING THE *URBAN* IN *URBAN TEENS*
PLACE-BASED DEFINITIONS

One common method of defining *urban* is to look at population statistics. In her book *Serving Urban Teens* (2008), Brehm-Heeger uses the U.S. Census Bureau's (2007b) definition to identify this group. The Census Bureau classifies an *urban area* as a community with a population center of at least 1,000 people per square mile at its heart and a number of surrounding blocks with a population density of at least 500 people per square mile. It classifies all other areas in the country as *rural*.

Using this definition, as of the year 2000, 79 percent of U.S. residents lived in urban areas and 21 percent lived in rural areas (U.S. Census Bureau 2000), making nearly four-fifths of the U.S. population urban—and making urban teens the majority rather than a specialized population.

Perhaps a more useful definition is the Census Bureau's breakdown of those living "Inside and Outside Metropolitan Areas" (U.S. Census Bureau 2000). Within the population of those living in major metropolitan areas, the Bureau classifies more than 85 million people, or just over 30 percent of the U.S. population, as living in a "central city." Here *urban teens* are a more select group, those living in the densely populated centers of major U.S. cities.

Instead of relying solely on population statistics, most dictionary definitions include some form of reference to cities as central to the concept of *urban*. Examples include "pertaining to or characteristic of, occurring or taking place in, a city or town" (*Oxford English Dictionary Online*) and "of, relating to, characteristic of, or constituting a city" (*Merriam-Webster Online Dictionary*).

Thus, population-based definitions and common dictionary definitions tie *urban* to living in or near large cities. For urban teens, growing up in or near cities typically shapes some, but not all, of their life experiences. Potential areas of impact include entertainment and leisure choices, ways of speaking, comfort with using public transportation, and interactions with strangers. Still, it seems as if there is something missing from these definitions, some key concepts that help to make urban teens a unique group in terms of their developmental and information needs.

POPULAR CULTURE DEFINITIONS

Another approach to defining *urban* is to look at some of the ways in which it is used in popular culture. In today's speech, *urban* is often used to describe a style, particularly of clothing or music. The *Oxford English Dictionary* added a newer definition of the term in 2007: "designating a type of music (esp. street music) that originates from a city, and typically reflects or is characteristic of urban life." A newly added subdefinition defines *urban sportswear* as "a style of casual clothing associated with urban culture and often regarded as stylish and contemporary. . . . such a style [was] originally associated with U.S. hip-hop culture and typically features baggy T-shirts with prominent logos, hooded tops, training shoes, and clothing associated with sports teams."

A significant part of this "urban culture" is the urban vocabulary. The existence of the online *Urban Dictionary* (www.urbandictionary.com) stands as proof of its importance and size. *Urban Dictionary* compiles definitions of words used in the urban style of speaking, as defined by users of the site. It boasts 3,790,761 definitions written since 1999 and offers thirty-eight definitions of *urban*; eleven of them refer to *urban* as a style, culture, or type of music. Together these definitions also point to another common connotation—a reference to African American culture. Of the thirty-eight definitions, eight include the words *black* or *African American* and three include additional references to race. One example is anything "associated with African-American or Hip-Hop culture."

Another popular culture source worth examining is *Urban Teen Magazine* (www.urbanteenmagazine.com/index.html), an online magazine written for and by teens from San Diego. Although much of the content focuses on entertainment, sports, school, and other issues of equal interest to urban, suburban, and rural teens, it also features pictures of teens showing off "urban fashions" and highlights stories of teens "making a difference" through service work in inner-city neighborhoods. It is these kinds of subtle cultural differences that define the *urban* in *urban teens* more than just population statistics.

Deutsch has pointed out that *urban* can have either a positive or a negative connotation, depending on context, and notes: "In the past few years, urban has taken on a new, hip connotation. 'Urban chic' is all the rage. There is an influx of young professionals into cities. Yet when paired with 'teen' or 'youth,' urban still conjures up an image of poverty. Today, a distinct separation exists between the 'urban' of gentrification and the 'urban' of public housing" (2008, 92).

DEMOGRAPHIC GROUP MEMBERSHIP DEFINITIONS

Urban can also refer to demographic group membership, such as race, ethnicity, socioeconomic status, or linguistic group. One defining characteristic of urban areas is diversity, in large part reflecting sheer population size. The *Encyclopedia of Urban America* (ABC-CLIO 1998) offers a useful explanation:

> A village might contain only one bookworm; a town can support a book club. In many towns, even today, a gay person might feel isolated. A city might support a gay book club whose members offer and receive mutual support. A city like New York might support gay book clubs that are differentiated by politics, ethnicity, or both. In large part, the emergence of such diverse communities within the city is a matter of simple arithmetic. With enough people, a community can form. In addition, and especially in the case of those who are viewed skeptically, or with disapproval, by the social mainstream, the very size of the large city offers an appealing anonymity. Where people do not know you, they cannot easily compel you to conform. Cities tolerate, and therefore attract, social minorities.

Obviously urban teens come from all types of racial and ethnic backgrounds, but most large cities do tend to have more racially and ethnically diverse populations than do rural and suburban areas. This is another one of the key concepts missing from definitions based purely on population statistics or proximity to large cities: race and ethnicity.

Race and ethnicity have had a strong influence on the growth of urban popular culture, especially the growth of hip-hop. Created in the mid-to-late 1970s by predominantly African American and Puerto Rican teenagers who lived in the South Bronx, hip-hop is now a billion-dollar subset of the music industry, and it has influenced other lifestyle and entertainment businesses including soft drinks, liquor, leisure wear, haute couture, automobiles, sports events, electronics, shoes, cigars, jewelry, and homes. But Tate (2003) points out, though hip-hop and the other aspects of urban popular culture discussed above have had an impact on teen culture around the world, they have not been able to erase the social realities of racism and discrimination that many urban teens face simply because of the color of their skin. As one young black teen notes, "Everyone says that race don't matter no more, but then they all ask us like what it means to be Black, and if it don't matter, then why does everyone want to know?" (Deutsch 2008, 106).

Just as urban teens represent various racial and ethnic groups, they also populate the full socioeconomic range, from wealthy to middle class to impoverished. That said, there is no denying that many urban communities have high rates of poverty and unemployment. The connection between the term *urban* and inner-city poverty is reflected in another of the *Oxford English Dictionary*'s (2007) newly added entries. It defines *urban regeneration* as "the process of improving derelict or dilapidated districts of a city, typically through slum clearance and redevelopment," referring largely to inner cities. In fact, *urban* is often used interchangeably with *inner city*. With this use generally comes the many negative implications of inner cities, such as crime, poverty, and social unrest.

For teens living in densely populated, impoverished inner cities, homelessness, crime, and related issues can be significant influences on their lives and life experiences. A passage from the *Freedom Writer's Diary* captures the reality of growing up in the projects: "I've spent most of my life living in poverty, being afraid to walk out my front door because of the risk of being shot. . . . I started to think about all of the horrific things I've witnessed. Crackheads getting high right in front of me, and drug dealers making more money in one day than a stockbroker makes in one week" (Freedom Writers 1999, 195).

Growing up in the projects can have a negative effect on urban teens' sense of self and on their future aspirations. For many urban teens the idea of attending college, of making a difference, is unimaginable (Deutsch 2008; Freedom Writers 1999). It is, however, important to remember that this is not always the case. Again, from the *Freedom Writer's Diary*:

> "Adversity makes warriors of us all," Cheryl said. "I grew up in the projects, and despite what others may have thought of me, I never let it bring me down. I've witnessed it all, and I didn't get caught up in the negativity surrounding my neighborhood. If I could make it in the projects I knew I could make it anywhere." (1999, 196)

MARKETING DEFINITIONS

The *Urban Dictionary* suggests that *urban* has become a marketing term as well. "The term is exploited by corporations such as MTV to refer to black music/culture, without mentioning race." It is a "marketing term used to hide the fact they are focusing on a racial group" and a "marketing buzzword used in urban renewal districts (run-down areas that the city has decided to restore into lofts, etc.)."

Again the term is connected to race/ethnicity, this time in connection with corporate advertising directed toward minority groups. To look at another example, the slogan of the Urban Marketing Corporation of America is to "Connect with Consumers of Color . . . All Colors." There is no reference to either population density or proximity to large cities in this slogan, just to "color."

There is some controversy over the use of the term *urban* for marketing to racial minorities. As Quinn and Pawasarat (2001) have suggested, "Marketing firms frequently use racial and class-based stereotypes to describe urban neighborhoods," and the resulting misrepresentations of urban neighborhood demographics often lead to lost economic development opportunities.

WHAT *URBAN* MEANS IN THE CONTEXT OF THIS BOOK

The point of examining all these definitions is that, no matter how we choose to define it, there is no one *urban*, and there is no one *urban teen*. Urban neighborhoods can be wealthy, middle class, or poor; majority white, majority Hispanic, majority black, or broadly diverse; located on the East Coast, the West Coast, or somewhere in between.

Throughout this volume we take a broad view of the term. Individual chapters represent different urban environments. For example, the *urban* in chapter 5, "Street Lit," refers to major metropolitan inner cities and to African American culture. On the other hand, the *urban* in chapter 13, "Following and Leading Teens Online," refers more to the Census Bureau's definition, based strictly on population density; its authors write about Worthington Libraries, in Worthington and Columbus, Ohio, both of which meet the Census Bureau's definition of *urban* based on population density, but which could also be viewed as suburban based on historical and cultural criteria.

URBAN TEENS AND LIBRARIES

What about urban teens and libraries? Does this population even use libraries? As the chapters in this book demonstrate, many urban teens do use their libraries. Many visit their public libraries on a regular basis in person or online or both. Many use their school libraries frequently during school hours or outside school hours or both. And much of this use is due to the thoughtful design and delivery of library services for this population.

That said, there are also many urban teens who do not use their public or school libraries, often because their libraries are not effectively reaching out to them. It is hard to say exactly how many urban teens do use libraries, both because of the difficulties of pinning down an acceptable definition of *urban* and because of a lack of good data. At least one recent study indicates that today's young adults (18–29 years) are the most frequent adult users of public libraries for solving government-information-related problems (Estabrook et al. 2007), so it does seem that young adults in general do use public libraries for certain purposes. But parallel statistics are lacking for younger teens, for urban teens in particular, and for the broader range of reasons why teens use public and school libraries.

Regardless of the numbers of urban teens using libraries, many librarians have not done a good job of making their services known to the public, and of making the public realize that many teens do use libraries. Just as the popular media often present negative images of urban teens as a troubled and troublesome population, often the public and the popular media assume that today's libraries do little more than circulate books, and that urban teens, and teens in general, do not use their libraries. For example, *Born Digital*, a recent book about the impact of the online information world on the newest generations of children and teens, suggests:

> These kids are different [from previous generations]. They study, work, write, and interact with each other in ways that are very different from the ways that you did growing up. They read blogs rather than newspapers. They often meet each other online before they meet in person. They probably don't even know what a library card looks like, much less have one; and if they do, they've probably never used it. (Palfrey and Gasser 2008, 2)

Of course, many of today's teens, including urban teens, do know what library cards look like, and many even use them. The authors of *Born Digital* seem to be thinking of libraries only in terms of traditional services, such as paper book circulation, and they casually dismiss libraries as physical buildings only, with no online presences or services and no connection to their communities. Most libraries offer a full range of services, but this message does not seem to have reached these authors, and it probably is not reaching the full population of urban teens either.

We cannot attribute this inaccurate mental image only to the public. The fault also lies with public and school librarians who need proactively to provide the public with a better understanding of today's libraries and the role they can play in urban teens' lives. It is not enough for librarians to offer the same kinds of services that they always have, hoping that urban teens will seek them out. They must design innovative new services that appeal to urban youth. According to Meyers (1999), for teens to be drawn to programs or services, they must be "relevant and desirable, and take advantage of the teens' desire to aspire to their next goal of achievement or accomplishment."

Finally, it is crucial for librarians, teachers, and others who want to reach these groups to go to the places where these teens feel the most comfortable, including both community and online venues, and to involve teenagers in making library decisions. One of the key lessons learned from the Public Libraries as Partners Youth Development program was the desire of urban teens to be involved in planning and promoting library services. Teens wanted to "showcase their talent and the talent of their peers" (Meyers 1999). As this volume shows, by working with urban teens, libraries can provide new and exciting spaces, resources, programs, and services—all of which can support the personal, academic, and career development of the youth we are trying to serve.

CHAPTER 2

MOVING BEYOND THE STEREOTYPES
Seeing Urban Teenagers as Individuals

SANDRA HUGHES-HASSELL, LEWIS HASSELL, AND DENISE E. AGOSTO

> That's what happened to brothers in the hood. People check us out and ran down who we was without even seriously checking us out.
>
> —Slam, in Walter Dean Myers, *Slam*

SLAM'S LAMENT IS ONE that can be heard throughout urban communities across the United States. Thanks in part to the media, the terms *urban teen* and *urban young adult* almost always conjure up images of racial and ethnic minorities, poverty, teen parenthood, gangbanging, and drug use (Deutsch 2008; Leadbeater and Way 1996; Michie 1999; Tatum 2005; Tatum 1997). Though it is true that many urban teenagers do grow up in troubled communities, not all of them "confront trouble at home, violence in the streets, and/or problems at school" (Massey et al. 2005, 73). And not all of those who do grow up in troubled communities succumb to the challenges presented there. Instead, many of them "push against the environments" (Tatum 2005, 22) in which they live and negotiate a safe passage through the difficulties they face into adulthood. Still, the media tend to focus on urban teens as a monolithic group, with very little focus on them as individuals, each with unique life experiences and influences.

All too often, many of us are unable to move beyond the distorted media images of urban teenagers. Viewing urban teens through this lens, we see them as either at risk, without hope, or "out of control and dangerous" (Tatum 2005, 28). To provide library services successfully to urban teens, we must move beyond the racial and socioeconomic biases that pervade the popular culture, as well as our own preconceptions (misconceptions), and see them as individuals, not as members of a stereotyped group. This chapter seeks to enable us to do just that by providing a broader lens through which to view urban teens. Informed by research in the areas of critical race theory, racial identity development theory, and education for social change, it offers alternative perspectives and expanded views of the lives of urban teenagers.

Writing this chapter was difficult because to have the conversation, to offer a different lens, requires presenting data about urban communities and urban teenagers that *could* be used to reinforce the stereotypes. The key to developing another lens, however, is not to deny reality but to explore the alternative stories—the stories the data alone do not tell. Because of the power of narrative to "counteract or challenge the dominant story" (Dixson and Rousseau 2006, 35), each section of this chapter begins with a quote from a young adult novel set in an urban community. The voices of the teenage characters serve to remind us of the need to reframe the conversation, to move beyond the stereotypes, and to develop library services that are truly responsive to the needs of urban teenagers.

DEMOGRAPHICALLY RICH

This place nestled at the edge of Prospect Park. Calling itself Flatbush on a good day. Full of noise and music. "Qué día bonita," the old men sing on the first warm day. And I echo them, "What a pretty day." I learned the language of the other people here. "What for yuh wanna be a-dobering she?" The liquid fire of the West Indies. Mrs. Shirley's southern, "Boy I'll go upside your head so hard you gonna wish you was never born."

—Melanin, in Jacqueline Woodson, *From the Notebooks of Melanin Sun*

From a demographic perspective, today's urban communities are increasingly multiethnic and multilingual. The Council of Great City Schools (www.cgcs.org/about/statistics.aspx), a coalition representing sixty-six of the nation's largest public school systems, estimates that 37 percent of urban students are African American, 35 percent Hispanic, 21 percent white, six percent Asian/Pacific Islander, and 1 percent Alaskan/Native American. Additionally, 29 percent of children attending urban schools are English-language learners. In New York City, for example, 170 languages are spoken, and in nearly half of all households English is not the primary language (Santos 2008). This trend toward diversity is expected to continue. According to the Population Reference Bureau, minorities are projected to make up over 50 percent of the U.S. population under age 18 by 2023 and 62 percent of all U.S. children by 2050 (Mather and Pollard 2008). Many of these children will be teenagers and many will live in urban communities.

Though multilingual diversity certainly presents a challenge for educators and government agencies, and even for the teens themselves, it can be viewed as an asset. Urban teenagers for whom English is not the first language have already learned or are in the process of learning their "second language." Because of their dual language abilities, many are taking on the role of language brokers or intermediaries between their parents or other limited-English-speaking adult family members and monolingual individuals such as teachers, store clerks, and government officials (Jiménez 2001; McQuillan and Tse 1995; Valdés 1996). This role places great responsibility on teens to relay messages accurately or to assist with crucial transactions, but it also gives them skills such as audience awareness, "real world" literacy skills, math skills, civic responsibility, and social maturity, skills that are valuable in today's increasing global society (Orellana 2003). And, as Sautter (1994, ¶9) argues, "Taken as a talent, their multilingual abilities may one day give these students a distinct advantage in the global marketplace."

Similarly, cross-cultural knowledge and understanding are critical to success in the twenty-first century. Business people, government officials, military personnel, diplomats, and educators are all required to be "'citizens of the world'—in their vision, their horizon, their information" (Drucker 1993, 195)—as they increasingly interact with multicultural clients, customers, students, and colleagues. When it comes to cross-cultural knowledge and understanding, however, Americans appear to be somewhat behind the global curve. Comparing the cross-cultural knowledge of Argentineans and Americans, for example, Westerfield and Jones (2008) noted that "higher levels of intercultural contact in the backgrounds of Argentine participants were consistent with higher aptitudes towards seeking international contact. . . . Argentines seem to have greater factual knowledge about the United States than do U.S. participants about Argentina." As Drucker (1993, 191) points out, "Knowledge is not impersonal like money. . . . Knowledge is always embodied in a person."

In other words, true cross-cultural competency requires more than just information about another culture. It requires "process knowledge"—being able to function effectively within another culture (McAllister and Irvine 2000). Urban teens, insofar as they interact within and across cultures every day, would seem to have—indeed, embody—such "process knowledge," and thus their multicultural backgrounds can be viewed more as advantages than as disadvantages.

ECONOMICALLY AND SOCIALLY DIVERSE

> We rolled past the legendary house that was once owned by James Brown, and turned deep into the seclusion of Addesleigh Park. Addesleigh Park was a neat triangle of beige Tudor houses and Swiss chalets. The block association saw to it that every yard had a weeping willow tree, a lamp post, and matching garbage cans.
>
> —Denzel, in Rita Williams-Garcia, *Fast Talk on a Slow Track*

> Where do you live? she asked.
> There, I said, pointing up to the third floor.
> You live *there*?
> *There*. I had to look to where she pointed—the third floor, the paint peeling, wooden bars Papa had nailed on the windows so we wouldn't fall out. You live there? The way she said it made me feel like nothing. *There*. I lived *there*. I nodded.
>
> —Esperanza, in Sandra Cisneros, *The House on Mango Street*

As the two epigraphs above demonstrate, urban communities are economically and socially diverse. In some U.S. cities, some urban households report an annual income of more than $700,000 (Roberts 2007). In the 2007 American Community Survey Report, the median household income in principal cities was reported to be $45,590, slightly less than the median household income in the United States, which was $50,700 (Bishaw and Semega 2008, 6). At the same time, the poverty rate in U.S. cities averaged 17.2 percent, with cities like Detroit and Cleveland reporting much higher poverty rates, 33.8 percent and 29.5 percent respectively (Bishaw and Semega 2008, 25). The Council of Great City Schools estimates that 64 percent of the children who attend public urban schools qualify for free or reduced lunches.

Within this social and economic diversity, many urban teenagers are faced with hardships and risks, especially poor teenagers of color. The disadvantages experienced by children who live in low-income communities and who are racial or ethnic minorities are far more common than the risks and hardships experienced by children in this country as a whole (Sautter 1994, ¶14). Research has found, for example, that children and teens living in poor families are more likely to experience parental divorce, live in single-parent homes, experience violent crime, drop out of school, and develop chronic health problems (Mayer 1997).

According to Taylor, however, the risks and hardships they face do not necessarily doom urban teens to failure, a life of poverty, or drug-related crime and violence: "Despite their overrepresentation among poor and 'at risk' adolescents, the majority of Black youths stay in school, avoid drugs and premarital pregnancy and childbearing, are employed or are eager to work, are not involved in crime or other forms of self-destructive behavior, and grow up to lead normal and productive lives, in spite of serious social and economic disadvantages" (1995, 6).

Leadbeater and Way reiterate this point: "The drop-out, the teenage welfare mother, the drug addict, and the victim of domestic violence or of AIDS are among the most prevalent public images of poor and working-class urban adolescent girls. . . . Yet, despite the risks inherent in economic disadvantage, the majority of poor urban adolescent girls do not fit the stereotypes that are made about them" (1996, 5).

It would seem that many urban teens who face obstacles and adversity in their lives demonstrate resiliency. Researchers have identified factors that enable urban teens to persevere, including not only a belief in their own capabilities but also the ability to rely on others, to access knowledge and resources in the community, and to cultivate supportive networks (Erkut et al. 1996). The influence of natural mentors, such as an aunt, neighbor, minister, or teacher, has also been consistently identified as an important factor in the lives of teens who have adjusted well in spite of profound, ongoing stress (Rhoads and Davis 1996). Intergenerational relationships are especially important for urban African American and Hispanic teens (de Anda 1984; Martin and Martin 1978; Organista 2003; Wilson 1986).

This resiliency is reflected in several books that describe the academic journeys of young urban teens: *A Hope in the Unseen* (Suskind 1998), *We Beat the Street: How a Friendship Pact Led to Success* (Davis et al. 2005), and *Teach Like Your Hair's on Fire* (Esquith 2007). *A Hope in the Unseen* and *We Beat the Street* focus on the experiences of African American males. In *Teach Like Your Hair's on Fire*, Esquith tells the stories of his students, who are predominantly Hispanic and Asian immigrants living in poverty in an East Los Angeles neighborhood. This resiliency is also apparent in *Holler If You Hear Me: The Education of a Teacher and His Students* (Michie 1999), which chronicles the experiences of a teacher and the African American and Hispanic middle school students he taught in a South Side Chicago neighborhood. The final passage of Michie's book sums up the strength many urban teens possess:

> The kids I teach know full well that the odds are stacked against them. They can find reasons to give up, to stop caring, to *not* go to school, almost anywhere they look. But I know that despite all that, come 9:00 A.M. tomorrow, Quincy's opening bell will sound and, as if by a miracle, they will be there, ready for a new beginning, a fresh start, a chance to be seen and to be heard anew. (1999, 181)

CULTURALLY STRONG

> It [the placement in a remedial class] just seems like more than a coincidence when it happens to me. Like what made them think I needed remedial anything. Nobody tested me. Nobody asked me. They just threw me in to it and then looked surprised when I knew it all. I mean, it makes you wonder—is it my hair?
>
> —Miah, in Jacqueline Woodson, *If You Come Softly*

The economic and social challenges urban teenagers face have caused many to view them through a deficit-oriented lens—one that represents their race, culture, socioeconomic status, language, and other characteristics as limitations. As Harry and Klingner (2007, 20) point out, interpreting cultural and racial differences as a deficit "loads the deck" against urban teens, especially poor urban teens of color. It often leads schools to lower their academic expectations of urban teenagers of color, to track them into remedial classes, or to place a disproportionate number in special education (Catsambis 1994; González et al. 1993; Harry and Klingner 2007). As Sautter (1994, ¶28) notes, urban teens react negatively to this deficit-oriented view of themselves, often becoming "disenchanted when they find that their home language and community culture are not valued." This disenchantment can turn into confusion, mistrust, and anger, leading urban teenagers to live up to the low expectations by underperforming, becoming disruptive, or even dropping out of school (Tatum 2005). This should hardly be surprising, given Rosenthal's (1995) work in self-fulfilling prophecies.

Many researchers reject this deficit-oriented model, focusing instead on the concepts of funds of knowledge or cultural wealth. Funds of knowledge are "those historically developed and accumulated strategies (e.g., skills, abilities, ideas, practices) or bodies of knowledge that are essential to a household's functioning and well being" (González et al. 1993, ¶13). In the case of Mexican immigrants, for example, they may include information about agriculture, construction and building, folk medicine, and trade, business, and finance on both sides of the U.S.-Mexican border (Moll et al. 1992). For African American families they may include the solidarity of the African American community as well the preponderance of family traditions and spiritual values that are passed on from generation to generation (Foley 1997). The specific funds of knowledge a family possesses are dynamic in content, vary from household to household, and change according to the current reality. According to Vélez-Ibáñez and Greenberg (2005, 54), for funds of knowledge to transfer from one generation to another, "the younger generational cohort must learn their substance and have the opportunity to experiment with them in a variety of settings."

The concept of cultural wealth is similar to funds of knowledge and is a key component of critical race theory. According to Yosso, communities of color nurture cultural wealth through at least six forms of capital:

Aspirational capital: the ability to maintain hopes and dreams for the future despite real or perceived barriers. For example, researchers have found that while the educational outcomes for Hispanics are lower than those of any other group in the United States, Hispanic parents consistently maintain high beliefs for their children's futures.

Navigational capital: the skill of moving through institutions that are not necessarily designed with communities of color in mind, including the educational, health care, and judicial systems. Navigational capital involves individual resiliency, but also the ability to draw on social networks.

Social capital: supportive social networks of people and community resources. These networks often help build, and are built on, navigational capital. For example, social networks and community resources might help an urban teenager apply for and successfully complete the SAT exam, a first step in applying for college.

Linguistic capital: the intellectual and social skills attained through experiences with more than one language or style of language. Linguistic capital refers to skills such as storytelling, communicating via visual art, music, or poetry, or "code switching" (moving from one dialect or language to another within a single conversation).

Familial capital: the cultural knowledge and connection nurtured through relationships with immediate and extended family members. Familial capital expands the concept of family and leads to a commitment to community well-being. Familial capital allows individuals to feel that they are not alone in dealing with issues, but instead are connected to others around them who have similar problems.

Resistant capital: knowledge and skills fostered through oppositional behavior that challenges inequalities such as racism, capitalism, and patriarchy. Resistant capital provides the tools and motivation necessary to continue to work to transform society. For example, both African American and Hispanic mothers often consciously raise their daughters to assert themselves as intelligent, beautiful, strong, and worthy of respect despite social messages to the contrary. (2006, 78–81)

Both of these concepts, funds of knowledge and cultural wealth, shift the lens away from viewing urban communities—especially those made up of working-class or lower-class families of color—as places of cultural, social, and intellectual poverty and disadvantage. They challenge us to see these communities as places of multiple strengths, to focus our attention on what we can learn from the cultural assets, wealth, and funds of knowledge that exist within them, and to build our programs on the strengths and interests of today's urban teens. As Barrera (quoted in Sautter 1994, ¶34) states, "We need to mine the gold of the communities in which students live. It is time for us to bring those cultural treasures into [our work] to benefit our children."

RACIAL IDENTITY DEVELOPMENT

Lucy writes proverbs too:
Dime con quien andas y te dire quien eres.
Tell me with whom you walk and
I will tell you who you are.

—César, in Juan Felipe Herrera, *Crashboomlove*

Who am I? The search for identity is a critical task of adolescence and involves multiple aspects of a teen's life, including religious beliefs, values, gender roles, and ethnic and racial identity. Though all teens explore each of these facets of identity, researchers have found that adolescents of color are more likely to be actively engaged in exploring their racial and ethnic identity than are white adolescents (Phinney 1990; Tatum 1997). As Tatum explains, teens of color think of themselves in terms of race because that is how the rest of the world sees them. On a daily basis they must navigate in a world where other people are making assumptions about who they are and what they can achieve based on their race. White teens, on the other hand, tend to "think of racial identity as something that other people have, not something that is salient for them" (Tatum 1997, 94). Instead, they view their whiteness as neutral or as a norm (Erkut et al. 1996; Phinney 1990; Tatum 1997).

Psychologist William Cross (1991) has proposed a theory of racial identity development that contains five stages: pre-encounter, encounter, immersion/emersion, internalization, and internalization-commitment. The first two stages are pertinent to this chapter. In the pre-encounter stage, children of color absorb many of the beliefs and values of the dominant white culture, including the belief that it is better to be white. Stereotypes, omissions, and distortions, combined with an image of white superiority, to some degree socialize children of color to value the role models, lifestyles, and images of beauty of white culture over those of their own cultural group (Tatum 1997).

In the encounter stage, children of color become aware of the impact of racism. This stage usually occurs during late adolescence, but it may begin as early as middle school. In this stage, children of color begin to wrestle with what it means to be a member of a group that is targeted by racism. Often this awakening is precipitated by an event or series of events. Examples include seeing a Hispanic parent asked to provide proof of citizenship when he is leaving his place of employment, being followed around by security guards at the mall, or viewing media images of the shooting of Oscar Grant, an African America man, by the Oakland BART police.

As Tatum (1997, 165–166) points out, "To find one's racial or ethnic identity, one must deal with [these] negative stereotypes, resist internalizing negative self-perceptions, and affirm the meaning of ethnicity for oneself." This entails answering questions like these: What does it mean to be a black (Hispanic, Asian, American Indian, etc.) person? How should I act? What should I do? For biracial teens, this process is further complicated by the question *What* am I? As teens struggle with these questions, they often seek support from other teens who belong to the same racial or ethnic group—others who understand their perspective and who have experienced similar stereotypes or prejudices.

In their journey to find the answers to these questions, many teens of color express anger and resentment at the racial discrimination they face and react by adopting an oppositional social identity. As Tatum (1997, 61) explains, this stance protects them from the impact of racism and keeps the dominant group at a distance. "Certain styles of speech, dress, and music, for example, may be embraced as 'authentically Black' and become highly valued, while attitudes and behaviors associated with Whites are viewed with distain."

Unfortunately, this stance can also be used to reinforce the negative stereotypes of urban teens of color. For example, academic achievement is one of the behaviors associated with whiteness that is often deemphasized or devalued by teens of color during this stage of identity development. Rather than question why academic achievement came to be viewed as a "white behavior," many educators blame the teens themselves for the academic decline that subsequently occurs (Tatum 1997). Tatum notes that if young urban teens were exposed to images of academically successful urban teens of color early in their lives they might be less likely to define school achievement as an exclusively white behavior. Similarly, if schools restructured the curriculum to allow students to view concepts, issues, themes, and problems from different perspectives, they might expand their definition of what it means to be black, Hispanic, Indian, or Asian American (Banks 1999).

Another example of oppositional social identity is reflected in the "cool pose" many black teen males adopt—dressing in beltless pants that hang below the waist, listening to gangsta rap, and greeting each other with special handshakes (Tatum 2005; Tatum 1997). Although this pose may allow the teen to "convey a strong impression of pride, strength, and control," it can also get him into trouble with authorities who do not understand this behavior as a coping mechanism, make it difficult for teachers and others to engage with him, and prevent him from becoming involved in activities that could expand his personal and social perceptions (Tatum 2005, 29).

Tatum (1997, 94) argues that white teenagers must also explore their racial identity actively. As she explains, whereas the task for teens of color is to resist the negative stereotypes and develop an empowered sense of self, the task for white teens is to develop a positive white identity based on reality and not on assumed white superiority. She argues that this is critical to the development of a just society. Erkut et al. (1996) concur and also believe that this is especially important for the health and well-being of working-class and poor urban teenage girls. Unfortunately, they do not provide additional information on how this might be accomplished.

VOICE

> I scream it out, too. "Call me by my name! I am not ugly. I am not stupid. I am Maleeka Madison, and, yeah, I'm Black, real Black, and if you don't like me too bad 'cause Black is the skin I'm in!" I yell.
>
> —Maleeka, in Sharon Flake, *The Skin I'm In*

One of the central tenets of critical race theory is the concept of voice. The theory demands "recognition of the experiential knowledge of people of color" (Matsuda et al. 1993, 6). It is through the use of personal narrative and story, these theorists argue, that we not only shift the lens through which many in the dominant culture view people of color (i.e., see them as sources of knowledge) but also empower people of color to enter the conversation—to tell *their* stories, stories that counteract the stories of the dominant culture (Dixson and Rousseau 2006).

Many researchers and authors are providing avenues through which urban teens can tell their stories. In addition to the books noted above, *Pride in the Projects* (Deutsch 2008) examines the construction of teen identity as it occurs in urban contexts. Based on four years of fieldwork with teenagers and staff members at a Boys & Girls Club in a large midwestern city, the book features the voices of seventeen urban teenagers, ten who identified themselves as black or African American, two as African American and Hispanic, two as African American plus two additional ethnicities, and one each as Hispanic, white, or other. In the first chapter of the book, Deutsch recounts a particularly powerful conversation with one of the teens:

> Inside the empty TV lounge, BJ and I sit, an African American teen and a white woman, shoulder to shoulder. Her 16-year-old body, athletic and strong, claims its space next to mine. Photographs are scattered across the table in front of us, the bright faces of BJ and her friends contrasting with the solemn tones of the buildings and landscapes of their urban neighborhood. One particular photo catches my eye. "What about this one?" I ask, pointing to a photo that shows nothing but sky, and in the center, a soaring bird. "Why did you take this one?" "Cause you wouldn't usually see, people think of the projects as bad," BJ says, looking me in the eye. "And that you wouldn't see birds or anything over here. So that's why I took that." (2008, 1–2)

In her analysis of this conversation, Deutsch points out that the interaction not only demonstrates BJ's awareness of media portrayals of public housing projects but also highlights her resistance to this image. By taking the photo, BJ is presenting a counterstory to the one told by the media and indicating her refusal to let them define who she is by where she lives.

Just encouraging urban teen voice, however, is not enough. What adults do with teen voice is equally important. In a revealing study of autobiographical narratives written by Latino eighth-grade students, Quiroz (2001) brings to light important factors and implications in collecting voice. The narratives, written by the teens at the end of the year for their high school academic files, revealed a diversity of thoughts, attitudes, and feelings about school and life, inequitable or dismissive treatment, and future aspirations. One student wrote: "My father was in the delivery room when I was born. My mom says that when my father had me in his arms tears started coming out of his eyes. He never hits me or screams at me. He only explains things and talks about them" (333). Another commented on the inequity of the schools she attended: "After Mrs. R. we had another teacher who we thought was going to be our permanent seventh grade teacher. She lasted about two days I think. Then she left for an eighth grade class . . . and the teachers kept changing. That seventh grade was so confusing I didn't learn a thing but I tried" (326).

As Quiroz discovered, however, rather than use these narratives to reveal and facilitate change, the educators rarely read them before filing them away, in effect silencing the students' voices. As she points out, "Language is merely the tool through which voice is expressed. For voice to be empowering, it must be heard, not simply spoken" (2001, 328). Encouraging teens to share honest feelings and thoughts becomes a failed and counterproductive endeavor when teens feel that doing so really makes no difference—that no one will really listen, nothing will change, and their voice does not matter. As critical race theorists point out, stories should be solicited *only* if they are intended to move us to action, to improve the experiences of urban teens.

CONCLUDING THOUGHTS

It is not our intention to deny the economic hardships many urban teens face, to explain away violent or antisocial behavior as a stage in identity development, or to romanticize the potential urban teenagers have to succeed. Instead, it is to expand the lens through which we view urban teens, to consider alternative explanations—alternative stories with alternative endings. If we want to foster positive outcomes for them, we must hear their voices, affirm their identities, validate their perspectives, see them as individuals, *and* find ways to help them get their voices heard. We must remember that although urban teens as a group do have some commonalities, as with any group of people, each urban teen is first and foremost an individual, and we must think of them as individuals first and as members of their demographic groups second. Rather than focus on urban teens as causes of conflict, we should include them as participants in research, in theory development, and in the design and delivery of library and information services. And we must continue to work to interrupt the social conditions that place them at risk. Critical race theory demands that social activism be a part of any of its projects (Dixson and Rousseau 2006). We believe that, if we incorporate social activism into our research and into the design of our library services and programs, we will be able to tap the full potential of urban teenagers, to work *with* them, to improve their world qualitatively and materially.

We end this chapter with the voice of an urban teen who feels empowered, who recognizes her potential, because of her interactions with her teacher and mentor, Erin Grunwell.

> For the first time, I realized that what people say about living in the ghetto and having brown skin doesn't have to apply to me. So when I got home, I wrote this poem.

> ## They Say, I Say

> They say I am brown
> I say
> I am proud.

> They say I only know how to cook
> I say
> I know how to write a book
> So
> don't judge me by the way I look.

> They say I am brown
> I say
> I am proud.

> They say I'm not the future of this nation
> I say
> Stop giving me discrimination
> Instead
> I'm gonna use my education
> To help build the human nation.

> I can't wait to read it to the class tomorrow.
>   (Freedom Writers 1999, Diary 103)

PART II
FOCUS ON RESEARCH: RESEARCH RELATING TO URBAN TEENS AND LIBRARIES

CHAPTER 3

REVAMPING LIBRARY SERVICES TO MEET URBAN TEENS' EVERYDAY LIFE INFORMATION NEEDS AND PREFERENCES

DENISE E. AGOSTO AND SANDRA HUGHES-HASSELL

MANY OF US BECAME librarians and library educators because we love books, reading, and looking for information of all kinds, and we base library services on the premise that reading and looking for information promote healthy youth development. There is a sizable body of research that has examined youth information seeking and use for school-related purposes, and we now have a fairly good idea of how youth gather, organize, and evaluate information for school reports and assignments. Much less is known about the kinds of information adolescents need for their nonschool, or "everyday life," activities, and about how everyday life information seeking and use contribute to adolescent development.

This chapter describes a three-year research project, funded by the Institute for Museum and Library Studies, that we undertook to fill in this gap in the research and to provide YA librarians with a clearer understanding of how library services can support urban teens' healthy transition to adulthood. But learning about the role of information in urban teens' development is not enough to ensure that libraries can support adolescent development to the fullest extent possible. We must also work to make library use a more significant part of teens' lives. Consequently, we include in this chapter a discussion of some of the barriers that keep urban teens from becoming frequent school and public library users, and we conclude with specific ideas for making public and school library services more appealing to urban teens.

BACKGROUND AND RELATED RESEARCH

Before we can design and deliver library and information services that promote urban teens' healthy development into adulthood, we must first understand the connection between information seeking and adolescent development. Although there is a relatively large body of library and information science research that has investigated the information behaviors of adults and children, the information behaviors of teens have received much less research attention. The bulk of the work that has been done has focused on how adolescent students go about looking for information for school-related purposes. Much of this work has built on Kuhlthau's (1991, 2003) model of the information search process, which she built largely on data collected from high school and college students engaged in school research projects.

Other adolescent information behavior research has studied how teens go about getting information related to future careers (e.g., Edwards and Poston-Anderson 1996) and the barriers that prevent them from finding all of the information they need when making career decisions (Julien 1999). Still other studies have considered teens' information resource design preferences, especially Internet and web-based resources (e.g., Agosto 2002; Fidel et al. 1999). Another group of studies has identified common information topics and the types of information teens typically need and seek as well as the information sources they most often choose to use (e.g., Agosto and Hughes-Hassell 2005; Latrobe and Havener 1997; Martin and Murdoch 2007; Shenton and Dixon 2003). More recently, Connaway et al. (2008) found that young adults identify Google and human sources as their most common first choices when looking for information and that expediency is a key factor in their selection of information sources.

Together, these studies provide a general picture of teens' information needs and information seeking and use for school and of their use of the Internet for school and, to a lesser extent, for personal use. They show us that teens are active users of information of various types and from various sources (e.g., Agosto and Hughes-Hassell 2005); that teens often turn first to humans as sources of information (e.g., Shenton and Dixon 2003); and that the Web, especially Google, is rapidly becoming a first choice for adolescent information seekers (e.g., Connaway et al. 2008).

Less research has examined teens' information behaviors outside of school, in their everyday lives. Research into everyday life information seeking is a growing subset of the information behavior research within the field of library and information science. Savolainen (2008, 2–3) defines everyday life information practice (an alternative term for everyday life information seeking) as "a set of socially and culturally established ways to identify, seek, use, and share the information available in various sources such as television, newspapers, and the Internet." Everyday life information seeking studies do not exclude the examination of information behaviors related to work and school but take a broader look at the purposes of information seeking and use throughout a person's daily life. The study presented in this chapter builds on past work in adolescent information behavior as well as the range of research into everyday life information seeking to move the understanding of teen information behaviors beyond the limited realm of information seeking for academic purposes into the arena of urban teens' everyday lives.

As limited as this body of research into teen information behavior is, there is even less library and information science research devoted specifically to the information behaviors of urban teens. Looking to the research literature beyond library and information science, most studies of urban teens and information resources have considered urban adolescents' access to computers. For example, Bleakley et al. (2004) found that 62 percent of urban teens and young adults have home computer access and that 66 percent use the Internet a few times a week or more. The U.S. Census Bureau estimated that, as of 2003, 76 percent of U.S. households with children between the ages of 6 and 17 years had one or more computers in the home (Day et al. 2005), a significantly higher figure than the Bleakley et al. finding. This suggests that urban teens are less likely to have access to computers in their homes than teens in general.

In another study of home computer use, Kupperman and Fishman (2002) presented four case studies of urban Hispanic middle school students who had gotten home Internet access for the first time. These case studies showed that the students and their families used the Internet for multiple purposes, including schoolwork, game playing, and online socializing.

Focusing more on personal attitudes and feelings associated with computer use, Tsikalas and Gross (2002) studied the emotional effects of urban adolescents' use of computers, particularly computers used in the home. They found home computer use to have positive impacts on students' attitudes about school, themselves, and computing.

Together, these studies of teens' and urban teens' information behaviors paint an emerging picture of the kinds of information teens typically need and seek and of some of the methods and sources they use for finding information. They fall short, however, of showing us how information seeking and use can support adolescent development and promote urban teens' healthy advancement from adolescence to adulthood, and how libraries can best support this growth process.

THE STUDY: URBAN TEENS AND EVERYDAY LIFE INFORMATION SEEKING
RESEARCH QUESTIONS

Three research questions guided our study:

- What are urban teenagers' most frequent everyday life information needs?
- What information sources and channels do urban teens favor?
- What types of media do urban teens most commonly use?

THE TEENS

We recruited two groups of Philadelphia teens, ages 14–17, to participate in the study. Sixteen of the students were employed with the Free Library of Philadelphia's Teen Leadership Program, providing homework assistance for children and planning and delivering afterschool programs for children. The remaining eleven teens were participants in the Boys & Girls Clubs of Philadelphia afterschool programs, where they played organized sports, used the clubs' computers for homework and entertainment purposes, and took part in organized social activities. Of the twenty-seven students, twenty-five were African American, one was Asian American, and one was Caucasian. About two-thirds of the participants had computers at home, a figure that corresponds closely to the Bleakley et al. (2004) figure. As a group these teens used public and school libraries infrequently for their own purposes, even though more than half of them were employed at the Free Library of Philadelphia at least two days a week.

STUDY METHODS

Since we were primarily interested in nonschool information behaviors, we asked the study participants to collect data mainly outside of school hours for the period of one week, using four data collection methods:

Written surveys. Students completed one-page surveys with questions about their age, grade in school, access to computers, frequency of school and public library use, reasons for using school and public libraries, and computer skills levels.

Audio journals. We gave the teens hand-held tape recorders and asked them to record, at least once a day, a discussion of the kinds of issues that came up each day that required them to get information. We also asked them to describe any efforts they took in addressing their information needs and to discuss their level of satisfaction with the results.

Written activity logs. We gave the participants log sheets on which to write down at the end of each day any questions that had arisen, whether or not they actually sought related information. We also asked them to write down where they had gone or with whom they had talked if they did seek answers to their questions.

Camera tours. We gave the participants disposable cameras. We asked them to take pictures of the places they commonly went for information and to snap a picture any time during the week when they found themselves gathering information.

We chose these four different data-gathering methods to represent a range of learning and self-expression styles: written, spoken, and visual. In doing so, we hoped to enable students with variant learning preferences to find at least one comfortable method of describing their information behaviors.

After the initial one-week data collection period had ended, we analyzed the data from the written activity logs to form a general picture of the teens' information behaviors. We used the constant comparative method (Glaser and Strauss 1967; Lincoln and Guba 1985) for data analysis. Data analysis led to the creation of a coding scheme (a list of categories and subcategories) representing the various topics the teens had recorded on their logs. The initial coding scheme included three major categories: places/sources of information, people consulted, and types of questions (see figure 3.1, left column).

The coding scheme represented our interpretation of the teens' everyday life information behaviors as recorded on their logs. Since this was a user-centered study, and since our main goal was to learn directly from the teens about their information behaviors, we next presented the coding scheme to them in a series of four group interviews. In each interview we asked the teens if they thought the coding scheme accurately represented their information behaviors and preferences and, if it did not, to work together to revise the coding scheme as necessary.

Each teen took part in one of the four group interviews. Each interview lasted roughly an hour to an hour and a half. Discussion and revision of the coding scheme generally took up about half of each interview session, and the coding scheme had changed considerably by the end of the fourth interview. The final coding scheme, which includes the combined suggestions and revisions from all four interview groups, can be seen in the right-hand column of figure 3.1. The items within each category appear in order from most frequent to least frequent information resources, channels, or topics. This means that under category 2, "media," for instance, the teens used telephones most frequently and phonebooks least frequently when looking for information.

For the next part of each group interview, we asked the teens to describe the time that stood out most in their minds when they had needed information, either during the week of the study or during the few weeks prior to the study. The teens told us a range of stories, from brief stories about needing to find bus or subway departure times to detailed stories about shopping trips, homework assignments, vacation planning, and so on. We concluded each of the four group interview sessions by asking the teens for suggestions for improving school and public library services.

After the four interviews were completed, we analyzed the full body of data—surveys, audio journals, activity logs, photographs, and interview transcripts. We then developed both a theoretical and an empirical model of the role of everyday life information in urban teen development based on what we learned. The next section of this chapter focuses on that theoretical model.

THE MODEL OF EVERYDAY LIFE INFORMATION SEEKING AND URBAN TEEN DEVELOPMENT

When we first undertook this project, we looked for a theory or model that would help us to understand teen development and serve as a background for the study. We examined several developmental theories, but none was a good fit for what we needed. The closest was Havighurst's (1972) list of developmental tasks of adolescence—eleven "tasks" that describe developmental changes that occur during adolescence:

FIGURE 3.1
PROJECT CODING SCHEMES

INITIAL SCHEME	FINAL SCHEME

INITIAL SCHEME

1. PLACES/SOURCES OF INFORMATION
    1.1 Television
    1.2 School
    1.3 Telephone
    1.4 Internet/Web
    1.5 Newspaper
    1.6 Other printed materials
    1.7 School material
    1.8 Magazine
    1.9 Boys and Girls Club
    1.10 Phonebook
    1.11 Computer (not Internet/Web)
    1.12 Books
    1.13 Library
    1.14 Product packaging
    1.15 Radio

2. PEOPLE CONSULTED
    2.1 Friends
    2.2 Teacher/school employees
    2.3 Parents
    2.4 Siblings
    2.5 Cousin
    2.6 Boys and Girls Club employee
    2.7 Librarian
    2.8 Sports coach
    2.9 Telephone operator
    2.10 Store clerk

3. TYPES OF QUESTIONS
    3.1 School homework questions
    3.2 Time of day/date of an event
    3.3 Meal selection
    3.4 Shopping/product information
    3.5 Current events/history
    3.6 Clothing selection
    3.7 Self-help information
    3.8 Television schedule
    3.9 Weather
    3.10 Traffic/transportation
    3.11 School activity
    3.12 Leisure activity
    3.13 Job information
    3.14 Information on specific people

FINAL SCHEME

1. PEOPLE
    1.1 Friends/family
    1.2 School employees
    1.3 Mentors
    1.4 Customer service staff
    1.5 Librarians
    1.6 Passers-by

2. MEDIA
    2.1 Telephones
    2.2 Television
    2.3 Computers
    2.4 Radio
    2.5 Newspapers
    2.6 Product packaging
    2.7 Personal communication systems
    2.8 Printed school materials
    2.9 Product catalogs
    2.10 Printed ephemera
    2.11 Books
    2.12 Magazines
    2.13 Phonebooks

3. TOPICS
    3.1 Schoolwork
    3.2 Time/date
    3.3 Social life/leisure activities
    3.4 Weather
    3.5 Daily life routine
    3.6 Popular culture
    3.7 Current events
    3.8 Transportation
    3.9 Personal finances
    3.10 Consumer information
    3.11 Personal improvement
    3.12 Job information

1. Adjusting to a new physical sense of self
2. Adjusting to new intellectual abilities
3. Adjusting to increased cognitive demands at school
4. Expanding verbal skills
5. Developing a personal sense of identity
6. Establishing adult vocational goals
7. Establishing emotional and psychological independence from his or her parents
8. Developing stable and productive peer relationships
9. Learning to manage his or her sexuality
10. Adopting a personal value system
11. Developing increased impulse control and behavioral maturity

Havighurst's list of tasks could be correlated to some of the behaviors reflected in the final coding scheme, such as tying information relating to sexual safety to Havighurst's ninth task, "learning to manage his or her sexuality." But Havighurst's list proved inadequate to support all of the information needs topics shown in figure 3.1. For example, seeking information to increase one's physical safety—that is, to deal with dangerous aspects of life in an urban environment—did not map clearly to any of Havighurst's eleven tasks.

It was therefore necessary to create twelve additional tasks to supplement Havighurst's original list:

a. Understanding and negotiating the social world
b. Seeking emotional health and security
c. Establishing relationships with adults other than parents/guardians
d. Developing a sense of civic duty
e. Establishing a cultural identity
f. Questioning how the world works
g. Developing physical self-sufficiency
h. Seeking physical safety and security
i. Expressing artistic preferences
j. Expressing aesthetic preferences
k. Understanding the physical world
l. Learning to recognize and accept his or her sexuality

The newly expanded list of twenty-three developmental tasks covered the range of information behaviors the teens had reported for the study, but it fell short of providing a theoretical overview of the role of everyday life information in urban teens' lives. Analysis of the expanded developmental task list combined with further analysis of the original data resulted in the development of an underlying model of the role of everyday life information in urban teen development. This theoretical model includes seven areas of development: the social self, the emotional self, the reflective self, the physical self, the creative self, the cognitive self, and the sexual self (figure 3.2).

Each of the seven "selves" represents a different area of adolescent development and comprises one or more of the developmental tasks from the expanded list of twenty-three tasks. These seven areas of teen development are not mutually exclusive. They often overlap, with some information needs supporting the development of multiple "selves." For example, a teen might want information about homosexuality to support her developing sexual self (in learning to recognize and accept her sexuality), her developing reflective self (in forming a personal sense of identity), and her developing cognitive self (in acquiring a basic understanding of what homosexuality is). Descriptions of each of the seven areas of teen development follow:

Social self. The social self refers to a teen's understanding of the human social world and to learning how one fits into that world. Developmental tasks corresponding to the self include developing stable and productive peer relationships and understanding and negotiating the social world. The types of information the teens needed to support their developing social selves during the week of data collection included information related to friend/peer/romantic relationships, social activities, popular culture, fashion, and social/legal norms.

Emotional self. The emotional self refers to a teen's inner world of feelings and emotions. Developmental tasks corresponding to the emotional self include establishing emotional and psychological independence from parents, developing increased impulse control and behavioral maturity, seeking emotional health and security, and establishing relationships with adults other than parents/guardians. The types of information the teens

FIGURE 3.2
EVERYDAY LIFE INFORMATION SEEKING (ELIS) AND THE SEVEN AREAS OF URBAN TEEN DEVELOPMENT

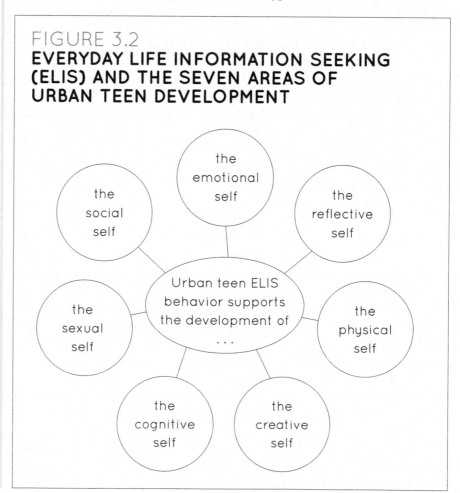

needed to support their developing emotional selves during the week of the study included information concerning familial relationships, emotional health, and religious practice.

Reflective self. The reflective self also refers to a teen's inner world but differs from the emotional self in that the focus is more introspective. Developmental tasks corresponding to the reflective self include developing a personal sense of identity, establishing adult vocational goals, adopting a personal value system, developing a sense of civic duty, establishing a cultural identity, and questioning how the world works. The types of information the teens needed to support their developing reflective selves during the week of data collection included information related to self-image, philosophical concerns, heritage/cultural identity, civic duty, college, career, and self-actualization.

Physical self. With the physical self, the focus returns to the external world. It refers to activities that support daily life, such as eating and shopping, and activities to support one's physical health and safety. Developmental tasks corresponding to the physical self include adjusting to a new physical sense of self, developing physical self-sufficiency, and seeking physical safety and security. During the week of data collection, the teens needed information about daily life routine, physical safety, goods and services, personal finances, health, and job responsibilities.

Creative self. The creative self refers to fulfillment of aesthetic needs. It involves either the creation of a creative product, such as a painting or a dance performance, or the judgment or appreciation of a creative work. Developmental tasks corresponding to the creative self include expressing artistic preferences and expressing aesthetic preferences. The kinds of information the study participants needed to support their developing creative selves during the week of the study included information related to creative performance and creative expression.

Cognitive self. The cognitive self refers to intellectual processing and understanding of the environment in which the teen lives. Developmental tasks corresponding to the cognitive self include adjusting to new intellectual abilities, adjusting to increased cognitive demands at school, expanding verbal skills, and understanding the physical world. During the week of data collection, the study participants needed information about academics, school culture, and current events to support their developing cognitive selves.

Sexual self. The sexual self refers to the broad range of issues involved with sexuality, both the concepts of sex and sexuality and the teen's own sexual behaviors. Developmental tasks corresponding to the sexual self include learning to manage one's sexuality and learning to recognize and accept one's sexuality. The teens in the study needed information related to sexual safety and sexual identity to support their developing sexual selves.

WHAT DOES THE MODEL MEAN FOR LIBRARIANS WHO SERVE URBAN TEENS?

Clearly the essence of urban teens' everyday life information seeking is the gathering of information to facilitate their teen-to-adult maturation process. For these teens everyday life information seeking is self-exploration and world exploration that helps them understand the world and their positions in it, themselves now, and who they aspire to be in the future. If libraries work to support the full range of teens' information needs, they can help teens to develop their healthy social, emotional, reflective, physical, creative, cognitive, and sexual selves. Figure 3.3 provides a planning model librarians can use as they set policy, select resources, and develop programs and services based on urban teens' everyday life information needs and behaviors.

But if teens do not frequent their school and public libraries, then the ability to support healthy teen development is greatly reduced. In the next section, we turn our attention to the teens' perceptions of libraries and their recommendations for improving public and school library services.

URBAN TEENS' SUGGESTIONS FOR IMPROVING PUBLIC AND SCHOOL LIBRARY SERVICES

When we first set out to conduct this study, we intentionally chose two groups of teens with fundamentally different relationships to libraries. We assumed that since they worked in public libraries, the Free Library of Philadelphia teens would be relatively frequent library users and have fairly positive views of libraries. We thought it likely that the Boys & Girls Clubs teens, who had no formal relationships with libraries, would be less frequent library users with less positive views of libraries. We were surprised to learn that neither group were frequent library users and that both groups had overwhelmingly negative views of libraries and librarians. We probed these issues in the group interviews to try to understand why both groups had such unpleasant perceptions of libraries and librarians. Each of the four interview groups discussed their reasons for these perceptions in detail.

At this point it is important to note both the dearth of school librarians in the School District of Philadelphia and the shortage of young adult librarians in the Free Library of Philadelphia. The School District of Philadelphia has 270 schools serving 180,000 students (SDP 2008), but it has

FIGURE 3.3
MODEL FOR PLANNING POLICIES, COLLECTIONS, SERVICES, AND PROGRAMS FOR URBAN YOUNG ADULTS

STEP 1:	STEP 2:	STEP 3:	STEP 4:	STEP 5:
Understand urban teen developmental needs	Use urban teen developmental needs to set priorities and establish goals	Evaluate capacity	Set policies; select resources; develop services and programs	Evaluate

only eighty certified school librarians (APSL 2008). Many of the schools in the district have no library, and others are staffed with paraprofessionals or parent volunteers. The most recent statistical report compiled by the PLA shows that the Free Library of Philadelphia has fifty-five YA librarians serving more than 74,000 teens (PLDS 2007). As noted in the teens' discussion below, many of their perceptions of libraries and librarians are based on interactions with nonprofessional staff or with librarians who are more comfortable serving children or adults. Their negative perceptions of libraries, coupled with the lack of YA library professionals in Philadelphia, reinforce the critical need for more librarians in both schools and public libraries who understand the developmental needs of teenagers and specialize in YA resources and teen programming.

When asked the interview questions "How could a school or public library make your life easier when you're looking for information?" and "If you could change your school and public libraries in any way you wanted to, what kinds of changes would you make?" the study participants provided a wealth of suggestions for improving school and public library services to urban teens. Their suggestions fell into four main categories: staff, collections, policies, and services. Figure 3.4 shows each of these four main categories and the corresponding subcategories for each area, discussed below.

STAFF

A few of the teens told stories of kind, helpful librarians and other library staff at their public and school libraries. Many more reported negative experiences with librarians and library staff, and these experiences had turned them away from using their school and public libraries. Critiques of library staff fell into two subcategories: knowledge and attitudes.

Knowledge

A recurring theme across the interviews was the teens' desire for library staff to be more familiar with urban teens' resource preferences, especially their leisure reading preferences. Over and over again the teens stressed that as members of inner-city communities they were interested in reading about people living in similar situations, and for this reason they were avid readers of "street lit" (also called "urban fiction"; see chapter 5). They wished library staff knew about this genre and could provide related readers' advisory. One of the boys wished that the librarians could "help me to find a good book, like, telling which book would be good to read and stuff," but the librarians with whom he had interacted were all unfamiliar with the kinds of books he liked to read: "Every time I ask them for a book, they never heard of it."

The teens also wished that library staff were more knowledgeable about local community characteristics. They suggested that collections should not be duplicated from library to library, and that librarians should know the particular interests of those in their communities in order to build appropriate collections. As one of the boys explained, "They really need—they *really* need—to have a hip-hop section where books specifically focus in on one topic: hip-hop. If [the library is located in] a real urban area . . . they would need to have a whole lot of African American hip-hop stuff." These teens did not see their librarians as members of their communities, holding instead a "them" versus "us" perspective.

Attitudes

In addition to wishing that library staff had deeper knowledge of teens' reading preferences and a better understanding of their local communities, many of the teens felt that library staff lacked tolerance of teens and their natural behaviors. As one of the boys explained, "I just think that the librarians should stop being so hard on us . . . over stuff that's not really important. When [we] are just trying to have a good time but not being too loud. I think they need to stop being so hard on everybody."

FIGURE 3.4
SUGGESTIONS FOR IMPROVING LIBRARY SERVICES TO URBAN TEENS

STAFF	Knowledge	Urban teens' resource preferences Local community characteristics
	Attitudes	Tolerance Kindness Mutual respect
POLICIES	Computer	Flexible time limits Free printing Reduced game restrictions
	Behavioral	Fewer library use restrictions Space for socializing
SERVICES	Teen programs	More programs More relevant and interesting topics
	Teen input	In planning and developing programs In selecting resources
COLLECTIONS	Books	More urban fiction More popular fiction Multiple copies
	Movies and Magazines	More popular titles More relevant titles More up-to-date titles
	Computers	More accessibility More computer games
	Music	Ambient music In-house listening stations

The teens explained that even in libraries where the YA staff had positive attitudes toward teens, often librarians and staff in other parts of the library had negative attitudes that made them hesitant to visit their libraries. The interview participants suggested that staff in all parts of the library should be trained to be more acceptant of teen behavior. As one of the girls explained, non-YA librarians and staff "are just real petty."

The participants also wished that librarians and library staff would treat them with respect. For example, one of the boys had tried on several occasions to find homework resources at his public library. Each time he had asked, "Excuse me, do you know where I can find this?" librarians had responded with terse comments such as "No, uh-uh. I'm busy." This lack of respect for his information needs led him to stop going to his public library. It is unclear how many times he had been treated in this manner, but even one such incident can tarnish a person's entire opinion of libraries.

Related to a lack of respect was the idea that library staff needed to treat teens with more kindness. Over and over again, the participants expressed the simple wish that their librarians would just be "nice."

COLLECTIONS

The next major area of suggestions for increasing the appeal of libraries to urban teens is library collections. These teens were active information seekers and information users, but libraries were rarely their first choices when looking for information, due in part to their view of library collections as mismatched to their information needs and preferences.

Books

Just as adults tend to think of books first and foremost when they think of libraries (OCLC 2005, 6-3), these teens tended to think of books first when thinking about libraries and library services. They offered several suggestions for making library book collections more appealing. They particularly wanted more urban fiction titles and more copies of popular titles.

Over and over again the teens stressed their desire to read books about adolescents living in urban environments similar to their own. They rejected much of mainstream YA literature, which they viewed as telling stories of teens living privileged, suburban lives:

> **Teen #1:** [The public library needs] more teen books, because most of the books at my branch, they're . . . [written] to one kind of teen, and all teens aren't the same.
>
> **Teen #2:** They don't have real broad selection.
>
> **Teen #3:** I don't like the teen books at my library.
>
> **Interviewer:** Can you think of what kinds of teen books are missing? Or what you'd like to see?
>
> **Teen #4:** Realistic types. Most of them there are fairy tales, come-and-get-me-on-a-pony type books.
>
> **Teen #1:** That's why most people, they don't read as much—books—because most of them aren't as realistic. The teen books aren't realistic.

Here is another similar conversation excerpt:

> **Teen #1:** My library needs more books. They need more books with teen-agers like us. People who care for us.
>
> **Teen #2:** They need, like, multicultural books. Books about our culture. They need books for *our* culture.
>
> **Interviewer:** Can you think of any examples?
>
> **Teen #2:** Black books. With girls, like teens growing up, like *Flyy Girl, True to the Game* . . .
>
> **Teen #3:** We don't be readin' that in school, books like *True to the Game*.
>
> **Teen #4:** We need more books for our age. Something that we can relate to!

Long waits on hold lists were another deterrent to library use. The teens wished for more copies of popular reading titles and described frustration with not being able to find books they were looking for on library shelves. They found it more convenient to borrow a popular book from a friend or family member or to buy a copy from a bookstore than to wait for a library copy to become available. They suggested that both school and public libraries should "get more copies of books," both popular reading titles and books needed for homework assignments.

Movies

The teens also critiqued their public library movie (DVD) collections. They wished for more movie offerings, particularly more recent releases. As one of the girls lamented, although the interview took place during the spring, her local public library still had "the same DVDs from the summertime." The phrases "up-to-date movies" and "new DVDs" were repeated throughout the interviews.

Magazines

Many of the teens reported magazines as a favorite type of reading material, but few considered their school or public libraries to be good places to find the kinds of magazines they enjoyed reading. As a group, they wanted more titles, especially urban-interest publications, and more up-to-date issues of existing subscriptions. For example, one of the girls spoke of her frustration in trying to find current issues of her favorite magazine at the branch library where she worked. Although the library supposedly had a subscription to *Twist*, every time she wanted to read it, she could find only the same outdated issue that she had already read:

> **Teen:** I like to read *Twist*.
>
> **Interviewer:** Does the public library have a subscription?
>
> **Teen:** They have it, but every time I go it's the same magazine. . . . I never see the updated one. It's like somebody picks them up and takes them home.

Music

The teens often mentioned music as a potential draw to libraries, both ambient music playing in libraries and individual in-house listening stations. Those who wished for ambient music in their school and public libraries were quick to qualify this suggestion by adding that teens—not library staff—would need to choose the kinds of music to play. Though a minority of the teens felt that music should be played only in separate teen "noisy" rooms to keep from bothering those interested in studying, many agreed that even when studying at home they had background music playing: "A lot of us teens, we listen to music all the time."

In addition to ambient music, many of the teens wished that their libraries would provide headphones for listening to music in the library, both music from the libraries' collections and music that could be downloaded from other sources. Teens in two of the four interview groups imagined individual listening stations that they could use to select music to check out to take home or to listen to while in the library.

Computers

Another theme that ran through all four focus groups was the desire for more computers in both school and public libraries. Many of the participants had had to wait in lines to use library computers, and many had subsequently given up using their school or public library computers. As one teen explained, "A lot of kids don't use [the school library] if they have to use a computer [because there are] only four computers in our library, where the school has over a thousand kids." The teens also wished for better access to computer games in libraries. A few even imagined library-owned game systems for playing with friends in public libraries.

POLICIES

The interview participants objected to library policies that served as deterrents to school and public library use.

Computer Policies

The teens saw limited hours when they could use school library computers and short time use limits for public library computers as problematic. Long wait times and printing fees were additional barriers to library computer use, as seen in the following discussion excerpt about the computers at school libraries:

> **Teen #1:** Yeah, I wait a long time for the computer.

> **Teen #2:** And you gotta sign up just to use the computer. It's like jail. And it costs ten cents a page to print!

Ten cents a page might be affordable for most adults, but to many of the teens in the interviews it was prohibitive. Other teens mentioned not wanting to use school and public library computers because of library policies against computer games. They objected to librarians' viewpoints that only reading and research were legitimate uses of library computers. Together, these various computer policies turned the teens away from using library computers and reinforced their negative perception of libraries.

Behavioral Policies

Restrictive behavioral policies were equally unpopular. The interview participants repeatedly lamented the strictness of the public library security guards and the frequency with which guards and other staff members told teens to leave the libraries. As one of the girls explained, "If they would stop being so harsh at the library—kicking people out—more [teenagers] would want to come."

One of the boys explained that policies against talking and socializing kept him from using his public library. He did go to the library twice weekly to work there, but he chose not to use it as a patron:

> People talk about it constantly: "We're going to try to treat you like adults." But they don't. So kids don't want to go to the library. I haven't been going to the library since I was in first grade. Some kids come in hollering, trying to purposely make the guards mad. But a lot of kids come in, sit down, just want to have conversation. Where would you rather have them? Outside, doing something bad, or in the library, just talking?

Getting permission from teachers to visit the school library proved to be an equally powerful barrier to school library use. One of the girls explained that at her school students could not enter the library without a note from a teacher. She wished that the library would start "letting me in without a note." Another told a story that shows how such a policy can serve as a roadblock to school library use:

> Yeah, for example, like today. I went [to the school library] to print this paper at the computer. I needed a special log-in, and that takes time. Since I was already late for school, I was asking her [the librarian], "Can I please come in here, please, please, and just type my name and print this paper? Less than five seconds, then I be out of here." [She replied in a nasty voice:] "No! You need a note."

Though policies such as requiring a note from a teacher to use the school library might help to preserve order within a school, they send the message that students are not welcome in their school libraries, and they create the unintended consequence of reduced library use.

SERVICES

The teens offered suggestions for improving library services to urban teens, including ideas for more teen programs and methods of increasing teen input in program design and collection development.

Teen Programs

The teens noted that their public library branches offered programs for children and programs for adults but very few programs for young adults. Worse yet, the few teen programs that were offered did not appeal to them. As one of the girls explained, "They need to have things that teens will really want to come to." The lack of programs targeted to teens sent the message that public libraries welcome adults and children but not those in the middle age group.

Teen Input

The interview participants also wished that the library staff would give them some power to decide the kinds of teen library services, programs, and materials offered at their libraries. In three of the four interview groups, the teens suggested surveying or interviewing teens to gather their input. One of the boys commented, "I think they should have meetings [with teens] and things like that so that everybody can express their opinions." Another teen suggested that "they could do surveys to find out who wants to do what, when do you want to do it." Not only would increased teen input lead to programs and services better suited to teens' needs and interests, it would also develop feelings of increased ownership in their libraries.

Some teens suggested that, to find out what types of programs would be popular among teens, librarians should try "talking it out" with them. The teens explained that they would feel honored and respected if the library would value their input. In addition to surveys, a few quick and easy techniques for "talking it out" with teens include holding informal focus groups to brainstorm programming ideas; putting up anonymous suggestion boards or suggestion boxes for programming ideas; providing book, magazine, music, and movie purchase suggestion forms; and holding programming idea contests.

PUTTING IT ALL TOGETHER: THE IDEAL LIBRARY FOR URBAN TEENS

For both public and school libraries, these recommendations show that listening to teen input about collections and services is key to increasing libraries' reach and influence. They further indicate that public libraries should, whenever possible, create a teen room that is separate from the rest of the library. There teens can listen to music, socialize, read magazines, play computers games, and so on. The teens' suggestions for school library changes are a call to school librarians to make their buildings and resources more available to students by removing unnecessarily strict policies and by expanding operating hours to enable teens to use their school libraries outside of school hours.

When thinking about their ideal library, the teens moved beyond the traditional view of libraries as book providers to envision full-service community centers. As one of the girls said, "The library is not only about books and computers. They should have more programs on Saturdays and Sundays, more programs to get the teenagers into the library. Because if they don't those kids [are] gonna be on the street." With a little bit of creative planning and organizing, public and school libraries can fulfill this vision of libraries as full-service community centers for urban teens (see chapter 7). Teens would then come to hold more favorable views of libraries and librarians, and libraries would ultimately see their teen patronage increase.

Finally, in describing their ideal library the teens demonstrated the importance of involving teenagers in planning and implementing services designed for them. This is another way that librarians can support teens' maturation into adulthood: by giving them voice and empowering them to mold their libraries around their needs. These teens were excited that we were showing interest in their ideas and opinions, and they responded with care and thought. It is important for librarians to respect teens' ideas and to show young adults that they can make valuable contributions to "adult" endeavors.

Ultimately, by understanding and implementing teens' recommendations libraries would be much more able to provide the kinds of information and information services necessary to support the healthy growth of urban teens in the seven areas of adolescent development: the social self, the emotional self, the reflective self, the physical self, the creative self, the cognitive self, and the sexual self. The teens have given us the vision. It is now up to us to work with them to make it a reality.

CHAPTER 4

DEVELOPING A LEISURE READING PROGRAM THAT IS RELEVANT AND RESPONSIVE TO THE LIVES OF URBAN TEENAGERS
Insights from Research

SANDRA HUGHES-HASSELL

IN RECENT YEARS RESEARCHERS, policymakers, and educators have devoted increasing attention to the literacy needs of adolescents. Many schools have begun to tackle the problem of reading in the middle and high school years by initiating adolescent literacy initiatives. A common element found in well-regarded programs is a focus on building the habit of leisure reading (McGrath 2005). Leisure reading is the reading students choose to do on their own, as opposed to reading that is assigned to them (Mellon 1990). It involves personal choice, choosing what one wants to read, and reading widely from a variety of sources—not just from books.

Both qualitative and quantitative studies have demonstrated a correlation between success in school and the amount of leisure reading students do (Allington and McGill-Franzen 2003; Kaczmarek and Stachowiak 2004; Krashen 2004). The amount of leisure reading done outside of school has consistently been found to relate to achievement in vocabulary, reading comprehension, verbal fluency, content knowledge, and writing ability (Reutzel and Hollingsworth 1991; Short 1995; Stanovich and West 1989). Students who read in their spare time become better readers, score higher on achievement tests in all subject areas, and have more content knowledge than those who do not (Cunningham and Stanovich 1991). As Krashen (1993, 84) notes, "Although free voluntary reading alone will not ensure attainment of the highest levels of literacy, it will at least ensure an acceptable level."

Developing a leisure reading program that is relevant and responsive to the lives of urban teenagers requires an understanding of the unique motivations, interests, attitudes, influences, and preferred reading materials of urban teens. Although researchers have studied the leisure reading habits of adolescents, urban youth have accounted for only a small percentage of the respondents. In this chapter, we discuss the findings of a three-part study investigating the leisure reading habits of 826 urban middle and high school students (Hughes-Hassell 2008).[1] The study investigated five aspects of urban teen leisure reading: (1) Do urban teenagers read in their leisure time? (2) If they read, what do they read, when do they read, and why do they read? (3) What topics and types of characters or people do they like to read about? (4) How do they obtain their reading material? (5) Who encourages them to read?

METHODOLOGY

This study was conducted in three parts. Table 4.1 provides demographic data for the study participants.

Part 1 was conducted in a small urban middle school in a large northeastern U.S. city. Two-hundred forty-five students attend the school, which serves grades six through eight as an alternative middle school. Twenty-one percent of the students are Caucasian, 73 percent African American, 3 percent Hispanic, and 3 percent Asian American. Sixty-one percent of the students qualify for free or reduced lunch. Results on the most recent state assessment of reading indicate that 67 percent of the students are scoring at basic or below basic levels.

Part 2 was conducted in a large urban middle school in the same northeastern city. The school serves approximately 1,340 students in grades five through eight. The student body is largely Latino (66 percent) and African American (27 percent). Eighty-six percent of the students qualify for free or reduced lunch. Results on the most recent state assessment of reading indicate that 68 percent are performing below basic, 23 percent basic, and 9 percent proficient.

Part 3 study participants were twenty-eight tenth- and eleventh-grade students enrolled in three English classes at a small urban high school in the southern United States. Fourteen percent of the students were African American, 18 percent Hispanic, and 68 percent Caucasian. Four were enrolled in English 10A, a standard-level college prep English course; one

TABLE 4.1
STUDY PARTICIPANTS

PARTICIPANTS	SCHOOL 1 MIDDLE SCHOOL	SCHOOL 2 MIDDLE SCHOOL	SCHOOL 3 HIGH SCHOOL	TOTAL
Female	119 (56%)	309 (53%)	14 (50%)	442 (54%)
Male	95 (44%)	275 (47%)	14 (50%)	384 (46%)
Total	214	584	28	826

in English 10B, a lower-level English class; and twenty-three in Honors English 11.

To collect data for parts 1 and 2 of the study, middle school teachers administered a five-page, twenty-item questionnaire focused on factors related to leisure reading: whether or not adolescents read in their leisure time; if they did, what, when, and why they read; the topics and types of characters or people they liked to read about; how they obtained their reading material; who encouraged them to read; and if they did not read, why not. The questionnaire, adapted from the 1999 Smartgirl.com/YALSA survey, contained sixteen multiple choice questions and four open-ended questions: (1) What was your favorite book when you were in elementary school? (2) In middle school? (3) What is the best book you've read this year? (4) Is there anything else you'd like to tell us about reading? Students were also asked to indicate their gender and age.

Part 3 employed a range of qualitative and quantitative data collection methods. First, the twenty-eight high school students who volunteered to participate completed a survey designed to assess how they spent their leisure time. The survey included questions about their activities outside of school and their reading practices and materials. Next, nineteen of the students volunteered to keep reading logs for one week in February, March, and April 2008, in which they recorded the title of anything they read (including websites, social networking sites, instant messaging, e-mail, and text messaging), along with the approximate time spent reading each item. Finally, these nineteen students participated in individual interviews, which focused on their history as readers.

FINDINGS AND DISCUSSION

The data collected in this study provide a snapshot of urban teens' reading behaviors, attitudes, and interests. Several themes emerged.

If we expand our definition of reading beyond "literary fiction," these urban teenagers appear to read in their spare time despite the time pressure and social pressure they experience. In general, 72 percent of them indicated that they read in their leisure time, although for some readers it might be only an occasional pursuit. Twenty-two percent said they read "constantly," and 51 percent indicated they "read when they get a chance." Six percent indicated that they did not read, and the other 21 percent said they read only for school. Females were more likely to read for pleasure than males (79 percent vs. 65 percent). The majority of the students indicated that they read in their spare time for three main reasons: fun and relaxation, because they can relate to the characters they are reading about, and to learn new things.

Those who did not enjoy reading seemed to prefer other activities rather than simply rejecting the act of reading. This was especially true for the high school students. Spending time with friends, participating in sports, playing video games, listening to music, and surfing the Web were more compelling to them than reading. As one young man stated, "There are just too many temptations like the computer, the Internet, and talking to my friends." Their reading logs showed that these high school students spent an average of two hours and forty-five minutes per day using My-Space, instant messaging, and text messaging to keep in touch with their friends.

All of the students, even those who reported not reading for leisure, appeared to recognize the value of reading. In their comments to the open-ended survey questions and to the interview prompts, many of the students acknowledged the importance of reading to their success in school, college, and the workforce. Though the majority seemed to view reading as a "quest for information" or "means to an end," some took a more aesthetic approach to reading and talked about "getting lost in a book" or "identifying with the characters." For example, several of the female high school students were reading Stephenie Meyer's *Twilight*. When asked what was appealing about the book, one replied, "Oh my! Those books . . . the characters! Edward is . . . oh, my!" Another young woman explained, "Reading moves me emotionally. I develop relationships with the characters and they don't argue back!"

Most of the students view reading as a solitary activity. For the most part they do not see themselves as belonging to a community of readers. When asked if they ever talked to their friends or family members about the things they were reading, most responded that they did not, although several mentioned passing good books on to their friends. One exception seemed to be series books, such as Twilight, Harry Potter, and Gossip Girl. One explanation for this could be that the voices of the teenage protagonists are so strong in these series. Another could be the media frenzy surrounding these three series in particular. All three have been adapted to film. The only discussions our students reported having with teachers revolved around the books they were reading for class. Only one student mentioned seeing a teacher reading for pleasure at school.

Not surprisingly, the students prefer reading materials that are relevant to their lives—magazines that deal with topics of interest to them, books about teenagers like them, and the Internet, which they view as not only providing more relevant, up-to-date information but doing so in a "social" manner. This is consistent with Hynds's (1990) research, which found that when teenagers read for pleasure they are searching for materials that will entice them to engage and maintain their interests.

Overall, the students appear to read very little during the summer. Only 22 percent reported that they continued to read for pleasure during the summer months. This is particularly troubling since research shows that summer reading is critical to summer learning, especially for low-performing and disadvantaged students, like those in the two middle schools (Allington and McGill-Franzen 2003; Kim 2004; Schacter 2003).

Although the teenagers in the two middle schools reported that they were engaged in leisure reading, their reading scores remained low. Why? The simplest explanation may be that they were not reading as much in their leisure time as they reported. Another explanation might involve the type of leisure reading they were doing. Although there is evidence that light reading provides motivation for more reading (Krashen 2004; Ross 1995), perhaps the reading of magazines (by far their preferred material) does not correlate positively with higher levels of literacy. Several researchers have noted that light reading does not automatically result in an ability to read advanced material—the material presented on standardized tests (Hafner et al. 1986). Thorndike (1973) found that for middle school students the types of reading that correlated best with improved reading comprehension were (1) humor, (2) history and biography, science fiction, myths, and legends, and (3) adventure and current events. Yet another explanation might focus on how educators are using, or not using, these students' preferred reading materials in the classroom. And, finally, perhaps the assessment instruments we use do not provide a way for students such as these, who primarily read magazines, comic books, and Internet documents, to demonstrate their strengths as readers. As educators we need to consider how we can (1) expand our assessment strategies to allow us to understand the strengths developed by the materials urban teens prefer to read and use the results to develop instructional strategies that help them become better readers, and (2) change the canon to include more culturally relevant titles.

Librarians seem to have minimal influence on the leisure reading behaviors of these teens. The high school students reported that they got most of their reading material from bookstores, visiting libraries primarily to complete research projects for school. This means their interactions with librarians are most often related to the research process—locating and evaluating resources that support the curriculum—rather than to leisure reading. Although the middle school students indicated that they got most of their leisure reading material from libraries, when asked who influences them to read, only 30 percent mentioned a school or public librarian.

IMPLICATIONS FOR LIBRARIANS

What did we learn from these teens that can be used to support the literacy development of urban teenagers?

MODEL THE SOCIAL NATURE OF READING

As Short and Pierce (1990, 84) note, "Literacy is a social endeavor." We become literate by acting as readers and writers within authentic social contexts. Social experiences are especially critical to the literacy development of teens. Adolescent literacy grows out of relationships—whether these are teen-to-teen, parent-to-child, sibling-to-sibling, teacher-to-student, or mentor-to-mentee (Zirinsky and Rau 2001). According to Hynds (1990, 255), when students "do not envision themselves as members of a literate community, they generally do not develop literate behaviors."

Librarians must provide a variety of options for urban teenagers to explore literature and language on a daily basis. One way to do this is to capitalize on students' interest in and use of information and communication technologies. The Internet has made it possible for students to interact with readers from around the world and to communicate with authors. Many African American and Latino authors and illustrators have developed web pages for teens to explore (e.g., Nikki Grimes, Gary Soto, Jacqueline Woodson, Jess Mowry, and Sandra Cisneros). Nikki Grimes extends the following welcome to visitors to her site (www.nikkigrimes .com):

> There's no cooler place to be than the land of poetry.
> Thanks for stopping by. So glad you found my site.
> Now that you're here, I hope you'll stay awhile.
> There's lots to see and do, so explore to your soul's content.

Jess Mowry uses his website (http://timoun.tripod.com/index.html) to empower the readers of his books to become critics and writers themselves. He showcases the views, opinions, and reviews of his work that come from the young people who read it, and he offers advice to them about writing and getting published.

On Sharon Flakes's website (www.sharongflake.com), students can watch a video featuring African American teens reading from *The Skin I'm In* (1998) or listen to a podcast of Flake reading from *Begging for Change* (2003). Equally important, Flake, Grimes, and Mowry include a series of photographs of African American teenagers engaged in reading and writing on their websites.

Many school and public libraries offer extensive opportunities for teens to take part in communities of readers through their library web pages or MySpace pages. Hennepin County (Minnesota) Public Library (www .hclib.org/teens/) and Charlotte and Mecklenburg County (North Carolina) Public Library (www.libraryloft.org), for example, provide ways for teens to not only discuss books with other teens and adults but also share their own writing with a broader audience. Podcasts, YouTube videos, blogs, and social networks are just a few of the Web 2.0 technologies they employ.

Finally, it is critical that librarians themselves be readers and that they make their reading visible to students. Librarians need to display the books they are currently reading, visit classrooms to talk about books with teens, and, most important, be passionate about our love of reading. Cullen (n.d.) reminds us:

> If we, as teachers, are not passionate about our subject then we cannot expect to [inspire passion in] others. It has been my experience that the cynical adolescent pose is merely a thin veneer and that what lies beneath is a desire to safely give vent to those feelings of excitement and enthusiasm as they discover the world. English teachers [and librarians] can provide important role models of people who are unashamedly passionate about words, books, poetry, drama, and above all, their work.

GIVE STUDENTS TIME DURING THE SCHOOL DAY TO READ

Providing time for students to read during the school day is particularly important for economically disadvantaged urban students who often have to work to improve financial conditions at home, and who may not have a place or the resources to read materials of their choice outside of school (Fisher 2004). This means librarians "need to be stronger advocates in middle schools and high schools for incorporating free reading time into the school day" (Chance 2000, 22). Sustained silent reading programs have been found effective if they are thoughtfully designed and consistently implemented over a prolonged period. Key factors include professional development for teachers, access to a wide variety of appealing reading materials, follow-up activities that encourage further voluntary reading, modeling by teachers and administrators, and informal accountability (Fisher 2004; Pilgreen 2000).

PROVIDE THE TYPES OF READING MATERIALS STUDENTS PREFER

Adults often send the message that the only reading that is *reading* is reading literature (Beers 1996; Mellon 1990). As we invite urban adolescents to read, we must remain open to their reading interests by providing and promoting reading materials that are of interest to them. Magazines are clearly a favorite leisure reading material. Adolescents are drawn to magazines for a variety of reasons, including the number and quality of pictures, the speed with which information can be gathered from magazines, the "coolness" factor, and the reading level (Jones et al. 2004). Librarians can promote magazine reading by providing and circulating magazines in public libraries, in school libraries, and as part of circulating classroom collections. The best way to select magazines is to involve students. Survey students, but also browse grocery stores, department stores, and local bookstores to observe the magazines adolescents are buying. *Black Beat, Jet, Latina, Low Rider, Sister to Sister, Slam, Teen en Español, Urban Latino, Word Up, WWE,* and *XXL* are among the magazines popular with urban adolescents. Many of these magazines are also available online, thus increasing accessibility, interactivity, and reader participation.

Comic books were also listed as a favorite reading material by many of the teens in our study. Many teachers and school library media specialists have successfully used comic books to engage reluctant readers (Norton 2003; Versaci 2001). Marvel and CrossGen have comics available on DVD that include original comic book art, enlarged word balloons, voice-overs reading the text, and music. This format not only appeals to visual learners but also makes it easier to circulate comics.

Two other popular formats related to comic books are the graphic novel and manga. Both are good for youth who read English as a second language or are reading on a lower reading level, because the simple sentences and visual cues allow the reader to comprehend the story (Jones et al. 2004). Selecting graphic novels and manga has become easier now that *Voice of Youth Advocates, School Library Journal,* and *Booklist* regularly feature reviews.

Reading about sports figures, musicians, and other celebrities is also popular with urban teens. In addition to magazines and the Internet, non-fiction books can provide students with avenues for exploring pop culture.

For many adolescents, nonfiction serves the same purposes as fiction does for other readers (Sullivan 2001). Nonfiction books published today contain high-quality pictures, lots of captions, and sidebars—features that make them especially appealing to students who have short attention spans, prefer visual media, or are reluctant readers. Graphic nonfiction is also popular with adolescents. Similar in format to graphic novels, graphic nonfiction covers a range of subjects, as demonstrated by the following titles: *Malcolm X: A Graphic Biography* (Helfer and DuBurke 2007), *Still I Rise: A Cartoon History of African Americans* (Laird and Laird 1997), and *Dignifying Science: Stories about Women Scientists* (Ottaviani et al. 2000). Visual cues make graphic nonfiction especially appealing to reluctant readers and English-language learners. Although many professional journals contain reviews of nonfiction, the real "pop" stuff often does not get reviewed (Jones et al. 2004). The best way to locate it is to visit a bookstore or, better yet, have students select titles from an online bookstore.

Finally, it is critical to respect urban students' culture and heritage by providing culturally relevant resources. The kinds of materials that have been found to be most effective with adolescent students of minority groups are those containing authentic portrayals that students can identify with—including characters, settings, and situations—or themes that students are keenly interested in and that are relevant to their lives (Harris 1993; Henry 1998). Young adults appreciate interesting reading materials that make sense to them (Au 1993; Harris 1993). Texts should reflect reality, but they should also point the way to a different, and better, reality for urban teens (Collins 1993; Guild and Hughes-Hassell 2001).

The number of multicultural titles published each year, though still inadequate, has increased steadily over the past decade. Authors such as Walter Dean Myers, Jacqueline Woodson, Sandra Cisneros, Gary Soto, Rita Williams-Garcia, Jess Mowry, and Sharon Flake are specifically writing YA novels set in urban communities. Novels such as these offer confirmation and validation of the lives of urban youth as well as legitimization of their inner-city cultures. The best of these books also counteract stereotypes of urban adolescents by creating characters who in the details of their lives challenge social expectations borne of stereotype. They do this by featuring adolescents—both male and female—who, for example, are successful in school and plan to attend college, understand and choose to avoid the dangers of drug use, and leave gang life behind (Collins 1993; Guild and Hughes-Hassell 2001; Tatum 2005).

Many of the students in our study indicated that they read best in Spanish. If our goal is to foster their love of reading, then we need to provide materials in their first language. Given their preference for magazines, educators who work with urban youth should consider acquiring not just books in Spanish but magazines and newspapers as well. This has the potential to accomplish two goals—to get students to read, and to engage them in conversations about reading with their parents, many of whom may speak only Spanish. There are several professional resources that feature reviews of multicultural and Spanish-language materials, including *Críticas*, an all-Spanish periodical with articles and book reviews; *Multicultural Review*, a journal focused on race, ethnicity, and religious diversity that provides reviews of books and other media with multicultural themes and topics; and the Barahona Center for the Study of Books in Spanish for Children and Adolescents (www.csusm.edu/csb/). Created by Isabel Schon, the Barahona Center is a comprehensive, bilingual database for books published in Spanish-speaking countries or translated into Spanish from other languages.

AGGRESSIVELY MARKET BOOKS AND OTHER READING MATERIALS TO URBAN TEENS

Many of the students in our study indicated that they enjoyed reading but were unable to locate materials they liked. Book talks, podcasts, YouTube videos, and book trailers are all excellent ways to introduce teens to appealing reading material. Tatum (2005) suggests that educators develop lists of "must-read" texts for black adolescent males whose literacy needs are intertwined with cultural, social, and emotional factors. He argues that to develop their literacy black male teenagers need to read texts that address their concerns as young black men living in turmoil and can help shape their ideas and their identity. His list includes both fiction and nonfiction, among them Walter Dean Myers's *The Beast; There Are No Children Here* (Kotlowitz 1991); *A Hope in the Unseen: An American Odyssey from the Inner City to the Ivy League* (Suskind 1998); and *And Still We Rise: The Trials and Triumphs of Twelve Gifted Inner-City Students* (Corwin 2000). Librarians might develop similar "must-read" lists for other cultural groups.

Another strategy that has proven effective is to use street literature as a bridge to more mainstream YA titles. Many of the teenagers in our study indicated that they wanted to read about teenagers like themselves. Street literature fulfils this need, but these titles are not often found in most school library media centers because of their controversial content. Librarians can use students' interest in books like Omar Tyree's *Flyy Girl* and Teri Woods's *True to the Game* to introduce them to urban YA titles that are less sexually graphic, violent, or morally derisive (Morris et al. 2006). (See chapter 5 for a continued discussion of street lit and urban teens.)

ADEQUATELY FUND SCHOOL AND CLASSROOM LIBRARIES IN LOW-INCOME URBAN COMMUNITIES

For students in low-income areas, school is the primary source of reading materials, yet urban school districts are less likely to fund school libraries adequately than their suburban counterparts. Neuman and Celano (2001) analyzed school libraries in both low-income and middle-income neighborhoods, assessing them in three categories: resources (including quantity and condition of books and computers), staffing, and availability. Their findings showed that the students who were most likely to benefit from school libraries were offered the poorest services and resources and the least access. Low-income schools were less likely to have a certified school library media specialist. Low-income schools had only two books—

in either good or poor condition—per student, whereas there were twelve books per student, with nearly all the books in good or excellent condition, in middle-income neighborhoods. In addition, for every computer in the library in low-income schools there were three in middle-income schools. Finally, school libraries were open approximately three days per week for students in low-income neighborhoods compared with five days a week in middle-income neighborhood schools. School districts need to recognize that investments in school libraries reach all students in the school and that the payoff is improved student achievement.

Similarly, classroom libraries in low-income communities tend to be smaller. Duke (2000) found that classroom libraries in low-income school districts were about 40 percent smaller than those in high-income school districts, with fewer new books being added every year. In high-income neighborhoods there are often many bookstores, a fully stocked library, and books in the homes. Poor neighborhoods are likely to have fewer books and resources in the public library and few, if any, bookstores. As a result, students in high-income areas have four thousand times the number of books available to them as students in low-income areas (Neuman 1999).

ACTIVELY PROMOTE SUMMER READING

We know summer reading is critical to summer learning (Heyns 1978; Kim 2004), yet only 22 percent of the students we studied reported that they continue to read in the summer. Perhaps the first step is to increase access to books and other reading materials in the summer for urban youth. Access to books has been found to be positively associated with the amount of independent reading students do in the summer, yet there is large disparity across socioeconomic status and ethnicity (Ferguson 2002; Kim 2004; Neuman and Celano 2001; Schacter 2003). To address this disparity, school districts might consider keeping school libraries open in the summer—parents could be trained to oversee the libraries—asking private foundations for funding to purchase literacy materials for low-income youth, and developing packets of materials that students can borrow for the summer.

Public libraries can continue to expand their summer reading programs to include initiatives that have been found to be effective with urban teens. For example, book clubs focused on the reading interests of urban teenagers have potential for promoting summer reading. The Teen Street Lit Book Club, for example, formed at one of the branches of the Free Library of Philadelphia, ran for a total of sixteen weeks—four times as long as originally promoted. When asked, "Why do you still want to have the book club?" one teen explained that the book club was fun and "kept them off the streets with something positive to do" (Morris et al. 2006). Programs like this could be offered in the summer at various times during the day and evening.

Another program that has proven extremely popular with urban adolescents is the Free Library of Philadelphia's Teen Author Series (McCaffrey 2005). This program connects adolescents with a Who's Who list of American writers, including minority authors like Ilyasah Shabazz and Julia Alvarez. Adolescents receive free copies of the authors' books and get to interact with the authors as they speak about their books, their lives, and the process of writing.

Write On! a partnership between the University of North Carolina Writing Center and the Durham County Library, is another program that could be adapted to support summer reading. The goal of Write On! is to promote fun, freedom, and focus through the act of writing for teens in grades seven through twelve in order to encourage "intellectual and creative abilities in the company of other teens and with the guidance of writing coaches" (Gregg 2008, 3). Each eight-week session culminates with publication of a book of poetry and an author party where the teens share their writing with their families (see chapter 12 for a detailed discussion).

PARTNER WITH PARENTS TO PROMOTE AND ENCOURAGE LEISURE READING

Studies show that parents are important in developing and sustaining the leisure reading habits of children and adolescents (Kim 2004; Strommen and Mates 2004). Chandler (1999) found that this was particularly true for students from working-class backgrounds, who often experience confusion because of a disconnect between literary experiences at home and school. Effective readers see reading as a recreational activity, something that can be done outside of school for enjoyment. They have homes with books and other reading materials and family members who visibly read frequently. Chandler suggests the following strategies to enlist parents as "literacy-teaching partners" and to create a culture of reading at home: survey or interview parents to gather data that will help you select texts that match the interests/cultures of the students, design family literacy programs in which parents can participate, and invite parents to join literature discussion groups with their children.

BE IN THE STUDENTS' CORNER

Input, stimulation, and encouragement from adults are key factors in helping urban teens develop into successful readers. Alvermann (2001) found that teachers enhance students' sense of competence and self-worth when they are able to convince them that they care about them as individuals and want them to learn. Perhaps more important, the "largest major factor protecting young people from emotional distress, drug abuse, and violence—other than the closeness they were able to achieve within their families—was 'perceived school connectedness'" (Pollack 1998, 250).

Well-trained, caring librarians can also help close the literacy divide. In a study of Philadelphia public libraries, Neuman and Celano (2001) identified five qualities of excellent librarians:

1. They make an effort to know students, call them by their first names, and develop a personal relationship that extends beyond the child to the family.
2. They push students to reach beyond their current abilities and to read beyond their current level.

3. They often do "over-the-shoulder" teaching, helping children as they learn to use computers and as they work on their homework.
4. They do not just point to materials, they teach children how to use the materials.
5. In the most difficult circumstances, they form writing clubs, chess clubs, and reading groups. They plan fieldtrips and other activities to attract and retain their young patrons.

Librarians who adopt these qualities as part of their professional practice can better understand and respond to the unique needs of urban teens.

As Tatum (2005, 153) points out, "There are no simple solutions; one method cannot fix all that needs to be fixed." However, by collaborating with urban teenagers to understand and address their leisure reading interests, librarians can have a transformative effect on their lives and the lives of their families. Giving voice to urban teens—taking seriously their ideas and opinions about leisure reading and literacy—may not only help educators better meet their literacy needs but also empower these teens to take an active role in their educations and in their communities.

Note
1. Aside from the complete study (Hughes-Hassell 2008), the results of part 1 (Hughes-Hassell and Lutz 2006) and part 2 (Hughes-Hassell and Rodge 2007) have been published separately.

CHAPTER 5
STREET LIT
Before You Can Recommend It, You Have to Understand It

VANESSA J. IRVIN MORRIS, WITH DENISE E. AGOSTO AND SANDRA HUGHES-HASSELL

URBAN FICTION ("STREET LIT") is a subgenre of African American literature. It initially gained popularity with readers in the 1970s with authors such as Donald Goines and Iceberg Slim, whose fiction chronicled the realities of inner-city living. In the past decade, this genre experienced a renaissance and gained significant readership among urban African American readers, particularly women ages 18–35 and teenagers ages 14 and up (Morris et al. 2006). The genre claims its literary lineage from pulp fiction, with its melodramatic plot lines, trite characterizations, and scandalous book covers. Some critics question the teen readership of urban fiction because of its graphic depictions of inner-city life, involving drugs, sexual exploits, domestic violence, incarceration, and death.

I have seen firsthand the power of urban fiction in promoting multiple literacy benefits for teen readers, such as enhanced critical analysis skills, the ability to make sociocultural connections between fiction and reality, appreciation for the collaborative writing process, and, perhaps most important, the development of the reading habit. Since 2005 I have been working with inner-city teenagers reading urban fiction novels at a North Philadelphia public library branch. We have formed a teen book club that currently has ten core members, ages 15 and up, grades ten and up. Many of the members have participated over a period of years—discussing, exploring, *and critiquing* their own tastes and understandings of this literary genre that often pushes the limits of socially acceptable norms. In 2007 the book club moved beyond discussing our reading to collaborating on our own urban fiction story. Meeting biweekly for two-hour sessions from September 2007 to March 2008, we were able to shape outlines for protagonists, an antagonist, supporting characters, setting, and plot as a working framework for an urban fiction narrative.

This chapter explains my journey into learning about the literacy benefits of inner-city teens reading street lit in a library book club. It explains the contextual importance of street lit, and through the voices of the teen readers themselves we learn how important the genre is to them as readers of literature, as readers of their lives, and as readers of the world.

MY INTRODUCTION TO STREET LIT

When I was an adult/teen librarian with the Free Library of Philadelphia during the late 1990s into the 2000s, I served in some of the poorest and most crime-ridden neighborhoods of North Philadelphia. It was not unusual to see drug paraphernalia on the sidewalks and in neighborhood parks or to see African American and Latino teens and adults bringing the private (e.g., having sexual relations, doing drugs, acting out domestic disputes) into the public sphere. Teen patrons who frequented the libraries were often malnourished, bad tempered, nervous, anxious, angry, and yet resilient.

The teens who frequented the library were usually latchkey kids looking for a safe haven off the streets after school and on weekends. The kinds of books that were popular with inner-city teens back then were the Sweet Valley High series, Walter Dean Myers's novels such as *Scorpions* and *Monster*, and Sharon Flake's *The Skin I'm In*.

Then one spring day in 2000, an African American teen girl walked into my branch, stood in front of my desk, and the conversation went like this:

Teen: Do you have *The Coldest Winter Ever*?

Me: Who? What? No, I never heard of that book.

Teen: Y'all should get that book. It's really good.

Me: Well, who wrote the book?

Teen: Sister Souljah. You know, the rap lady from that old hip-hop group?

Me: Public Enemy. She was a member of Public Enemy.

Teen: Yeah! HER! You gotta get that book!

I blinked at her. Number one, she was a new patron. I knew the teens who frequented the library, and this girl had never been in my branch before. I was struck by her recommendation; it made me curious about what she knew about this book.

I already had Sister Souljah's autobiography, *No Disrespect*, in the teen collection. It had enjoyed a nice circulation run in urban libraries across the country over the preceding years. Also, I remembered Sister Souljah as a fellow undergraduate in my African studies classes at Rutgers University in the early 1980s. So it was not a hard sell for me to order this new novel of hers. I ordered two copies.

I got the books, processed them, and put them on the shelf. By the end of the next day, both copies were gone. A few weeks later, a group of teen girls came in and asked me, "Do you have *True to the Game*?" I peered at them quizzically and said, "No, never heard of that one." They all oozed:

"Ooooo! You gotta get that book!" So within just a few weeks I was getting kids into the library I had never seen before asking for these novels that I knew nothing about. I ordered two copies of Teri Woods's *True to the Game*, along with two more copies of *The Coldest Winter Ever*. Within three days, all of the books were checked out; none of them ever came back. It was then that I knew that something was going on with inner-city teens and their reading habits, and I was intrigued to understand and to accommodate it.

The next title that was constantly requested was Omar Tyree's *Flyy Girl*. After that it was Shannon Holmes's *B-More Careful*, Solomon Jones's *Pipe Dream*, and Vicki Stringer's *Let That Be the Reason*. Urban fiction was fast becoming a popular genre, bringing in teenagers who had never been to the library before. These teens were knowledgeable about their books and were demanding more, and more, and more. We couldn't order them fast enough. By 2005, I began the Widener Branch Library Urban Fiction Teen Book Club to promote the genre as a cluster collection within the library and to learn what teens were getting out of reading this genre. The club was also my opportunity to learn about the genre through readers' eyes. This meant that I, too, became a reader of urban/street fiction.

MEET THE CLASSIC NOVELS OF URBAN FICTION

I consider *The Coldest Winter Ever*, *True to the Game*, and *Flyy Girl* classics of the street lit genre because they were among the first books on the market within this genre and the first titles to be heavily requested by library patrons in my library and other branch libraries across the city and beyond. Another reason I deem these three titles a "holy trinity" of sorts is that, although they were published almost a decade ago, they are still popular and heavily read by urban readers (and now some suburban readers) today. In Philadelphia, but also in every city or town where I have lectured about this genre, librarians and teachers report that patrons and students are still requesting these same titles.

The Coldest Winter Ever is a tale about a teen girl named Winter Santiaga. She is the daughter of the most successful drug kingpin in Brooklyn during the 1980s. Winter is accustomed to a high lifestyle, which her father easily affords. After the family moves to a Long Island mansion, federal authorities catch up with Mr. Santiaga, who is incarcerated for drug dealing. The mansion and all his other possessions are seized, and the family is left homeless. As her mother succumbs to drug addiction and prostitution and her sisters are absorbed into the foster care system, Winter spends a year trying to live on her own. Ultimately she is framed for a crime she did not commit and is sentenced to twenty-five years in jail.

True to the Game is the love story of Gena and Quadir, two young adults from the inner city who are seeking to make it out of the 'hood. Quadir is a handsome and smart young man who gets caught up in the drug game and becomes the biggest drug dealer in North Philadelphia. They fall in love, and Quadir showers Gena with all the possessions and money she desires.

Unknown to Gena, Quadir is making arrangements to quit the drug game altogether. He hides millions of dollars as his retirement fund but is killed in a shootout at a club on New Year's Eve. Gena finds the safe containing the money and drives into the sunset with millions of dollars in the trunk of her car.

Flyy Girl is the story of Tracy Ellison, a teenage girl coming of age in the middle-class neighborhood of Germantown in Philadelphia. With her parents newly divorced, Tracy has a violent relationship with her mother but an understanding one with her father. She spends her teenage years flirting, dating, and sexing undeserving young men. Life gets even more complicated for Tracy when she meets a drug dealer named Victor, with whom she falls in love. She hides the relationship from her family, seeing the thuggish young man in secret. Victor is jailed for his illegal activities as Tracy graduates from high school. During her freshman year in college, Tracy still pines for Victor, even visiting him in prison. The book ends with Tracy writing a letter to her father admitting her love for Victor.

These titles set the tone for the urban fiction genre as we know it today. All three are still in print and have extended their life spans by morphing into sequels and trilogies. *Flyy Girl* became a trilogy with two subsequent titles: *For the Love of Money* and *Boss Lady* (2005). In November 2007, Teri Woods published the long-awaited sequel to *True to the Game*, *True to the Game II: Gena*; soon after publication it appeared on the *New York Times* Best Sellers list three weeks consecutively. Sister Souljah published *Midnight: A Gangster Love Story*, the long-awaited sequel to *The Coldest Winter Ever*, in 2008.

THE GENRE IN GENERAL

Using Brooks's (2006, 375) conceptualization of African American literature, we can agree that urban fiction is a part of the overarching genre of African American literature because it is predominantly written "both by and about African Americans." Just as Brooks specifies that African American children's literature is a small representation of African American life, the same is true for urban fiction. Street lit is not meant to represent all of African American life. It specifically deals with the harsh everyday realities of lower-class and lower-middle-class inner-city neighborhoods and the various dramatic activities that take place there in the name of survival.

All of these elements are familiar to the inner-city teen reader. They are also familiar to the writers of urban fiction. Sister Souljah was a hip-hop rap artist when *The Coldest Winter Ever* was published in 1999. Teri Woods was an "ex-wifey" (an inner-city drug dealer's girlfriend) and wrote from that stance in *True to the Game*. Omar Tyree was born and grew up in the streets of Philadelphia, and it is this world that he recreates as the setting for *Flyy Girl*. Thus, the tone for the genre begins with the authors and the locations from which they come, as well as with sociocultural stances based on their own past experiences.

TEXTUAL FEATURES OF STREET LIT

In this section I discuss the textual features that serve as a blueprint for the street lit genre, taking inspiration from Brooks's (2006) categorizations as realized in the three classics of street lit described above.

1. Recurring themes
    a. Teen/young adult protagonist
    b. Realistic fiction as bildungsroman
    c. Signifying serializations
    d. Surviving street culture
    e. Exposure to cultural history as a source of pride

2. Formats/packaging
    a. Genre blending (poetry, rap or song lyrics, letters, etc.)
    b. Titles: Double entendres
    c. Moral inclinations: Dedications, notes, and excerpts

3. Linguistic patterns
    a. African American English (AAE)
    b. Regional dialect
    c. Standard English

Reader response theory focuses on the reader as the interpreter of a text, as opposed to focusing on the author's intent. It suggests that readers use their own experiences and knowledge bases to make meaning from written texts, and that meaning varies from reader to reader, just as life experiences and knowledge vary from person to person. By focusing on the readers and their authentic responses to the novels they read, reader response theory serves within this chapter to illustrate how urban teen readers respond to street lit from an *aesthetic stance*, in which they glean personal under-standing and enjoyment from the texts. It also illustrates how they may respond with an *efferent stance*, in which they pull the text, moral render-ings, and cautionary warnings from the stories (Rosenblatt 1996).

RECURRING THEMES

Protagonists

In all three novels, the protagonists are female teens. Many street lit novels have female protagonists, which is possibly why this genre attracts pre-dominantly female readers (Morris et al. 2006). That said, male readership of street lit continues to grow, especially as male hip-hop rap artists are beginning to publish their own urban fiction novels based on their lived experiences, such as 50 Cent's *Blow* and Snoop Dogg's *Love Don't Live Here No More*.

Realistic Fiction as Bildungsroman

Realistic fiction in YA literature is typically about characters coming of age. They generally go through trials and tribulations and emerge socially and morally transformed, usually having learned valuable life lessons. Such stories are also regarded as bildungsromans, a term nearly synonymous with coming of age.

In each of the three classic novels, the protagonist goes through a coming-of-age journey. As with problem novels within the realistic fiction genre, urban fiction tells realistic stories about realistic characters in real places. These kinda-tragic-reality-based realistic stories hit close to home for many of their readers because of the familiarity with the settings, styles of the characters (e.g., hip-hop lingo, name brand clothing popular in the inner city), and themes that are recognizable in everyday life (e.g., going to school, dodging violence in the streets, dramatic family interactions). But it is the protagonists' journey of identity formation that pulls readers into the story and takes them on a journey of aesthetic and efferent stances. In these terms, reading street lit can be said to be a quest for literary pleasure and personal maturation.

Teens' literary responses to these novels take on a "personal act of enjoyment [that] has social and political consequences. . . . Students need to make sense of the literary dimension of their reading experience and to relate it to their extraliterary experience in complex and subtle juxtapositionings between the world of the imagination and the 'real' world, between the ideology of the text and that of the reader's sense of self" (Bogdan 1990, 134).

I have yet to meet a teen girl who has read *The Coldest Winter Ever* and not identified with the protagonist. They see themselves in Winter, or they understand Winter because she is reminiscent of someone they know or see in their daily lives. One book club attendant said, "If I read a book and I'm reading about this girl who is dark-skinned, long, dark hair, clothes like this and like that, I know that is not me. But [then] I *see her* when I'm walking down the street, so [then] I can relate to it."

In *The Coldest Winter Ever*, Winter comes of age by learning at the end of the story that her choices are what land her in jail. Still, her own sense of inadequacy stops her from counseling her sister, Porsche, who has taken on Winter's old ways of being a ghetto princess. Winter decides she will not help her sister by rationalizing:

> I wanted to warn her about certain things in life. Usually I'm not at a loss for words. But I didn't feel good enough to tell her what I really thought. I knew what she would think: "Winter, you're just saying that 'cause you're in jail." . . . "Winter, you're just saying that because you're jealous." So instead of saying what I had learned, what was on the tip of my tongue, I said nothing at all. Hell, I'm not into meddling into other people's business. I definitely don't be making no speeches. . . . She'll learn for herself. That's just the way it is.

In *True to the Game*, Gena goes through many trials and tribulations, such as the murder of her best friend, the isolation her lifestyle imposes, and the death of her love, Quadir. Gena witnesses shootings, funerals, and the rape of a friend as life lessons leading to greater maturity. In this way, urban fiction is accurately mirroring the accelerated maturation process that many inner-city young adults experience in their daily lives. By the end of the story Gena is not as naive as she used to be, and she is a survivalist thinker in terms of what her next steps should be after the death of Quadir. Here Gena's emotional journey is complete, but the author leaves her riding off into the sunset of the unknown. We can see in this bildungsroman technique that, as in *The Coldest Winter Ever*, the author is setting the story to continue as a sequel.

For Tracy Ellison in *Flyy Girl*, the coming-of-age journey begins at the age of 6 and ends when she is a freshman in college. Tracy is focused on her emerging sexuality and the choices she makes to understand her personal power. We see Tracy and her girlfriends date and break up with quite a few young men. Because of a stable family life, Tracy is able to come out on the other side of her adolescent exploits and enter college. Even though she is still smitten by her drug dealer boyfriend, she is able to reflect via a letter to her father on her past mistakes and make plans for her future. Again, the author uses the quest journey as a device to set up the two sequels to the story.

Signifying Serializations

The serialization of street lit has become commonplace within the genre. Though readers had to wait from 1999 to 2007 for a sequel to *True to the Game*, Woods published other titles such as the Dutch series, which was introduced to the reading public as a trilogy. Readers read *Dutch, Dutch II: Angel's Revenge*, and the third installment, *Dutch III: The Finale*. Other popular urban fiction series include T. N. Baker's *Sheisty* and *Still Sheisty, Part 2*; Chunichi's series about her protagonist, Ceazia Devereaux, in *Gangster's Girl, Married to the Game*, and *The Naked Truth*; and short story compilations such as *Around the Way Girls*, vols. 1–4, and *Girls from da Hood*, vols. 1–3. Signifying within a novel that additional installments will come is almost like a game between the authors and readers in terms of gaps that are left in the story to be filled by the readers (Iser 1978); the authors return with new stories to fill in those gaps, and readers can see if they guessed right or wrong, if their imaginations and own authorial intents are in sync with the authors of the texts. It is a constant conversation—a dance, if you will—between author and reader.

This serialization creates a wide community of readers who are having conversations about characters, themes, and plots across regions, dialects, and worldviews. These conversations are being held all over the Internet on website message boards such as www.aalbc.com, www.allreaders.com, and www.streetfiction.org. These conversations are also being held via author panel discussions and group interactions in high school hallways, phone conversations, personal discussions, and other social outlets, like the Widener Library Teen Book Club.

To punctuate this point, I cite a book club meeting at Widener Branch Library in North Philadelphia on November 30, 2007:

> **Ashley:** I've been reading urban fiction for a long time, ever since I was like twelve or thirteen, and it's true that a lot of the stories are the same. You see the same stories over and over again. . . .

Eddie: But it seems to me that in black literature [the authors] are afraid to veer off course, like doing something drastically different with their characters, like having maybe a, I dunno, an anorexic, light-skinned-lookin' boy on the cover.

Interviewer: That's because you're not going to find any anorexic-lookin' light-skinned boys in the 'hood.

Multiple teens: You sure not!

Deena: Maybe one or two! [Laughter]

In this exchange, the teens are critically discussing street lit and connecting books in the genre to what is typically observed in their daily lives in the inner city (in terms of quantity of reflective identities). We can see that Ashley is a "practiced reader" (Harding 1962, 140) of the genre, and that Eddie, who freely admits earlier in the discourse that he is not experienced, indeed is not. Focusing on Ashley's comment, we can see that "the reader discriminates; and this is true even at the low levels of trivial fiction, though there the discriminations may depend on criteria that better educated or more practised readers have discarded" (Harding 1962, 140).

To take it a step further, we can perceive the serialization of urban fiction as a style of signifying, which is described as an African American literary tradition by Gates in the seminal work *The Signifying Monkey* (1988). Gates talks about repetition and revision of black texts as a means of talking to one another in the form of intertextuality. This intertextuality as expressed within the urban fiction genre manifests itself in the form of serialization of stories where the familiar is made strange and "the strange made familiar" (Shklovsky 1966), further inscribing readers with text. This leads authors to produce more texts with familiar characters and stories, which further inscribes readers and the text. Couple this intertextuality of "talking texts" (Gates 1988, 217) with social talk *about the genre*, via avenues such as book clubs, and the contribution of urban fiction to the literacy competencies of its readers becomes clear.

African Americans, via a shared history of cultural discourse, are so familiar with signifying that such a literary performance on the part of African American authors and readers can be said to be intrinsic at various levels of artistic expression (Gates 1988). Signifying on the part of the urban fiction reader within a book club environment can be looked at as a kind of literary response akin to Eeds and Wells's (1989) breakdown of talk that goes on in literature discussion groups: interpreting, hypothesizing, predicting, and verifying. In the Widener Teen Book Club, we are interpreting the genre of street lit. We are also interpreting each other; we hypothesize and mediate authors' intent with our own intent in reading and making sense of the genre. We predict how culture informs literature; we predict action in the story; we even collaborate in writing. We verify individual knowledge into a collective knowledge, especially when the kids are the experts (e.g., on hip-hop culture, the street lit genre). We signify.

Surviving Street Culture

Street culture is evident in all these novels. In *The Coldest Winter Ever*, Winter's story is about her navigation of the streets while trying to recover from her father's incarceration and loss of his drug empire and income. In *True to the Game*, Gena falls in love with Quadir, a young adult African American male who has been a drug lord for a long time and is now trying to retire from the drug game. In *Flyy Girl*, Tracy falls in love with a drug dealer who is ruthless in his treatment of her, yet in her youthful naivety she doesn't see it. All three protagonists have this youthful naivety, bordering on stupidity, in common. Because they delude themselves about the realities of their situations, they make unintelligent choices with dire consequences.

Female book clubbers often question the maturity and intelligence of these kinds of protagonists, responding that they would not make the choices the characters did. Just as in reading other literary genres, Widener book club members use the reading of street lit as an opportunity to *not* engage in living the inner-city life for the moment, and to "perch" and reflect on that life. Britton (1984, 325) sees this reflection as critical for identity formation. He states that by taking up a spectator's role in the reading of literature "we give shape and unity to our lives and extend our experiences in an ordered way." The book clubbers do engage in gossip about their favorite characters at book club meetings. Britton says that gossip is a literary stance in this sense because it is linked with evaluation.

In street lit the stories usually take place during the 1980s and 1990s, coinciding with the upturn of the hip-hop movement and also with the U.S. government's stepped-up drug war (Skolnick 1994). Thus the stories retell instances of drive-by shootings, disenfranchised residents of urban poor communities during the Reagan/Bush era, and the pulse of the hip-hop industry as well as chronicling the aftermath of the civil rights (1960s) and black power (1970s) movements. Our three classic novels are all set during that time frame as well. *The Coldest Winter Ever* is set in the 1990s. *True to the Game* covers a two-year span, from 1988 to 1990. *Flyy Girl* takes place during the 1980s, as illustrated clearly with Tyree's dedication "to all sisters and brothers, in memory of the glamorous and exciting '80s." Iser (1978, 74) notes that literature is a "recodification of social and historical norms," which enables readership to see beyond their usual perceptions of the everyday—even when the book may reflect their everyday experiences (as in street lit). Many street lit authors such as Washida Clark, Vicki Stringer, and Shannon Holmes penned their first novels while serving jail time for drug-related offenses. Thus, they are telling the stories of their lived experiences *in history*.

There is much repetitiveness in urban fiction, with multiple titles having the same themes and plotlines. Following Bogdan's viewpoint, as these kinda-tragic-reality-based stories are crystallized into a literary form they become a cathartic framework, as opposed to a "pessimistic" or stereotyped presentation. Bogdan confirms that "a tragedy helps us to objectify this knowledge and come to terms with it within the safe confines of the imagination" (1990, 111). The Widener book clubbers confirm this notion. They commonly say that urban fiction is valuable to them because "it teaches us what not to do" (Morris 2007, 12).

So, although surviving street culture is a prevalent textual feature of the urban fiction genre, teen readers are not responding to this theme in an aesthetic way, as in "Wow! I want to be a drug dealer or drug addict!"

Rather, they respond to this kinda-tragic-reality-based textual feature in an efferent way, coming to an understanding of "what not to do" (Rosenblatt 1996).

Expressing Cultural History as a Source of Pride

There are many ways in which the protagonists in street lit can be characterized as representing cultural history as a source of pride. In *Flyy Girl*, it is through the influence of the college girls she meets that Tracy learns to appreciate her identity as a young African American woman. She attends cultural functions such as the Black Family National Reunion, where she wears a kinte cloth outfit reminiscent of traditional African attire.

Sister Souljah inserts herself as a character in *The Coldest Winter Ever* to serve as the conduit for exposure to culture as a source of pride. Souljah (the character) lives a moral lifestyle and tries to help Winter by allowing her to live in her ethnically decorated home. Souljah (the character) is a community activist and knows a popular hip-hop artist. Souljah (the character), her sister, and Winter share a large brownstone townhome with another African American woman who is a medical doctor. In this way, Souljah (the author) exposes Winter to cultural history via role models and community involvement to foster cultural pride. Readers bring their own cultural knowledge to what they read. Thus they see aspects of their culture reflected back to them in literature, which serves as a bridge to heightened understanding of self and the world.

As a case in point, at the Widener teen book club meetings I facilitate discussions that bring out members' personas and cultural knowledge, questions, and misunderstandings, which are then connected to texts to serve as a bridge for answering questions. Copenhaver (2001, 346) cites Louise Rosenblatt's admonition: "If we wish young people to participate in literature, we have to be concerned about the world they live in, the experiences they bring to the text. We must offer them works to which something in their own lives, their own preoccupations, and their own linguistic habits can serve as a bridge."

True to the Game incorporates cultural elements via the characterization of Quadir. Woods makes Quadir a fully rounded person, aware that what he is doing is morally wrong. Woods characterizes Quadir as a Black Muslim, one educated in African American history and social politics. At one point in the story we see Quadir musing about the slave history of African Americans and connecting that historical fact to the conditions of inner-city dwellers in the current day of the story. He is anxious to be out of the drug game once and for all, although the storyline does not allow him to reach his goal.

FORMATS/PACKAGING

Genre Blending

One of the most interesting features of the street lit genre is its creative incorporation of different literary forms into the narratives. Poetry, letters, rap and song lyrics, and stream-of-consciousness vignettes are often blended into the stories. Such devices include a letter from Winter's father in chapter 11 of *The Coldest Winter Ever* as well as an exchange of letters between Sister Souljah and Midnight in chapter 16, bringing the epistolary element to the genre. Poetry is featured in *True to the Game*, in which Gena writes romantic poetry to Quadir throughout the story. Stream-of-consciousness snippets are interwoven throughout all three narratives, and Tracy's letter, including a poem to her father, ends the story of *Flyy Girl*.

Titles: Double Entendres

Titles with double meanings are characteristic of street lit. This literary strategy speaks to Gates's (1988, xxv) exploration of "double voicedness" in African American literary tradition. Gates says that double voicedness is another form of signifying with four textual traditions. The double meaning of titles is not new in African American literary tradition, as Gates makes clear. However, whereas African American literary tradition makes a play of its book titles against Western literary tradition by "signifying upon Western etymology" (1988, 221), urban fiction titles signify upon the dialect of African American English (AAE).

For example, the title *The Coldest Winter Ever* initially makes one think of the winter season. In colloquial discourse, *cold* in this context means "unfeeling and heartless," but it can also mean "something awesome or nice; something worthy of hatin'" (www.urbandictionary.com). In the context of the narrative, we see that Winter can indeed be emotionally cold. She is also cold in the "worthy of hatin'" sense early in the story because of her privileged "princess" status. As the story progresses we see how the double consciousness of Winter's coldness affords her a life experience that becomes deprived, leading us full circle to the dominant English meaning of the phrase "the coldest winter ever."

In *True to the Game*, this double voicedness again signifies on African American dialectal discourse. *True* in AAE is synonymous with *yes*, as in "yes to the game," denoting participation in "the game." *Game* means many things in AAE, such as the ability to get sex and the drug trade in the inner city.

The title *Flyy Girl* is a nod toward protagonist Tracy Ellison as a fashionable, high-maintenance, attractive ghetto girl. The word *flyy* in urban slang means "to look good." The phrase "flyy girl" signifies on lower-income African American young adult females who are focused on representing themselves as anything other than poor. This is achieved by meticulous attention to cleanliness, grooming, and fashionable clothing, shoes, hairstyles, and makeup. The extra *y* seems to signify on the traditional word *fly*, as if to ask a list of questions such as "Who is fly?" "What is fly?" "Where are you fly?" "When are you fly?" "How are you fly?" and "Why be fly?" A flurry of identity-forming questions can be presupposed to hint at the foundational theme of *Flyy Girl*, which is the protagonist's identity formation as an African American teen girl coming of age during the decadent 1980s. Other examples of double entendres in street lit titles include *B-More Careful* (Holmes), *Ride or Die* (Jones), *Dime Piece* and *White Lines* (Brown), and *Riding Dirty on I-95* (Turner).

Moral Inclinations: Dedications, Notes, and Excerpts

Critics complain that urban fiction stories are graphic, sensationalistic, and immoral. Still, patterns of moral cautionary messages appear throughout the genre in the form of poetic, foreshadowing dedications (e.g., *The Coldest Winter Ever*), author notes to moralize the story (e.g., *True to the Game*), and chapter excerpts of continuing volumes to show the development of the characters and story (e.g., *Flyy Girl*).

Many novels also provide moralistic insights or characters within the narrative (Wright 2006). In *The Coldest Winter Ever*, the moral tone is realized through the characterizations of Sister Souljah and Midnight. In addition to the author's note at the end of *True to the Game*, morality is actualized throughout the novel via the frustrated musings of the character Gah Git, Gena's grandmother. The lessons in *Flyy Girl* are exemplified via Tracy's appropriation of the character Mercedes' style as a "flyy girl" and Tracy's ultimate reflection and personal turnaround at witnessing Mercedes' downward spiral as a crack addict.

LINGUISTIC PATTERNS

Paralleling hip-hop's evolution from a marginalized youth cultural movement into a mainstream popular cultural commodity, street lit gained its momentum on the streets, out of the car trunks of the authors themselves. Woods popularized entrepreneurial publishing when she independently published *True to the Game* in 1999 and pursued book sales on 125th Street in Harlem as a street vendor (personal communication, 2007). Omar Tyree initially self-published *Flyy Girl* in 1993, but with minimal success until Simon and Schuster offered up the novel in reprint edition in 1996. *The Coldest Winter Ever* was also published by Simon and Schuster in 1999 via its imprint Atria Books.

Indeed, many later street lit authors have created their own best sellers on the streets (e.g., Solomon Jones, Vicki Stringer, and Kevin Weeks). Stringer and Woods were so successful in their entrepreneurial efforts that they went on to found their own publishing companies, Triple Crown Productions and Teri Woods Publishing. Although both are now writers with mainstream publishing imprints (Woods with Grand Central Publishing and Stringer with Simon and Schuster), they still run their publishing companies independently.

This entrepreneurial publishing has entitled authors to total control over their stories, writing them in their own language and presenting the text in their own way. Thus, urban fiction is generally written at least partially in AAE, with variant regional dialectal forms depending on the setting of the story and characters. The editing and literary fluidity may seem off-putting, but this alleged literary "sloppiness" adds to the authentic voice of the author telling the story. In fact, urban fiction is preserving AAE form in text, especially with expressions stemming from hip-hop culture.

One problem with urban fiction entering the mainstream publishing industry is the threat of the loss of authentic AAE. As a case in point, Tracy Brown's first two novels, *Black* and *Dime Piece*, were published by Stringer's Triple Crown Productions. Written in eloquent AAE style with some editing problems, *Black* is a great urban fiction love story about the trials and triumphs of protagonists Kaia and Aaron. Brown's next effort, *Criminal Minded*, was published by mainstream imprint St. Martin's Griffin.

Written in straight American Standard English, the result is a stale presentation compared to Brown's earlier works. As more urban fiction authors enlist with mainstream publishing houses, urban fiction may lose some of the language forms that give it its street quality and authenticity.

CONCLUSIONS

The textual features of urban fiction that Brooks (2006) identified—teen protagonist, bildungsroman, signifying serializations, surviving street culture, exposure to culture, genre blending, titles as double entendre, moral tone, and AAE—are consistently represented in the three street lit classics discussed here. It is this consistency that appeals to the genre's readership, especially urban teens, since the primary features include teen protagonists coming of age in similar settings and speaking similarly dialectal language.

This formula is a natural outcome of the experiences of authors who live or witness some of the experiences they write about. Most of the authors were born, raised, and lived in inner cities or have served time in prison. Discussions of the novels in the genre may actually be an important identity-formation tool that allows urban teen readers space and time to sort out their understandings of the disorganized environments in which they live. Allowing urban fiction to give them that space may be a catalyst for readers moving up and out of that space or, better yet, reorganizing that space.

Teen readers are responding to this genre in a variety of ways. One example is the Widener Teen Book Club. The members who have been attending the club for the past two years have moved beyond just reading the books and discussing how they reflect their own lives. They are now critiquing the books and evaluating the characters' decisions. The book club that started as a reading book club has become a reading, writing, and socially active book club. The members are meeting authors and challenging them in open forums.

These are just a few of the literacy benefits of reading street lit. Does engagement with these texts help urban teens succeed in school? This is an interesting question that we should explore. Do the teen readers go on to read something "better"? Probably not. I have learned from my book club members that they go on to read other genres while continuing to read urban fiction. As a case in point, at one meeting I asked the participants what they were reading now and what they had read in the past six months. The eight teens in the group listed forty-five titles, including science fiction, fantasy, and canonical classics. The titles were not all urban fiction titles. And they were not all required school texts. This indicated leisure-reading practices with the outcome of reinforced situated literacies (Barton et al. 2000).

This story is by no means over. As in the signifying serialization feature of street lit, the research for this genre needs to be sequeled, trilogized, and serialized, until we all understand and appreciate that transgressive literature such as street lit contributes to heightened literacies for its readers. To echo Copenhaver (2001, 356), "The students themselves have much to teach us."

Because the reading of this genre holds much promise for teen readers, it behooves librarians to learn as much as they can about street lit, approaching the genre with a professionalism that sees it as a literature that speaks to its readers in ways that create experiences that become literacy events. Titles should be purchased with knowledge and care about the stories that are told, because these stories are important to many young readers. They are important to their understanding of their environments, and they are important to their understanding of reading. Thus, street lit belongs on library shelves.

CHAPTER 6

URBAN TEENS, ONLINE SOCIAL NETWORKING, AND LIBRARY SERVICES

JUNE ABBAS AND DENISE E. AGOSTO

THE ONLINE SOCIAL NETWORKING trend is huge and growing. In June 2008, social networking websites received more than half a billion unique visits, with Facebook being the most popular and MySpace being the second most popular (www.comscorc.com). Ito et al. (2008) have argued that social networking and other modes of computer-mediated communication are common fixtures in the everyday lives of today's youth. As a result, public and school librarians must consider whether or not they should support their use in the library. In this chapter we discuss what we know so far about adolescents' use of online social networking, provide a snapshot of how public libraries are responding to the social networking trend, and present the results of a pilot study of urban teens and their use of these sites. We conclude with related recommendations for public and school librarians who serve urban teens.

WHAT IS ONLINE SOCIAL NETWORKING?

Online social networking is a relatively new phenomenon. Friendster, MySpace, and Facebook—three sites that have been especially popular with adolescent users—began in 2002, 2003, and 2004, respectively. But what is online social networking? Social networking utilities are a specific category of social technology: "Social technology refers to computer-mediated communication environments that connect people for collaboration, communication, and information sharing. The result is a dynamic online community. Weblogs, wikis, forums, instant messaging and e-mail are all social technologies that facilitate information sharing and online community formation" (Lamb and Johnson 2006, 55).

Each social networking site has a unique community of registered users who create profiles and web pages describing themselves and their interests, read other people's profiles and pages, and communicate with other users via a variety of technologies, including posting messages on friends' pages, e-mailing, instant messaging, blogging, and more.

The heart of social networking sites is the personal profile, which is a part of each user's personal web page. Typically only a small portion of a person's profile or page is open for public viewing, most commonly a user name and possibly a profile picture. After setting up a page, users can invite people to become a "friend." "Friending" someone enables both friends to see the full content of each other's profiles and pages, and friends receive status updates on their pages when their friends change their profiles, add new content such as pictures and blog posts, join new interest groups, and so on. Users often check their pages on a regular basis as a way to learn the latest news about their online friends.

Most people use social networking for building and maintaining relationships with old and new acquaintances and for expressing personal interests and personal opinions about society and the world. For example, users of Facebook can join groups to express their opinions about everything from fashion (by joining groups such as "Advocates for Eliminating Socks with Sandals!!!") to politics (by joining groups such as "I endorse Barack Obama—and I'm telling my friends!") to food (by joining groups such as the "Baked Beans on Toast Appreciation Society"). Often joining these special interest groups goes no further than simply signing up to express an opinion, but sometimes people use them to meet others with similar interests and opinions.

HOW WIDESPREAD IS THE SOCIAL NETWORKING TREND AMONG TEENS?

The popular press has often portrayed social networking utilities such as MySpace as dominated by adolescents, but these sites are popular with adults as well. In a study of MySpace users based on data collected in 2007, Thelwall (2008) found the median age to be 21, with slightly more female than male users. Other sites, such as Webkinz, serve mainly juvenile users and combine game play with social networking. Still other sites, such as Facebook, which was originally restricted to college students, serve a generally older audience. In the case of Facebook, users age 25 and older constitute more than half of the user community (www.comscore.com).

This is not to say that social networking has limited appeal to adolescents—quite the contrary. A 2007 Pew Internet and American Life Project survey found that more than half of U.S. youth ages 12–17 use social networking sites (Lenhart and Madden 2007). It also found that more girls than boys use these sites, and that more older teens than younger teens use them. According to the study, the most common reason for using social networking sites is to maintain existing friendships, with meeting new people coming in as a secondary purpose: "The vast majority of teens who use social networking sites say they use the sites to maintain their *current* friendships, while half report using the sites to make *new* friends" (2007, 5).

This study also found that "the most popular way of communicating via social networking is to post a message to a friend's profile, page, or 'wall'; more than 4 in 5 social network users (84%) have posted messages to a friend's profile or page" (2007, 6). Teens in the study who reported using these technologies reported doing so on a frequent basis, with about half visiting the sites at least once a day.

In the Pew study, MySpace was the most popular site, with 85 percent of responding teens using it more often than any other social networking site. Facebook was the second favorite, but it was the first choice of just 7 percent of the responding teens. No other site was the first choice of more than 2 percent of the respondents, indicating that MySpace had a near monopoly for adolescent users (Lenhart and Madden 2007). In the time since the study was conducted, however, Facebook has gained prominence over MySpace for users of all age groups, so it is possible that it is now more commonly the first choice of a greater percentage of teens.

HOW AND WHY DO TEENS USE SOCIAL NETWORKING SITES?

Since online social networking is a relatively new trend, studies of adolescents' use of these tools are limited. Some studies have examined young adults' motivations for using online social networking, such as the Pew study discussed above, which found maintaining existing relationships to be the most popular reason for use (Lenhart and Madden 2007). In a related study, Boyd examined high school students' use of MySpace; when asked why they used MySpace, respondents said that "the answer is simple: 'Cuz that's where my friends are'" (2007, 9). Boyd concluded that the use of social networking utilities is predominantly to further preexisting relationships with known friends.

Looking at a slightly older user group, Bumgarner (2007) surveyed undergraduate-age Facebook users and found that the most frequent reason for use was social activities. Common social activities included reading friends' profiles, making comments to friends, and looking at friends' photographs. The second most frequent reason for use was as a directory for compiling friends' contact information. In their analysis of research literature dealing with adolescents and online communication, Subrahmanyam and Greenfield (2008, 119) showed that for all kinds of online communication, from instant messaging to blogging to social networking, "adolescents use these communication tools primarily to reinforce existing relationships."

On the basis of interviews with more than eight hundred minors and more than five thousand hours of observing youth interacting online, Ito et al. (2008) came to the same conclusion: the main motivation for using digital communication technologies is to maintain preexisting relationships. Thus, all of these studies indicate that social contact is the prime motivating factor for adolescents' use of social networking sites, and much of this social contact is with existing friends.

WHAT ARE THE BENEFITS AND DRAWBACKS FOR TEENS WHO USE SOCIAL NETWORKING SITES?

Proponents of using online social networking when working with teens often point to its potential for supporting adolescents' healthy socialization: "Teens are particularly drawn to social technology because it meets many of their socialization needs. Young people talk about being unique and different from others, but at the same time they seek affirmation from their friends" (Lamb and Johnson 2006, 55). As Rapacki (2007) has pointed out, teens develop their personal pages as a form of personal expression, which is an important component of defining one's personal identity. Both the design and content of user pages enable self-expression and self-understanding. Rapacki also sees blogging as a modern form of journaling—again, a form of healthy self-exploration and self-expression. Hinduja and Patchin (2008) reinforced this idea of social networking as promoting adolescent identity building.

Ito and colleagues argued that, not only does engaging in online communication help youth learn rules for appropriate social behavior, it also increases their technical literacy and helps them develop self-directed learning skills. They concluded that "participation in the digital age means more than being able to access 'serious' online information and culture; it also means the ability to participate in social and recreational activities online" (2008, 35).

Although the scholarly research into teens' use of social networking is still limited, there have been many reports of adolescent social networking published in the popular news media. Many of these articles have profiled cases of online predators using social networking sites to prey on unsuspecting minors, such as "Sex Offenders Use MySpace, New Jersey Warns Parents" (*New York Times*, July 4, 2007) and "MySpace.com Subject of Connecticut Sex-Assault Probe" (Associated Press, February 6, 2006).

To investigate teen safety on MySpace, Hinduja and Patchin analyzed the content of 1,475 teen MySpace profiles to see how common it was for teens to make publicly available personally identifying information such as phone numbers and addresses. They found that "youth are including a variety of types of information on their public MySpace profiles, but that the vast majority of youth seem to be responsibly using the website. That is, only a small minority included personal or private information. In addition, approximately 40% of adolescents restricted their profiles so that only friends could access their contents" (2008, 140). As a result, these researchers suggested that "the popular media has been quick to demonize MySpace even though an exponentially small proportion of its users have been victimized due to irresponsible or naïve usage of the technology" (2008, 125).

In a related study of adolescent safety online and of identity building online, Livingstone interviewed teens about their use of social networking sites. She noted that "it would be mistaken to conclude that teenagers are unconcerned about their privacy. . . . Teenagers described thoughtful decisions about what, how, and to whom they reveal personal information, drawing their own boundaries about what information to post and what to keep off the site" (2008, 404).

In actuality, the number of dangerous incidents in online social networking communities is extremely small, and using these sites is generally safe, provided that teens are taught what kinds of personal information are safe to post and what kinds are not, and how to deal with potentially risky encounters with others online. Teaching this can be an important task for librarians.

HOW HAVE LIBRARIES RESPONDED TO THE ONLINE SOCIAL NETWORKING TREND?

The popular messages about the frivolous nature and dangers of social networking have in some cases led to adults' restricting teens' access. Many public and school libraries have blocked social networking sites from library computers because of worries that users, especially minors, might put addresses, phone numbers, or other identifying information on their pages, putting themselves at risk. Other school and public librarians who do not support the use of these tools in their libraries view them as lacking educational value.

These arguments are familiar. When e-mail first gained popular usage, many public libraries refused to support its use for the same reasons. Now that e-mail use is overwhelmingly popular and it is a familiar technology to the majority of library users, many public libraries that once blocked e-mail have reversed their decisions and now allow patrons to use library computers for e-mailing. It is possible that this pattern will repeat itself with social networking sites as they gain users and as the general public gains widespread familiarity and comfort with these technologies.

Indeed, the past couple of years have seen an increasing number of public, academic, and even school libraries creating library pages on social networking sites. Some libraries use their pages just for publicity purposes, but others use them as reference portals, for communicating library news and events to users, and for a host of other interactive purposes. For example, the Denver Public Library's MySpace page for teens offers basic information about the library, a virtual bookshelf with recommended titles, a blog, a reference portal, and more. As of mid-April 2009, 956 MySpace users had friended the library's page. The Belmont (New Hampshire) High School Library Facebook page, which features a monthly theme, lists new fiction and nonfiction acquisitions and has both a discussion board and a wall for posting comments. As of mid-April 2009, it boasted 94 fans (users who link the page to their profiles), most of whom were Belmont students.[1]

SNAPSHOT OF PUBLIC LIBRARY USE OF SOCIAL NETWORKING SITES

To gain a better understanding about how public libraries are responding to the social networking trend, and more specifically how they are using social networking with teens, we examined the social networking practices of a sample of public libraries serving small, medium, and large communities; we based our sample on Hennen's (2008) *American Public Library Ratings.*[2]

We examined the websites of the top ten libraries in each of Hennen's ten population categories, ranging from a service population of more than 500,000 to one of under 1,000. Although the size of population served does not directly correspond to the U.S. Census Bureau's definition of *urban,* which is based on population density (U.S. Census Bureau 2007b), it is logical to conclude that most of the libraries in the larger population categories are located in urban areas. (See chapter 1 for a detailed discussion of the definition of *urban.*) We searched these websites for references to library pages on any online social networking utilities. We also searched MySpace and Facebook to see if libraries that did not mention social networking on their websites nonetheless had pages on either of these sites, since they are currently the two largest social networking utilities. The results are presented in table 6.1.

As indicated in table 6.1, 60–80 percent of the larger public libraries reviewed (those serving populations over 100,000) have at least one social networking page on either MySpace or Facebook, with neither MySpace or Facebook dominant. It is interesting to note that all of these public libraries have library websites and at least 90 percent have teen library websites or web pages specifically for teens, but the majority do not have a link on their library websites to their social networking pages.

Social networking sites are used at roughly the same rate for the larger mid-range public libraries but at lower rates for the smaller mid-size libraries and at even lower rates for the smallest public libraries. Looking across the full range of public libraries by size of population served, roughly speaking the larger the population served, the more likely the library is to have a library social networking page on either MySpace or Facebook.

WHAT IS ON PUBLIC LIBRARIES' SOCIAL NETWORKING PAGES? HOW ARE THEY USING THESE TOOLS WITH TEENS?

Some librarians have argued that we can use social networking sites to advertise library services (e.g., Evans 2006) and to teach youth about online safety (Harris 2006). As Harris wrote, "MySpace and other social networking sites are among the fastest growing areas of the Internet. It is unreasonable to think that they'll simply go away. Our best bet is to become part of the conversation and help youngsters make good, safe decisions as they join the online community" (2006, 30).

TABLE 6.1
SNAPSHOT OF PUBLIC LIBRARY SOCIAL NETWORKING BY POPULATION

HAPL LIBRARY POPULATION	SOCIAL NETWORKING CHARACTERISTICS	HAS LIBRARY WEBSITE	HAS TEEN WEBSITE	LINK FROM LIBRARY WEBSITE TO MYSPACE OR FACEBOOK
500,000	80% have social networking 20% no social networking 10% MySpace only 10% Facebook only 60% both 20% teensite on MySpace	100%	100%	60% no links 40% have links 30% of the 40% have links from other social networking pages
250,000	80% have social networking 20% no social networking 10% MySpace only 30% Facebook only 40% both 20% teensite on MySpace	100%	90%	60% no links 40% have links 20% links to both 10% links from teen page
100,000	60% have social networking 40% no social networking 30% MySpace only 10% Facebook only 20% both 10% teensite on MySpace	100%	90%	80% no links 20% links to MySpace only
50,000	80% have social networking 20% no social networking 10% MySpace only 40% Facebook only 30% both 10% teen advisory board on Facebook 10% library book club on Facebook	100%	100%	80% no links 20% have links 10% links from teen page

(cont.)

TABLE 6.1 (cont.)

HAPL LIBRARY POPULATION	SOCIAL NETWORKING CHARACTERISTICS	HAS LIBRARY WEBSITE	HAS TEEN WEBSITE	LINK FROM LIBRARY WEBSITE TO MYSPACE OR FACEBOOK
25,000	70% have social networking 30% no social networking 30% MySpace only 10% Facebook only 30% both 20% teensite on MySpace	100%	90%	60% no links 40% have links 30% links to MySpace only 10% links to both 30% links from teen page
10,000	30% have social networking 70% no social networking 0% MySpace only 20% Facebook only 10% both	100%	90%	90% no links 10% have links
5,000	30% have social networking 70% no social networking 20% MySpace only 10% Facebook only 20% teen or YA social networking	100%	80%	60% no links 40% have links 40% links to MySpace only 20% links from teen page
2,500	0% have social networking	100%	30%	0% have links
1,000	0% have social networking	90%	20%	0% have links
<1,000	0% have social networking	80%	0%	0% have links

Perhaps the strongest reason for supporting social networking in libraries is its great potential for reaching teens (Chu and Meulemans 2008) and for making teens aware of library services. Social networking sites can be used to promote more traditional library services, such as book circulation, as well as online services, such as writing online book reviews. Many authors have set up MySpace pages where they blog about their current projects, let fans discuss their favorite books, and give biographical and other personal information about themselves. Libraries can link to these sites, post recommended book lists, and enable teens to review their favorite titles online—all methods of getting teens excited about reading and using library services.

To explore in detail how a specific sample of public libraries are using social networking sites to connect with users, we used the same public library sample as mentioned above. We combined some of Miller and Jensen's (2007) ideas for connecting with library users via social networking sites with some of the areas addressed in our survey (described below) to put together a list of potentially useful features and services public libraries could add to their social networking pages. We then looked at what features or services for teens these public libraries included on their MySpace and Facebook pages.[3]

Tables 6.2 through 6.5 provide a snapshot of features on these public library social networking pages. The most prevalent features were links to library websites, photos of the libraries and of activities that took place there, video clips of the libraries and library programs, links to other websites of interest to library patrons, blogs maintained by library staff, and announcements of current events being held at the library.

As seen in table 6.2, across the size categories 10–80 percent of the libraries had a link from their library social networking page to the library website. Of the libraries serving more than 100,000, more than half linked the two tools this way, indicating fairly strong linkage between the two types of

TABLE 6.2
FEATURES OF LIBRARY SOCIAL NETWORKING SITES BY POPULATION CATEGORY: TEEN PAGES AND LIBRARY INFORMATION

LIBRARY POPULATION	LINK TO LIBRARY WEBSITE	LINK TO LIBRARY TEEN WEBSITE	DESCRIPTION OF SERVICES	LIBRARY PHOTOS
500,000	70%	30%	30%	80%
250,000	60%	30%	30%	70%
100,000	50%	30%	30%	50%
50,000	80%	10%	20%	60%
25,000	60%	30%	60%	70%
10,000	30%	10%	30%	30%
5,000	10%	20%	10%	30%

online systems. Surprisingly, the majority of the public libraries' social networking pages reviewed did not include separate teen pages, even though social networking is often viewed as dominated by young adult users; on the average across all population categories, only 30 percent had dedicated teen pages. Also of note, only an average of 50 percent across all categories included a link to their other social networking pages, if they had pages on other sites. The percentages of libraries that included descriptions of library services or library photos on their pages varied widely.

Table 6.3 indicates that more than half of the libraries in the largest two categories included video clips on their pages, whereas less than half of those serving 100,000 or fewer included videos. Audio/MP3 files were much less common across the range of libraries. Links to other websites were generally more common.

Looking at table 6.4, a rough trend can be seen for library blogs: generally the larger the population served, the more likely a blog was included. There is less of a size-related trend for library event announcements. Photos and reviews of new books were rare across nearly all of the size categories, indicating that few of these libraries are using their social networking pages to promote traditional book circulation.

Table 6.5 shows that reviews of or information about library databases were even rarer. None of the public library social networking pages reviewed included any at all. Photos of library staff were fairly uncommon as well, and none of the library social networking pages reviewed included a library photo tour.

TABLE 6.3
FEATURES OF LIBRARY SOCIAL NETWORKING SITES BY POPULATION CATEGORY: MULTIMEDIA CONTENT AND EXTERNAL LINKS

LIBRARY POPULATION	VIDEO CLIPS	AUDIO/ MP3	LINKS TO MYSPACE OR FACEBOOK	LINKS TO OTHER WEBSITES
500,000	70%	10%	30%	80%
250,000	50%	20%	50%	70%
100,000	40%	40%	50%	60%
50,000	40%	10%	40%	70%
25,000	40%	10%	30%	70%
10,000	20%	0%	0%	30%
5,000	10%	10%	20%	20%

It appears from this analysis that public libraries in all population categories provide many different features and services on their social networking sites, but they do not focus on teens as their main user group, or even as a unique user group. Chu and Meulemans (2008), Evans (2006), Harris (2006), and Miller and Jensen (2007) present many good ideas for how public libraries can use social networking sites to connect with their adolescent users, but it appears that these ideas have been slow to carry over into practice.

WHAT ABOUT URBAN TEENS AND ONLINE SOCIAL NETWORKS?

The various studies discussed at the beginning of this chapter give us background information about why and how teens use social networking sites, how popular they are, and the library policies surrounding them. The study of library websites shows us how public libraries serving various population sizes are using social networking utilities such as MySpace and Facebook to advertise and deliver their services. But none of these studies addresses issues specific to urban teens and their online social networking behaviors. To learn more about how urban teens in particular are using social networking sites, we undertook a pilot study in which we surveyed teens in two urban public libraries.

This was a small pilot study ($n = 10$) to test the survey questions before giving the survey to a larger population for a full-scale study. Although

TABLE 6.4

FEATURES OF LIBRARY SOCIAL NETWORKING SITES BY POPULATION CATEGORY: LIBRARY NEWS AND BOOK REVIEWS

LIBRARY POPULATION	LIBRARY BLOG	EVENT ANNOUNCEMENTS	PHOTOS OF NEW BOOKS	REVIEWS OF NEW BOOKS
500,000	70%	40%	30%	20%
250,000	70%	50%	0%	0%
100,000	50%	30%	10%	0%
50,000	40%	50%	10%	0%
25,000	50%	30%	10%	0%
10,000	10%	20%	0%	0%
5,000	10%	10%	0%	0%

the findings presented below can shed some light on urban teens' online social networking behaviors, they should not be viewed as being statistically generalizable to the larger population of U.S. urban teens. It is interesting to note that, when the researchers spoke with parents about having their teens participate in the survey, many of the parents reported that their teens did not use social networking sites, because of parental concerns about online predators. Other teens mentioned that they texted their friends and had no need to use social networking to talk with their friends. Only teens who were users of social networking utilities completed the surveys, and their responses must be viewed as representative of online social networking users' behaviors only.

SETTING AND STUDY METHODS

With a 2007 estimated population of 540,321, Oklahoma City ranks thirty-first among the hundred largest U.S. cities (U.S. Census Bureau 2007a) and has a densely populated urban city center. Our survey was conducted in two branches of the Oklahoma City Metropolitan Library system. These branches, located in densely populated city areas, were selected in consultation with the YA coordinator of the library system. According to the system website, the Metropolitan Library System is one of Oklahoma County's premier information, education and entertainment resources. Its seventeen branch libraries serve about 600,000 people.

Data were gathered during two popular teen events: a gaming day and a library lock-in night. Teens ages 12–17 chose between taking the survey on paper, administered onsite, and taking it online at the library or at home.

TABLE 6.5
FEATURES OF LIBRARY SOCIAL NETWORKING SITES BY POPULATION CATEGORY: DATABASES AND LIBRARY PHOTOS

LIBRARY POPULATION	REVIEWS/INFO. ON DATABASES	PHOTOS OF STAFF	LIBRARY PHOTO TOUR
500,000	0%	20%	0%
250,000	0%	60%	0%
100,000	0%	20%	0%
50,000	0%	30%	0%
25,000	0%	20%	0%
10,000	0%	0%	0%
5,000	0%	0%	0%

Survey participation was voluntary and limited to teens who identified themselves as users of social networking utilities. Ten urban teens, nine females and one male, completed the survey. Two of the respondents were 12 years old, five were 13 years old, and three were 15 years old.

FOCUS OF THE STUDY AND FINDINGS

Overall, the focus of the survey was to determine how and why urban teens use social networking sites. Questions were related to the following:

1. The purposes and reasons for which urban teens use online social networking, and the frequency of their use
2. What other media or technologies they use
3. What kinds of activities they engage in when using these sites
4. What types of content they like to add to their own pages
5. What kinds of information they share about themselves on their pages
6. Whom they friend, how they decide to friend someone, and whether or not their friends are people they already know offline before friending them online
7. Whether or not their parents view their pages and, if so, how often
8. Their concerns about their safety or sharing of personal information, as well as what they do if they feel unsafe online

Although the pilot study included only a handful of urban teens, their responses to why they use these sites can give us a partial picture of the motivations for urban teens to use social networking utilities. Reasons for use included "to be with friends," "to talk to friends and to have fun," "It is fun and I can talk about homework or study for a test coming up," to "listen to music," and "to play games." When asked what kinds of things they do when they use social networking sites, the teens reported "chatting with friends" and "working on their own pages" as the top activities, along with "reading friends' pages" and "posting messages for friends."

The teens reported using not just social networking utilities but a wide variety of other information technologies, including communicating via e-mail, chat, and instant messaging; listening to music both online and offline; playing computer or video games; and sending text messages. The majority of the pilot study sample also reported that they had read a book or magazine recently.

The respondents often multitask while using social networking utilities. They indicated that they like to engage in other activities, such as listening to music, instant messaging, reading a book or magazine, doing homework, surfing the Web, watching movies, or texting on a cell phone while using social networking sites.

They reported having the following materials on their social networking pages: text about themselves, message board features, links to friends' pages, chat areas, photos, video clips, audio files, blogs, and links to other websites. On their website these teens like to share information about their hobbies and pets, books they are reading, their likes and dislikes, stories, movies they have seen or want to see, and school-related information.

Rather than limit their online friends to peers, the respondents have a broader base of friends, including parents, grandparents, and other family members. They also reported that they tend to know their friends in person before friending them online, as opposed to meeting them online. The majority of respondents indicated that their parents or guardians reviewed their social networking sites at least monthly.

Some of the study participants expressed concerns about their safety when using these sites or when sharing personal information. When they felt unsafe, they would either tell a parent, tell a friend, unfriend someone, or stop using the social networking site.

These pilot study responses are similar to the findings of the Pew (Lenhart and Madden 2007) and Boyd (2007) studies reported above. Our urban teen participants indicated that many of their activities on social networking sites were focused on communicating with friends, and that social connectivity was the prime reason they use these sites. Based on this very limited pilot study data, it seems that urban teens' online social networking behaviors are similar to those of teens in other demographic groups.

CONCLUSION: WHAT DOES THE SOCIAL NETWORKING TREND MEAN FOR LIBRARY SERVICES TO URBAN TEENS?

Chu and Meulemans (2008) explained that most young adults spend much more time on social networking sites than on library websites, suggesting that librarians can use online social networking to increase library reach and visibility. Social networking sites receive, literally, thousands of times more hits than library websites, and the two biggest, Facebook and MySpace, are two of the most popular sites on the Web. Chu and Meulemans concluded that "these data are a compelling reason . . . to meet students at their technology of choice—their choice is not the library's website" (2008, 70). This is not by any means to suggest abandoning the active creation and maintenance of library websites, but to highlight the fact that libraries need strong representation and services in multiple online arenas. It also suggests that library websites should be linked to libraries' social networking pages to offer increased online access points and to offer users multiple ways to interact online with their libraries.

A school or public library with a library website, library blog, MySpace page, or Facebook profile is a library that has moved into the Library 2.0 world. Bolan and colleagues have pointed out that moving toward a Library 2.0 format, that is, a format that involves patron interaction as well as patron creation and management of library information, means placing increasing trust in patrons. It also means giving some of the control over library content to users. "Essentially, librarians have to listen more, trust more, and be willing to relinquish some control to allow customers of all ages and backgrounds to have the best library experience possible" (2007, 41).

THE IMPORTANCE OF ONLINE UPKEEP AND MAINTENANCE

Creating a library profile is just the first step in using a social networking site to serve school, public, or academic library patrons. These tools are not static information resources. They require frequent monitoring, revision, and updating. The content should be kept current, and it should change as library events and library patrons' needs change. But what should a library do with a library page on a social networking site after it has been created? Miller and Jensen (2007) offer suggestions for academic libraries interested in using Facebook to connect with undergraduate students, and these suggestions can be applied to school and public libraries as well. They point out that, although many Facebook users are willing to join special interest groups to express an opinion or an allegiance, most users rarely return to group pages after initially joining them. These pages are consequently poor choices for library promotion and services. More effective, according to Miller and Jensen, is for libraries to set up profiles and then add friends:

> You have to connect with your patrons before you can effectively promote your services to them. Fortunately, there are a variety of ways to build your community on Facebook. We recommend the following:
>
> - Friend all of the student workers at your library. This will make you more visible to them and their Friends.
> - Facebook allows students to list their courses. Join the ones you are doing instructional sessions for and ask all of the students in them to be your Friend.
> - Display your Profile during instructional sessions and invite students to seek you out.
> - Friend new students at your fall welcome festival by making a laptop available or by taking names on a sheet of paper. Remember, many freshmen sign up for a Facebook Profile as soon as they receive their e-mail address at orientation. (2007, 20)

Miller and Jensen (2007, 20–21) also list ideas for librarians interested in getting started in promoting their services using Facebook, including posting descriptions of new databases or other new resources, uploading the library's blog, announcing upcoming library programs and events, posting photos of new books, posting staff photos and contact information, and creating a library photo tour.

The important point here is that merely creating a social networking page or profile is not enough to attract and maintain users. The library must also actively seek out users and provide them with reasons for wanting to use the library's online services.

A NEW ROLE FOR LIBRARIANS: PROMOTING TEENS' ONLINE SAFETY

Social networking is an important part of the healthy socialization process for many of today's teens, but online encounters can also be dangerous. Librarians can use their knowledge of responsible information practices to help teens become safer users. Some of this responsibility lies with the companies that host these utilities, some of which have taken increased safety measures. For example, the minimum user age for MySpace is 13 years, and users ages 13–15 are required to set their profiles as private (viewable only by friends, not the general public). All the same, most of the responsibility of teaching teens safe online practices falls to parents and adult intermediaries. Hinduja and Patchin note that

> adults can reduce the possibility of youth victimization [online] in multiple ways. These include supervising adolescents online whenever possible, promoting awareness of online safety and ethical use of computers and the Internet, and investigating incidents that are potentially injurious. Additionally, parents, educators, and other adults in supervisory capacities should work with teenagers to cultivate self-control, tolerance, and respect, as well as to learn conflict avoidance and de-escalation techniques. (2008, 139)

School, public, and academic librarians can do this, especially in urban settings where youth may encounter unfamiliar people on a daily basis and be more likely to friend them online.

As Lamb and Johnson (2006, 57) have said, "Social networks are something that educators cannot ignore. They have become part of the culture of young people." Librarians interested in serving teens—urban teens in particular—have much to gain from making them part of the library culture as well.

Notes

1. See the Denver Public Library's MySpace page for teens at www.myspace.com/denver_evolver, and the Belmont High School Library Facebook page at www.facebook.com/pages/Belmont-NH/Belmont-High-School-Library/19239766464.
2. We realize that the Hennen findings—the HAPL report, as they are often called—have been criticized by the some in the library community, who say that Hennen's methods for rating library services are flawed and that his selection of the "best" public libraries is inaccurate. We are neither validating nor disavowing his findings. We are simply using the ratings as a method of identifying libraries that serve a range of population sizes. To read more about the HAPL report, see www.haplr-index.com/HAPLR08_CorrectedVersionOctober8_2008.pdf.
3. For the purpose of this analysis, the population categories of 2,500, 1,000, and under 1,000 were not included, since the libraries in these categories did not have pages on social networking sites.

CHAPTER 7
URBAN TEENS AND THEIR USE OF PUBLIC LIBRARIES

DENISE E. AGOSTO

NEARLY ALL URBAN AREAS of the United States are served by public libraries, and many of these libraries offer targeted resources and services for young adults. But are we doing enough to support the full range of developmental roles that public libraries can fulfill in urban teens' lives? We cannot answer this question without knowing why teens choose to use to public libraries in the first place, but research on the topic is spotty. For many years, librarians have assumed that teens' two major reasons for public library use are schoolwork and leisure reading. It is possible that these are but a few uses in a much wider array that public libraries can support.

In this chapter I review the research relating to teens and public library use and report the results of a survey that asked urban teen public library users why they use public libraries. I then offer suggestions for librarians interested in expanding their support of urban adolescent development beyond just schoolwork and leisure reading into many other areas of urban teen life.

WHAT THE RESEARCH TELLS US ABOUT PUBLIC LIBRARY USE IN GENERAL

What do we know about why people of all ages use public libraries? Many studies have asked *how often* people use public libraries, but fewer studies have asked *why* they use them. A 2007 Pew Internet Life Project/University of Illinois survey showed that 53 percent of adults in this country had visited a public library during the prior year (Estabrook et al. 2007). In characterizing public library roles, the study focused on the public library as an information provider and on adults' use of library resources to address specific information problems, leaving the question of other reasons for library use largely unanswered.

This assumption that information needs—and reading and books in particular—are the driving force behind public library use is common. Wilson (2004, 28) explained, "It is a given that reading is fundamental to the business that libraries provide." Scrogham (2006) suggested that the future success of the public library in the United States depends on a continuing commitment to the library as a place for reading, for books, and for exchanging ideas.

It seems that the public agrees with this view of public libraries as book providers first and foremost. A 2005 OCLC survey of public attitudes toward libraries showed that the public overwhelmingly equates public libraries with books. The report concluded, "'Books' is the library brand. There is no runner-up" (OCLC 2005, 7-3). Certainly reading and information are fundamental to public library services, but there may well be other important functions for public libraries in their communities. Assuming that the public will mainly use libraries for information-related services is a backward approach to library planning. More effective planning would entail first asking people why they use libraries (and how they would like to use libraries if they could), and then designing services and programs to meet those needs and wishes.

WHAT THE RESEARCH TELLS US ABOUT TEENS' PUBLIC LIBRARY USE

There has been equally limited research regarding teens and their reasons for public library use. The bulk of what has been done points to teens' use of public libraries to check out books and other library materials, to gather information to support their schoolwork, and to use computers and other library technologies for information access. For example, Vavrek (2004) surveyed teens about their use of public libraries and found that their primary reason was to borrow books and other materials. Similarly, Bishop and Bauer (2002) found the top three reasons to be for research, for volunteer work, and for Internet use. Cook et al. (2005), surveying six hundred teens, learned that they visit public libraries for research purposes, to check out books, and to enjoy the restaurants. They found positive perceptions of libraries to decline as teens age, and they found girls to rate library services more positively than boys.

These studies might at first glance seem to represent an array of different roles that the public library plays in teens' lives. Looking at them more closely, however, shows that they focus predominately on teens' use of public libraries for information-gathering purposes.

A few studies have considered why some teens do *not* use libraries. They have produced evidence that teens tend to think of libraries just as information providers, and that some teens prefer to use the Internet to look for information. For example, Barack and Kenney (2006) reported that about one-sixth of respondents to a YALSA survey never used their public or school libraries. Many of the teens reported preferring to use the

Internet for information. Similarly, Abbas and colleagues found that the primary reason middle and high school youth did not use libraries was that they preferred to use the Internet to find information. Other top reasons included "I don't like having to return things," "I don't like to read," "Public library too far away to get to," and "I prefer to use the school library" (Abbas et al. 2008, 81).

WHAT THE RESEARCH TELLS US ABOUT URBAN TEENS' PUBLIC LIBRARY USE

Even less research has focused on the reasons urban teens use public libraries. As a part of the Public Libraries as Partners in Youth Development project, Meyers (1999) interviewed teens at urban public libraries about their views of libraries and librarians. She concluded that most teens thought of public libraries as unwelcoming and "uncool," keeping them from becoming more frequent library users.

My study with Sandra Hughes-Hassell (Agosto and Hughes-Hassell 2005) produced similar findings (see chapter 3 for details). We studied two groups of urban teens in Philadelphia. One group worked part-time at the Free Library of Philadelphia as homework helpers and programming assistants. The other group had no formal relationship with the library system. Surprisingly, the two groups expressed equally negative opinions of public libraries and public librarians, opinions that prevented them from using library services more fully. The teens felt that the libraries welcomed children and adults, but not adolescents. One of the Free Library student employees said:

> My personal opinion of the library? I do real well in school, but I never really had to go to the library. They should make it so it would welcome not only children but also teens. Because the children's section doesn't have much for us. [I wish they would] make it so it's not only for children. I never went to the library until I started working here. I couldn't remember the last time I went to the library for my own personal use.

These urban teens were also turned off by what they viewed as outdated library décor, excessively strict rules for library behavior, unfriendly staff, and a lack of books and other materials reflecting their own cultural backgrounds.

Kimball and colleagues asked more than four thousand students in grades five through twelve in the Buffalo, New York, area questions about their library and Internet use habits. The results showed that urban youth use public libraries somewhat less often than their rural and suburban counterparts, but that the urban youth who do use public libraries do so more frequently than rural or suburban youth. Survey respondents were asked to choose what they might do while in the library. Of the thirteen choices provided, all referred to information seeking and use except one: "attend library programs and exhibits." The five most frequently selected choices were "do research for school paper or project," "borrow books to read for fun," "study or work on homework assignment," "use reference materials such as dictionaries or encyclopedia," and "use computer, go online, or use the Internet" (Kimball et al. 2007, 54).

A SURVEY OF URBAN TEENS' PUBLIC LIBRARY USE

Against this backdrop, I designed a survey to investigate two main questions: (1) Why do urban teens use public libraries? (2) How can public libraries expand their services to better meet urban teens' needs? It was distributed to one hundred teens ages 14–17 at two urban public libraries. Part One of the survey included basic demographic questions concerning age, sex, frequency of public library use, frequency of school library use, and availability of home computer access. Part Two included three open-ended questions: "Why did you come to the library today?" "What kinds of information do you look for at the library?" and "What kinds of information do you need that you can't find at the library?" Part Three listed areas of information that teens might need and asked how well their public library could meet their information needs in each area. In this chapter I summarize the results of Part One to supply background information on the survey respondents, then focus on the question "Why did you come to the library today?" For a discussion of the remainder of the survey, see Agosto et al. (2007).

TWO URBAN PUBLIC LIBRARIES

The two urban public libraries were the Elizabeth Public Library, in Elizabeth, New Jersey, and the Sellers Memorial Free Public Library, in Upper Darby, Pennsylvania. Both areas are urban by U.S. Census Bureau standards and are densely populated throughout. With a population of 129,337, Elizabeth is the fourth largest city in New Jersey.[1] It is located 15 miles southwest of New York City. Its diverse population is an estimated 57 percent Hispanic and 20 percent African American. Slightly over half of the population is foreign born, and nearly three-quarters (72 percent) speak a language other than English at home. The median annual family income is $43,285, about 26 percent lower than the $58,526 national average. With its proximity to New York City, Elizabeth is an expensive place to live. The median home value is $385,100, more than twice the national average of $185,200. Elizabeth is therefore a very diverse community with a high proportion of English-language learners and a below-average typical income level.

The Elizabeth Public Library has one main library and three branches to serve this highly diverse urban community. Although the library's website and newsletters are written in English, the library does offer bilingual materials within the collection as well as a Spanish/English bilingual story hour and homework help in Spanish. The library website also includes links to the U.S. Immigration and Naturalization Service and links to common questions asked on U.S. citizenship exams. The survey was administrated in the main library, which employs a full-time librarian to supervise adult and teen services. The Elizabeth Public Library offers a wide variety of YA programs, including author visits, an anime club, and a teen advisory council.

Upper Darby, Pennsylvania, is 6 miles west of Philadelphia and has a population of 84,113. Its residents are an estimated 21 percent African American, 9 percent Asian, and 2 percent Hispanic. Just 15 percent of the population is foreign born, and 20 percent speak a language other than English at home. Across the nation, Americans are 13 percent foreign born, and 20 percent speak a language other than English at home, figures that closely mirror Upper Darby residents. Housing prices in Upper Darby average less than half of those in Elizabeth at an estimated $149,600, yet the median annual family income is $60,997, about 40 percent higher than in Elizabeth. Thus, both Elizabeth and Upper Darby are densely populated and located close to a major U.S. city, but Upper Darby's population is somewhat less diverse and somewhat better off economically than that of Elizabeth.

The Sellers Memorial Free Public Library has a main library and two branches. The survey was distributed in the main library, which employs a full-time YA librarian. The Sellers library offers several programs for teens, including a teen blog, a knitting club, and a teen advisory board.

The surveys were distributed to one hundred teens who were visiting the two libraries. Of the one hundred surveys, ninety-seven usable surveys were returned, for a 97 percent return rate. Although the two libraries serve populations that vary somewhat in basic demographic characteristics, the most notable difference being the large immigrant population in Elizabeth, there was little overall difference in the responses of the two groups of teens. Since teens at both libraries tended to use the two libraries for the same reasons, their responses are combined here for discussion.

WHO WERE THE TEENS IN THE SURVEY?

More girls than boys chose to complete the surveys. Of the 97 respondents, 54 (56 percent) were female and 43 (44 percent) were male. Accurate statistics are not available for the two libraries, but librarians at both libraries estimate that slightly more teen girls than boys use their services. The teens ranged in age from 14 to 17, with age 14 being the most common.

The teens were asked to select their frequency of public and school library use from four choices: "about once a week," "about once a month," "a few times a year," and "almost never." Table 7.1 summarizes their responses. Nearly all (97 percent) of the respondents reported using public libraries at least a few times a year, whereas only 65 percent reported using school libraries at least a few times a year. These figures indicate that the respondents tended to be frequent public library users, more frequent users as a group than the average U.S. teen. As a point of comparison, in the Kimball et al. (2007) survey of students in grades five through twelve in Buffalo, New York, just 69.5 percent of the students surveyed visited a public library during the previous year. It is not surprising that the current study found a higher average rate of public library use, given that the survey respondents were recruited within public libraries.

It is also not surprising that these teens reported much higher public library use than school library use, again because the study took place in a public library. There was also some gender-based variance in the reporting of library use, with the girls tending to use both public and school libraries slightly more often than the boys.

Seventy-six respondents (78 percent) indicated that they had access to a computer at home. This number is somewhat lower than the Kaiser Family Foundation estimate that 86 percent of 8- to 18-year-olds have access to a computer at home (Rideout et al. 2005, 10). This lower figure may reflect the lower-than-average economic status of the Elizabeth area, since fewer teens in Elizabeth reported having computers at home than teens from the wealthier Upper Darby. Or it may reflect the fact that some teens who did not have access to a home computer had gone to the library for access.

WHY DID THE TEENS USE PUBLIC LIBRARIES?

The question "Why did you come to the library today?" resulted in a wide range of responses from the teens, many of whom gave more than one reason. For example, one of the boys wrote that he had gone to the library "for a TAB [Teen Advisory Board] meeting and for borrowing books." One of the girls wrote that she had gone to the library "to go over the play and to watch a movie for the teen summer program." Multiple reasons within single answers were separated and counted individually, for a total of 163 reasons for library use.

TABLE 7.1
FREQUENCY OF LIBRARY USE

RESPONSE	PUBLIC LIBRARY NUMBER (%)*	SCHOOL LIBRARY NUMBER (%)*
About once a week	67 (69)	17 (18)
About once a month	14 (14)	27 (28)
A few times a year	13 (13)	18 (19)
Almost never	3 (3)	35 (36)

*Percentages do not total 100 due to rounding.

To analyze the responses, I first put all 163 answers into a simple database. I then used the constant comparative method (Glaser and Strauss 1967; Lincoln and Guba 1985) to organize the various reasons into groups. Also called "the cut and paste technique" (Stewart and Shamdasani 1990), the constant comparative method involves repeatedly reading through a set of data and cutting and pasting individual pieces of data into multiple sets of smaller groups until the set of groups that best answers the research questions is found. This set of groups becomes the coding scheme, and a model or other answer to the research questions is built from the resulting coding scheme.

After repeated rounds of analysis, I found that the best fit of the data to the research question "Why do urban teens use public libraries?" involved separating the 163 survey responses into thirty-one unique reasons for library visits, listed in figure 7.1. The numbers in parentheses after each

---

FIGURE 7.1
CODING SCHEME 1: INDIVIDUAL REASONS FOR LIBRARY VISITS

To participate in library club meetings (25)
To check out/return books (20)
To attend library programs/events (12)
To read books/magazines at the library (11)
To check out books for personal interest/needs (8)
To read books/magazines for personal interest/needs at the library (8)
To use computers (8)
To browse books/To see what new books are available (6)
To do homework (5)
To do volunteer work (5)
To socialize with friends (5)
To visit a librarian/library employee (5)
To find books for homework (4)
To make new friends (4)
To play computer games (4)
To find a safe environment (3)
To have fun (3)
To research a personal hobby/interest (3)
To socialize with boyfriend/girlfriend (3)
To use computers for homework (3)
To use computers for personal interest/needs (3)
To accompany friends (2)
To do research related to homework assignments (2)
To find a quiet environment (2)
To gain knowledge (2)
To get computer game codes (2)
To get academic tutoring (1)
To get unspecified information (1)
To improve oneself (1)
To please one's parents/guardians (1)
To work in the library (1)

library visit reason indicate the number of times each reason appeared among the 163 total reasons. For example, I separated the response "For a TAB meeting and for borrowing books" into two reasons for visiting the library: to attend the TAB meeting, and to borrow books. These two reasons fell into two of the thirty-one library visit reasons: "To participate in library club meetings" and "To check out/return books."

I then collapsed these thirty-one reasons into eleven categories of reasons for library visits (figure 7.2). Some of these eleven categories represent traditional uses of public libraries, such as using libraries for information related to schoolwork. Others are less traditional, such as using libraries for interaction with peers.

Although each of these eleven categories can be used for planning and developing library services and programs, they fall short of providing a model of the roles of public libraries in teens' lives. The final step in the data analysis process involved creating such a model. I continued to analyze the data, grouping the eleven categories by broader theme, and uncovered three main roles of the public library in urban teens' lives. I arranged these three library roles and the eleven library visit categories into a visual model, as shown in figure 7.3.

THE LIBRARY AS INFORMATION GATEWAY

Of the 163 total reasons for library visits, 52 percent corresponded to the *library as information gateway*, making it the most common role of the public library for these teens. This role refers to the library as provider of information and information access, from book circulation, to Internet and database access, to reference services, and so on.

Common activities under the library as information gateway included checking out and returning books, using library computers to look for homework-related and personal-interest information, reading books and magazines, and seeking homework assistance. For example, one teen wrote that she had gone to the library "to read magazines." One of the boys had visited his library "to do some researching on the computer."

FIGURE 7.2
CODING SCHEME 2: LIBRARY VISIT CATEGORIES

TEENS USED THE LIBRARIES:
  For information related to unspecified needs (40)
  For organized entertainment (37)
  For information related to personal interests/needs (30)
  For information related to schoolwork (15)
  For interaction with peers (14)
  For unorganized entertainment (7)
  For refuge (5)
  For community improvement (5)
  For interaction with library staff (5)
  For personal improvement (4)
  For financial support (1)

Within the library as information gateway, the most commonly reported category of library use involved looking for information related to unspecified needs (40 of 85 responses, or 47 percent). These reasons included "To check out books," "To get information off of the computer," "To read some good books," and so on. In these cases the teens briefly described the information-related activities in which they planned to engage, but they did not explain why they wanted information or what they planned to do with it.

The next most commonly reported use of the library as information gateway was to get information related to personal interests/needs (30 of 85 responses, or 35 percent). In these cases, teens wrote that they wanted "to find a good book to read this weekend," or that they wanted information related to hobbies and interests such as photographs of their favorite celebrities, computer game codes, music lyrics, and other similar items.

The remainder of the reasons for using the library as an information gateway described gathering information related to schoolwork (15 of 85 responses, or 18 percent). For example, one teen had gone to the library "to use the Internet to do a summer assignment." Another needed "to work on [his] AP English assignment." Still another wanted "to find a book for [her] summer reading assignment."

Of the three major library roles, this first one most closely corresponds to the traditional view of public libraries as information sources. But focusing on it alone is not enough to provide full service to young adults.

THE LIBRARY AS SOCIAL INTERACTION/ ENTERTAINMENT SPACE

Of the 163 total responses, 63 (39 percent) corresponded to the *library as social interaction/entertainment space*. In *Serving Urban Teens* (2008), Brehm-Heeger pointed out that urban teens use public libraries not just as

---

FIGURE 7.3
THE ROLE OF THE PUBLIC LIBRARY IN TEENS' LIVES

LIBRARY AS INFORMATION GATEWAY
 information for unspecified needs
 information for personal interests/needs
 information for schoolwork needs

LIBRARY AS SOCIAL INTERACTION/ENTERTAINMENT SPACE
 organized entertainment
 interaction with peers
 unorganized entertainment
 interaction with library staff

LIBRARY AS BENEFICIAL PHYSICAL ENVIRONMENT
 refuge
 community improvement
 personal improvement
 financial support

homework resources but as social gathering places. Indeed, for the teens completing this survey the libraries served almost as frequently as space for social interaction and entertainment as a place to seek information.

Responses corresponding to this library role involved creating and maintaining social relationships or simply seeking out opportunities for amusement. Common activities included participating in library club meetings, attending library programs and events, using the library as a place to socialize with friends, going to the library to meet new friends, using the library as a place to meet with boyfriends or girlfriends, playing computer games at the library, and going to the library to socialize with library employees. As one of the girls wrote, she went to the library "cuz I wanted to see my boyfriend and talk to my friends." Another one of the girls wrote that she "came to the library today so that I can have fun and meet new people."

Within the role of the library as social interaction/entertainment space, the most common category of library use was for organized entertainment (37 of 63 responses, or 59 percent). These reasons involved going to the libraries to attend programs and special events. For example, one teen had gone to the library "to watch a movie." Another was "there for a weekly meeting of the knitting/crocheting club."

The second most common category of reasons falling under this library role was for interaction with peers (14 of 63 responses, or 22 percent). These responses involved using libraries as a social meeting place, such as visiting the library "to meet my friends," "to hang out with my boyfriend," "to have fun and meet new people," and "to talk with my friends."

The third most commonly listed library use involved using the libraries for unorganized entertainment (7 of 63 responses, or 11 percent). These responses dealt with going to the library for entertainment purposes, but not to attend a scheduled library event. For example, teens wrote that they had gone to the library "to play on the computer and read anime books," "to play games," and "to look for a movie to watch."

The final category of library use as social interaction/entertainment space was the most unexpected: teens going to their libraries to engage in interaction with library staff members (5 of 63 responses, or 8 percent). For instance, one girl wrote that she had gone to the library to see the YA librarian, whom she mentioned by name and called her "Mommy #2." Three other respondents also identified their YA librarians by name, as in writing, "I came today to visit [librarian's name]."

THE LIBRARY AS BENEFICIAL PHYSICAL ENVIRONMENT

Of the 163 total responses, 15 (9 percent) corresponded to the *library as beneficial physical environment*; that is, nearly one out of every ten survey responses indicated that they went to their libraries to take advantage of the physical library, as opposed to seeking information, social interaction, or entertainment. Librarians should view the concept of the library as beneficial environment as a reminder that for urban teens the library building itself is an important resource.

One-third of the responses corresponding to this role fell into the category of using the library for refuge (5 of 15 responses, or 33 percent). These teens had gone to the library seeking to escape dangerous home environments, to flee unpleasant conditions at home, or to get away from noisy conditions elsewhere. For example, one of the boys wrote that he "love[s] to read and love[s] the library. It is a quiet place to get away from family." Another sought "a safe place to go after school."

The idea of public libraries as safe places has engendered controversy among librarians and library researchers. Most notably, Bernier (2003, 198–199) rejected the idea of public libraries as safe places: "Libraries cannot deliver safe spaces any better than we can insure that wisdom will come to those reading our collections. And we should not promise that we can." Although it is true that public libraries can never be entirely safe places, these adolescents felt that their libraries were safer than their homes, or safer than other places they could go during nonschool hours. For this reason, librarians should work to make their libraries as safe as possible with the help of community groups such as police and fire departments.

Another third of the answers falling under this role referred to teens' using their public libraries for community improvement by doing volunteer work there (5 of 15 responses, or 33 percent). As one boy wrote, "I came to help. I came for volunteering."

Still other respondents used the library for personal improvement (4 of 15 responses, or 27 percent), that is, as a place to gain personal knowledge. For example, one of the girls wrote that she had gone to the library that day "to improve [her] reading and communication skills." Another wrote that he was hoping to "advance [his] learning."

Finally, one of the teens was using the library as a place of employment and a means of financial support (1 of 15 responses, or 7 percent). She wrote that she had gone to the library "to come to work and earn some money."

WHAT DOES IT MEAN FOR LIBRARIANS?
RECOMMENDATIONS FOR PUBLIC LIBRARIES SERVING URBAN TEENS

Above all, public librarians should remember that urban teens use libraries for many reasons beyond just schoolwork and leisure reading. Looking back at the model of teen development discussed in chapter 3, we recall that there are seven major areas of teen development: the social self, the emotional self, the reflective self, the physical self, the creative self, the cognitive self, and the sexual self. The traditional view of the public library as an information resource clearly supports the development of the cognitive self, and it supports development of most of the other "selves" in part as well. But to support all seven areas of teen development to the fullest extent possible, librarians must broaden their views of public libraries beyond just that of information providers. We should think of our libraries as combined information gateways, social interaction/entertainment spaces, and beneficial physical environments, and we should think of them as important resources for supporting the broad range of teens' developmental needs, needs that extend beyond just schoolwork and leisure reading.

Public librarians who would like to support the fuller range of urban teens' developmental needs but are not sure how to go about it can use the model presented here as a guide for planning and delivering library services and programs. The next sections offer programming and service examples for each of the areas of the model presented in figure 7.3.

THE LIBRARY AS INFORMATION GATEWAY

Urban teens' use of the library as an information gateway reminds us that we must continue to make information and literacy services a cornerstone of public library service. Just like teens in any other situation, urban teens need and deserve access to high-quality information resources and services.

In addition to developing and maintaining high-quality collections of books, magazines, DVDs, audio materials, databases, and other computer resources, we should also provide literacy support services for teens. Examples of these services include read-alouds and readers' theater programs, tutoring help, hi-lo reading materials, and computer literacy classes.

Keep in mind that when creating and maintaining library collections for urban teens it is also important to include a wealth of culturally relevant information resources. This is especially crucial in urban areas with significant foreign-born populations, especially those with language difficulties. Teens from other cultures can find interpreting materials representing the predominant U.S. culture difficult. As Sandra Hughes-Hassell and I once wrote:

> The most responsive collections include not only multicultural books, but a wide range of materials including newspapers from the students' countries of birth, bilingual books and videos, music, English-language translations of stories from students' countries/cultures of birth, and links to websites that are culturally relevant and, if available, written in their native languages. (Agosto and Hughes-Hassell 2007, 145)

A diverse collection is also important for teaching all teens about our diverse world and for promoting tolerance of diversity. Diversity of materials applies to both fiction and nonfiction items, and to all media formats as well. The Web is an easily accessible, fertile source of authentic information representing all types of cultures. Librarians can create pathfinders that link to sets of resources from different cultures to bolster the multicultural offerings within their collections, and they can link these pathfinders to the library's website for easy access.

Urban librarians should also check their websites to make sure that they offer links to resources in all three of the information gateway subcategories: information for unspecified needs, information for personal interests/needs, and information for schoolwork needs. A web page offering access to resources related to information for unspecified needs might include basic information about library policies and procedures of special interest to teens, such as how to get a library card and whether parents or guardians can look at teens' library records.

To create a web page linking to resources relating to information for personal interests/needs, librarians can distribute short surveys within the library asking teens about their hobbies and interests. A simple three-question survey that asks, "What kinds of things do you like to do?" "What kinds of materials do you like to read?" and "What kinds of topics do you like to learn about at the library?" can produce a wealth of information about teens' personal interests. Librarians can then search for high-quality books, magazines, websites, and other resources related to these topics and create links to them on the library's website.

Even better is to create pathfinders on popular topics. Pathfinders are annotated bibliographies that briefly introduce a topic, such as skateboarding or science fiction, and then provide tips for searching for information related to the topic and suggest books, magazines, websites, and so forth, on the topic. They offer those interested in learning about a topic a place to start and guidance in investigating that topic.[2]

Finally, careful collection maintenance and frequent weeding are crucial for increasing teen use of the library as an information gateway. Out-of-date, torn magazines and books and dead links on the library's website are turn-offs not just to teens but to library patrons of all ages.[3]

THE LIBRARY AS SOCIAL INTERACTION/ ENTERTAINMENT SPACE

The heavy use of the library as a social interaction/entertainment space by the teens in this study tells us that librarians should promote and support the social and entertainment roles of their organizations if they want to provide the full range of services teens want and need from their public libraries.

Fulfilling teens' social and entertainment needs is not just fun or frivolous. Teens need social and entertainment opportunities for self-expression, to develop social skills, and to support their healthy development into adulthood. Providing book clubs, computer clubs, gaming clubs, and movie viewings can create badly needed opportunities for teens' healthy social and emotional development. Public libraries can provide these important social and entertainment opportunities for urban teens who lack transportation to other venues or who lack the funds to pay for activities such as movies, summer camps, and social clubs.

The greatest number of responses under the social interaction/entertainment category described teens visiting their libraries to attend organized entertainment events. Teens mentioned everything from movie showings to manga club meetings to fencing club practice as drawing them into their libraries. Many U.S. public libraries do provide organized events for teens, but most could expand these offerings. One of the best ways of starting new library programs is to learn about successful programs at other libraries. The fifth edition of YALSA's *Excellence in Library Service to Young Adults* (Alessio 2008) provides planning, staffing, funding, and materials details for a wealth of successful YA programs and can serve as a guide for increasing your library's organized teen activities. The chapter "Services under $100" is especially helpful for libraries with limited programming budgets.

If providing a range of programs other than literacy-related services seems beyond your area of expertise, there is no need to worry. This is where collaboration can really help librarians meet teens' needs. For example, if you learned from teens at your library that they are interested in sketching, you could contact your local museum to ask if a museum employee or volunteer would be willing to visit your library to offer sketching classes. You would provide the space and the access to the teens. The museum would provide the sketching knowledge. And you could work together to plan the program, find program funds, and advertise, increasing the staffing power and visibility of both your library and the museum.

Organized library programs provide teens with the chance to interact with their peers, but equally important is providing unstructured socialization time. This is why it is so important that teens have a space of their own in public libraries. Ideally, that space is a closed-off room where teens can play music, eat, play games, and interact without disturbing the rest of the library. But if physical space limitations preclude a separate room, then blocking off a corner of the library and placing a few comfortable chairs there can serve as a substitute for a separate teen space. Or, if the library insurance policy permits it, creating a teen garden space on the library grounds might serve as a pleasant substitute.

Unorganized entertainment is probably best supported by the library, again, by a space dedicated to teen use. Providing a teen space shows adolescents that they are welcomed in the library and gives them a sense of ownership. Yet, sadly, even though almost all U.S. public libraries provide space dedicated to adult services and to children's services, many fewer have spaces dedicated to serving adolescents. (See chapter 11 for a deeper discussion of library spaces for teens.)

Teens in this study visited their libraries because they liked their librarians and felt personal connections to them. It follows that another way to bring more urban teens into public libraries is to work to change their unfavorable perceptions of librarians. Recall the studies discussed earlier in this chapter that have shown urban teens' negative attitudes toward librarians and libraries to act as barriers to public library use. Both of the libraries in the study reported here had highly active YA librarians in place, librarians who were successful at connecting to their teen communities. As a result, their teen programming was generally well attended, and they had built up groups of regulars who frequented the libraries not just to use their services but also to visit their favorite librarians.

THE LIBRARY AS BENEFICIAL PHYSICAL ENVIRONMENT

Recall that teens in this study who used their libraries as beneficial environments had gone there seeking refuge, community improvement, personal improvement, and financial support. Support for this last major role of the public library in urban teens' lives can be done at several levels, from evaluating the safety of the library environment, to creating targeted programming related to safety issues, to increasing teen volunteering opportunities.

To bolster the library as a refuge for teens, librarians in urban areas should keep in mind that, although no public library is a completely safe place, it may be the safest place for some urban teens after school and on weekends. Library staff might look into ways to make the library building safer and more welcoming. Or they might team up with the local police department and use the physical space of the library as a place where teens can learn about personal safety issues.

The most logical method of supporting the library as a place where teens can engage in community improvement is by creating an active teen volunteer program. Several teens in this study were eager to volunteer at their libraries. Teen volunteer programs help teens (by enabling them to improve their communities and by giving them important early work experiences) as well as libraries (by providing inexpensive labor and by increasing teens' sense of ownership in their libraries). Teens can be instrumental in providing homework and technology assistance to children, in supervising children's programs, in organizing and running teen advisory boards, and in many more ways. Minkel (1999) suggested that most public libraries are short-staffed when it comes to keeping the library website up to date. Teen volunteers can be valuable library website maintenance assistants and help with link checking and other maintenance tasks. This kind of technical work can also provide teens with valuable work experience.

Writing in *School Library Journal*, Suellentrop (2007, 24) noted a "recent explosion of teens seeking to volunteer at libraries." She suggested that a teen volunteer program include a variety of volunteer roles and counseled librarians to match teens' talents with their tasks:

> Not every task fits every teen. Help teens discover their talents by offering them a wide array of possibilities. Outgoing teens can hand out programs, welcome patrons to an event, or help visitors with computer questions. Artistic teens would love reading to children, assisting with storytime, or designing programs and displays. Shy teens can make name tags, as well as develop scavenger hunts and word puzzles for younger children. Those who are more detail oriented can help with inventory supplies, labeling, making sure periodicals are in order, and preparing summer reading packets.

Providing volunteer opportunities is also a method of supporting urban teens' use of the library for personal improvement. However, most teens in the survey who had visited their libraries for personal improvement were seeking educational opportunities. Librarians can support these interests by providing high-quality, teen-friendly reference services and by developing and maintaining high-quality collections. Though most public libraries that target YA services work hard to develop and maintain their YA collections, many fewer have an information desk located within the YA area. This omission leaves teens to choose between the children's department and the adult department to ask for help. A desk dedicated to serving teens sends the message that teens' reference questions and other requests for help are important and valued, and it goes a long way toward making young adults feel included in library services.

Finally, teens' use of the library as a source of financial support tells us that librarians should hire teens from their communities when feasible to work in positions such as library pages and other part-time roles. Again both the libraries and the teens benefit. Teens can find valuable part-time work and early work experience, which can be difficult to acquire, and libraries can gain energetic new employees who know the library community from an insider's perspective.

CONCLUSIONS

Just as the OCLC (2005) survey showed that the overwhelming majority of U.S. adults tend to equate books with public libraries, this survey found that most urban teen public library users also strongly associate books with public libraries. More urban teens might use their libraries if they realized that libraries do much more than provide books. As a result, one of the most important things public librarians can to do to bring more urban adolescents into their libraries is to spread the message that libraries mean much more than books. It is important to advertise this message both within and outside the library with fliers, public service announcements, postings on the library website, and notices in blogs, Facebook, MySpace, and anywhere else teens are likely to notice. Also important is to deliver the message personally to teens by visiting schools, community groups, and other places where teens congregate, always repeating the message that the public library is much more than just books.

It is not enough just to expand our ideas of public library services beyond the library as information provider. We must also actively work to broaden the reach of the public library. Outreach, which means taking library services beyond the confines of the library building, is crucial to getting the message out to teens. Going to places where urban teens feel welcome can spread the message that the public library is much more than an information resource, and it can counteract teens' negative perceptions of libraries and librarians. As Brehm-Heeger (2008, 191–192) explained:

> Outreach activities raise the library's profile not only among teens but also among . . . other organizations serving teens and lead to invitations for the library to become a more active contributor to community discussions. This is vital in urban areas because though there are more organizations dedicated to serving teens in urban communities than in rural or truly suburban communities, the greater number of organizations does not necessarily translate into a coordinated, effective, community-wide approach to serving teens.

Librarians do not need to become experts in all areas of service and programming that teens need. This is where community collaboration becomes so important. Community collaboration expands the reach and breadth of the public library while taking advantage of the expertise and resources of all organizations involved. For example, a library wanting to expand its support of urban teens' social interaction/entertainment needs might consider teaming up with a local community theater to provide acting lessons at the library. Everyone involved gains something from the other partners: the library, the theater, and the teens themselves.

Once urban teens begin to understand that their libraries provide much more than schoolwork and leisure reading materials, and once they see that their librarians are excited about having them use library services, they are much more likely to become active library users and library supporters. Their healthy development into adulthood is likely to benefit from this change, and public libraries will then be playing a larger role in supporting the full range of urban teens' needs.

Notes

1. Demographic data cited in this section were drawn from http://fact finder.census.gov.
2. For more information on how to create pathfinders, visit the Wenatchee School District's "Pathfinders: Guides to Information Resources" at http://home.wsd.wednet.edu/WSD/Instructional/learn teach/libraries_media/Pathfinders/path.htm, and the Springfield Township High School Virtual Library's "Template for Creating Pathfinders" at www.sdst.org/shs/library/pathfinder.html.
3. For help in learning how to weed your collection, see Slote (1997).

CHAPTER 8

PUBLIC LIBRARY WEBSITES AND URBAN TEENAGERS' HEALTH INFORMATION NEEDS

SANDRA HUGHES-HASSELL AND DANA HANSON-BALDAUF

THINK BACK TO ADOLESCENCE. Sure, we know. If you are like most of us, that time of life is perhaps best left for distant, dusty, back-of-the-closet yearbook memories. Along with big hair, leg warmers (parachute pants for you fellas), and annoying flair-ups of acne (always on school picture day), life was filled with excitement and drama, embarrassments and insecurities, rebellious struggles for independence, and loads and loads of questions—questions about life, love, sex, and changing bodies.

Unfortunately, if you were growing up any time before the 1990s, reliable answers to sensitive and often embarrassing questions were often hard to come by. Eavesdropping on older sibling conversations and sharing stories around the middle school cafeteria table were often the mainstays of information retrieval. Thank goodness for young adult novelist Judy Blume. Although books such as *Are You There God? It's Me, Margaret* and *Then Again, Maybe I Won't* have earned her recognition as one of the most banned children's authors in the United States, for many of us they paved the way into adulthood by answering many of the questions we were too embarrassed to ask anyone else. Television was also significant in our education on life. Who could ever forget those great afterschool specials on ABC? Does anyone remember Helen Hunt's riveting performance as a strung-out teen barreling out of that plate glass window in *Angel Dusted*? It sure scared us!

HEALTH INFORMATION ON THE INTERNET

Fortunately, when it comes to finding answers, today's teens seem to have it a little easier than we did "back in the day"—thanks largely to Q&A collaborative websites like WikiAnswers and Yahoo! Answers and search engines such as Google, Yahoo, and Ask.com. A recent Pew Internet study (Estabrook et al. 2007) reported that more people, including teenagers, would rather turn to the Internet to find answers to everyday problems than seek advice or information from family members or professionals. A 2006 Pew Internet report indicated that at least 75 percent of today's teens utilize the Internet specifically to look up health-related information (Rideout 2001). A more recent study conducted by YPulse, ISIS (Internet Sexuality Information Services), and the market research firm Peanut Labs found that over 50 percent of young people ages 13–24 are accessing health and wellness information on the Internet (O'Malley 2008). WebMD was cited by over 15 percent of the respondents as their favorite source, and 17 percent indicated that they use online confessional sites or message boards to share personal health-related information.

The following, all pasted directly from answers.yahoo.com, is a small sampling of what some teens are concerned with and asking today in online environments, along with a few of the answers they are finding:

I'm fifteen and a freshman in high school. I don't want to sound stupid or something, but I'm really starting to hate my life. I've lost so many friends and I'm always feeling out of place. It seems like I can't even make friends, I don't even know what to do. I used to have so many, but now I feel like an outcast. Sometimes I just want to run away. What do I do?

> **Answer 1:** Just wait until you become a high school senior. That's when it all comes boiling down.

> **Answer 2:** Stay strong and start doing things that interest you. Never feel like you have to follow the crowd.

Answer 3: GET OVER IT!

My boyfriend is a drug user and I'm pregnant could the baby have problems? We both are seventeen years old, and I am pregnant. My boyfriend (who got me pregnant) chews tobacco, does pot and weed. I am so nervous that our baby will be retarded or be addicted to drugs. I have never done drugs before. But we have made out while he chewed several times and often times even swallowed his spit. On several occasions I had sore throats, stomachaches, and I was spitting blood. He smokes around me too and has had for a while now.

> **Answer 1:** YOU have the problem—him! I suggest you dump him and see a medical practitioner that can help you end the pregnancy immediately. Shouldn't you be in school somewhere, instead of throwing up from swallowing tobacco spit? PLEASE—find better things to do with your time!

> **Answer 2:** No probably not but I would just stay clear and try and convince your partner to stop taking drugs as if the social service find out your baby is going to have a surroundings of drugs then the baby may be taken away from you until the environment is safe for the healthy unborn child
> **good luck with your pregnancy**

What should I do if I am suffering from anorexia for the second time?

>   **Answer 1:** Eat a creamcake. If your sick, then your anorexic.

>   **Answer 2:** how did you become anorexic e-mail me plzzz

>   **Answer 3:** just stuff yourself with food

>   **Answer 4:** Eat more! Food is Good.

How do I come out to my parents as a gay teen? I'm fourteen so I need advice from older people. But no one try to make me straight

>   **Answer 1:** Congrats on knowing yourself at this age. As for coming out, start out simple, maybe with friends. They are usually more understanding at first. If you are positive that you want to though, go for it. I hope that they are intelligent individuals that will not go crazy. If you are unsure what their reaction may be there is no need to rush. If your living situation would be in trouble, wait until you live on your own. Do what you feel is best for you though and I wish you all the luck.

>   **Answer 2:** Jeez I feel for you . . . and your dad. . . . he's going to be devistated. . . . as a father that is one talk you pray never happens. . . . oh well, you gotta do what you gotta do. . . . I'd take a walk thru the mall and check out all the hotties in their short skirts one last time and make sure there isn't any hope for you first dude.

It is no surprise that the Internet has become an indispensable tool for individuals seeking health information. As lack of access to affordable and high-quality health care reaches levels of national concern, individuals, increasingly, are turning to health-related websites as a first-stop triage tool for diagnosis and treatment of conditions and ailments (Borzekowski and Rickert 2001). Among the most vulnerable and affected by the health care crisis are urban youth living at or below the national poverty level, who quite often have limited access to good information and resources regarding health care and health-related services. For example, McKee and Fletcher (2006) found that a disproportionate number of urban adolescent girls, especially non-U.S.-born girls, lack a usual source of care and regular health care provider. Similarly, with regard to urban adolescent males, it seems that very few inner-city health care facilities offer focused sexual and reproductive health information and services to young men. This is especially disconcerting given evidence of risky sexual behaviors among urban adolescent males and the increased risk of sexually transmitted diseases, HIV/AIDS, and unplanned fatherhood (Lindberg et al. 2006).

Despite the lack of health-related services geared toward urban youth, studies of everyday life information seeking have shown that information pertaining to health-related issues *is* a frequent need among urban teens. Hughes-Hassell and Agosto (2007) found that urban teens had questions not only about their own health, such as "What is more comfortable, a tampon or a pad?" and "How does one go about getting free insurance?" but also about the health conditions of their families and friends. Issues related to human sexuality, including sexual safety and sexual identity, were also common.

Although the search for answers to health-related issues has become much easier over the past few years given the availability and ease of the Internet, unfortunately (as you may have garnered from our informal online investigation), the "answers" found on websites such as Yahoo! Answers and WikiAnswers may be about as accurate and useful as the information we gathered around that cafeteria table years ago.

Although there are websites that offer high-quality health-related information, young adults continue to have difficulty with their searches. Keyword searches on various search engines such as Google and Yahoo may not yield reliable and informative answers teens are seeking either. Searching challenges are attributed to difficulty formulating questions because of broad use of terms or misspellings (Lyons et al. 1997; Wallace et al. 2000), random and unsystematic web searching (Bilal and Kirby 2002; Fidel et al. 1999), the inability to determine credibility of websites, and encountering blocks as a result of filtering software (Gray et al. 2005; Richardson et al. 2002).

Moreover, although many studies have highlighted the Internet's availability, anonymity, and affordability as key reasons teens turn to it for answers to their health-relate questions (Barak and Fisher 2001; Gray et al. 2005), issues related to online privacy and confidentiality remain a concern and prevent many teens from seeking sensitive information in the online environment (Vargas 2005).

So where do libraries fit in? A recent report indicates that young adults are some of the most prevalent patrons of library services, using libraries more for problem-solving information than their elders (Estabrook et al. 2007). Given this finding and the challenges teens face when searching for health information online, it seems obvious that public libraries might take the lead. Libraries, particularly public libraries, have a long history of providing consumer health information to adults in their communities. Over the past few years, this service has transitioned online as libraries provide Internet access to electronic consumer health information (Smith 2006). Additionally, many public libraries have developed websites specifically for teens serving as centers for reference, educational support, popular materials, community information, and library programming (Hughes-Hassell and Miller 2003; Jones 1997). Including links to useful health websites may alleviate some of the frustration teenagers face when searching for reliable health information on the Internet (Vargas 2005).

STUDY: PUBLIC LIBRARY WEBSITES AND HEALTH INFORMATION

Are urban public libraries using their teen web pages to provide health information for young adults? To answer this question, we conducted a study of 101 websites of some of the largest metropolitan public libraries in the United States to determine the extent and scope of online health-related information geared specifically toward teenage patrons.

STUDY DESIGN

Five research questions guided our study: (1) What percentage of urban public library websites for teenagers provide consumer health information? (2) Which health topics are commonly included? (3) Which websites are recommended? (4) What percentage of the recommended websites were designed specifically for teenagers? (5) Who are the primary sponsors of the recommended sites?

Our sample included public library websites from the two largest metropolitan areas in each of the fifty states and the District of Columbia. Each website was accessed between April and June 2007 to determine if it contained a link to a page specifically developed for young adults. If a YA page was found, we examined it for health-related information. For each recommended health-related website, we recorded the web address, sponsor, and topics covered. We also examined each of the recommended sites to determine if they were developed specifically for a teenage audience.

FINDINGS

To begin, we found that of the 101 library websites we surveyed, only seventy-two included a web page specifically geared toward their young adult patrons, and only thirty-six of those web pages included links to online health-related resources and information. The libraries most likely to provide health-related information for teens through their websites were those serving communities with low poverty rates (<10 percent) and those with poverty rates between 25 and 30 percent. Only 30 percent of the libraries in the highest-poverty communities had YA websites that featured health-related information. A regional comparison showed that libraries in midwestern states were less likely to provide health information for teens by means of the library's YA website than those in other areas of the country (table 8.1).

The topics included as health information by each library varied greatly. Table 8.2 presents the categories and specific health-related topics most frequently included on the websites. Some of the libraries recommended websites that clearly dealt with health-related issues, such as diet, disease, drug abuse, exercise, and pregnancy. Others included websites that at first glance might seem unrelated to health, such as Choosing a Piercer, which provides guidelines for ensuring that individuals have a "safe piercing experience," and Tattoo Facts, which includes a section entitled "What is bad for my tattoo?"

A total of 290 distinct sites were recommended to teens seeking health-related information. The number of health-related websites recommended by each library ranged from one to ninety-three, with the average being seven. The sponsors of the websites were primarily nonprofit organizations, including government agencies, community-based organizations, professional associations, foundations, universities, hospitals, public television stations, and youth advocacy and educational organizations. More than half of the recommended sites were developed specifically for a teenage audience. Table 8.3 provides the titles, web addresses, and sponsors of the ten most frequently recommended sites.

Many of the recommended sites not only provided factual information in the form of articles or answers to frequently asked questions but also included interactive components such as chats, threaded discussion forums, and hotlines that provide teens with the opportunity to communicate with experts and other teens about health issues. For example, Sex, Etc. provides a weekly live teen chat with sexual health experts, and Teen-Growth includes a section titled "Crisis Call" that includes phone numbers for various crisis hotlines across the United States.

IMPLICATIONS FOR PRACTICE

Now we return to the original question. How common is it for urban public libraries to use their teen web pages to provide health information? Unfortunately, not as common as we had hoped. Only slightly more than one-third (36 percent) of the library websites examined for this study included links to online health-related resources and information for teens. So where do we go from here?

Teenagers are making decisions every day that impact their health and well-being. The most recent Youth Risk Behavior Surveillance System report showed that during the thirty days preceding the survey 43 percent of the students surveyed had drunk alcohol, 20 percent had used marijuana, and 23 percent had smoked cigarettes (CDC 2006). Thirteen percent of the teens reported being overweight, 80 percent admitted that they did not eat healthy diets, and 67 percent said they did not attend physical education classes daily. Additionally, 47 percent of the high school students surveyed reported having sexual intercourse; 37 percent had not used a condom. Public libraries can support the needs of these teenagers by providing links to health-related materials and organizations as part of their YA library websites.

TABLE 8.1
LIBRARY YA WEBSITES AND HEALTH INFORMATION FOR TEENS, BY REGION

REGION	LIBRARIES WITH A YA WEBSITE	LIBRARIES PROVIDING HEALTH INFORMATION ON THE YA WEBSITE
Midwest	65%	23%
Northeast	66%	38%
South	63%	36%
West	75%	38%

TABLE 8.2
HEALTH TOPICS MOST FREQUENTLY INCLUDED

GENERAL CATEGORY	SPECIFIC TOPICS	
Growth and development	Anatomy Puberty (physical and emotional changes) Appearance and self-care (teeth, skin, hair, etc.)	
Self-expression	Body piercing Tattoos Identity	
General health and well-being	Activism Choosing a doctor College/career choices Dieting Disabilities Disease, infections, and conditions First aid Fitness and exercise Health care rights	Health insurance options Injury prevention Internet safety Media literacy Medicine safety Nutrition Racism Sports Steroid use
Emotional and mental health	Anger management Anxiety and stress Body image Bullying Counseling/therapy Dealing with death Dealing with divorce Depression Eating disorders Living in crisis Love and relationships	Peer pressure Phobias Relationships (family/friends) School/social issues Self-esteem Self-mutilation (cutting) Shyness Suicide
Physical safety	Bullying Date violence Domestic violence Gang-related activity Homelessness Incest Internet safety	Physical abuse Rape/sexual assault Runaways Sex trafficking School violence Terrorism
Sexuality and sexual health	Abortion Abstinence Adoption AIDS/HIV Anatomy Birth control Homosexuality Puberty Reproduction Reproductive rights Safe sex	Sex vs. love Sexual activity (intercourse, masturbation, etc.) Sexual identity Sexual violence Sexually transmitted diseases Teen pregnancy Teen parenting

(cont.)

TABLE 8.2 (cont.)

GENERAL CATEGORY	SPECIFIC TOPICS
Alcohol and drugs	Alcohol Dependency and addiction Drinking and driving Drug laws and legislation Getting help Recreational and prescription drugs Steroid use and abuse Tobacco

One of the factors that may be preventing libraries from using their library websites to support teen health information seeking behavior is concern about the quality of information. As Block (2001, 21) points out, "Librarians have always been extra-conscientious about handing out medical information because we know that the consequences of wrong information can be deadly." Though the quality of web-based health information is much higher today than it was a decade ago, it is still necessary to evaluate the websites that are recommended (Gillaspy 2005).

Fortunately, several organizations have established quality criteria. For example, the Health on the Net Foundation (HON) developed a code of conduct that addresses the principles of reliability and credibility of health information on the Web (www.hon.ch). Websites that post the HON icon are monitored for their compliance with these features. The Health Information Technology Institute of Mitretek Systems, Health Summit Working Group (www.ahrq.gov/data/infoqual.htm) developed a set of criteria that can used by health care professionals, librarians, and individuals to evaluate health information on the Internet. These include

Credibility. Includes the source, currency, relevance/utility, and editorial review process for the information.

Content. Must be accurate and complete, and an appropriate disclaimer provided.

Disclosure. Includes informing the user of the purpose of the site, as well as any profiling or collection of information associated with using the site.

Links. Evaluated according to selection, architecture, content, and back linkages.

Design. Encompasses accessibility, logical organization (navigability), and internal search capability.

Interactivity. Includes feedback mechanisms and means for exchange of information among users.

Caveats. Clarification of whether site function is to market products and services or is a primary information content provider.

TABLE 8.3
MOST FREQUENTLY RECOMMENDED HEALTH-RELATED WEBSITES FOR TEENS

WEBSITE TITLE	NUMBER OF LIBRARY WEBSITES RECOMMENDING	WEBSITE URL	WEBSITE SPONSOR
TeensHealth	22	http://kidshealth.org/teen/	Nemours Foundation
Go Ask Alice	17	www.goaskalice.columbia.edu	Columbia University's Health Promotion Program
TeenWire	14	www.teenwire.com	Planned Parenthood
TeenGrowth	12	www.teengrowth.com	TeenGrowth team comprises world-renowned pediatricians, educators, and Internet professionals committed to improving the lives of adolescents
SEX, ETC.	9	www.sexetc.org	Center for Applied Psychology at Rutgers University
Health Information for Teens	9	www.fda.gov/oc/opacom/kids/html/7teens.htm	U.S. Food and Drug Administration, Department of Health and Human Services
girlshealth.gov	9	www.4girls.gov	Office on Women's Health in the Department of Health and Human Services
i wanna know	8	www.iwannaknow.org	American Social Health Association
freevibe.com	6	www.freevibe.com	National Youth Anti-Drug Media Campaign, a program of the Office of National Drug Control Policy
National Eating Disorders Association	5	www.nationaleatingdisorders.org	National Eating Disorders Association

There are also resources that librarians seeking to provide health information for teens can use to identify appropriate sites. Among these are *Health Information for Youth: The Public Library and School Library Media Center Role* (Lukenbill and Immroth 2007), the Internet Public Library's Teenspace (www.ipl.org/div/teen/), and the Health Information Project at the Mid-Hudson Library System (http://hip.midhudson.org). In her monthly column in *School Library Journal*, Gail Junion-Metz often reviews health-related websites for youth as well.

Limiting the number of recommended health-related websites so that they can be carefully screened and monitored is also important. For example, one of the libraries included in our sample provided links to ninety-three different websites. Among those was Teenadvice.org (www.teen advice.org). This site consists of sponsored links to websites that at first glance appear to be appropriate. On closer inspection, it becomes apparent that, although many of the sites are sponsored by reputable organizations, others are not. For example, there is a link to Love.Dada.net (a.k.a. Intimate Dating), which enables individuals to "flirt, chat, and meet millions of singles online or on your cell."

Another strategy to consider is providing links only to community-based organizations. The Public Library of Charlotte and Mecklenburg County's Life Info site (www.libraryloft.org/needHelp.asp) contains the following note to teens: "As a young adult, it may be hard to find accurate helpful information about issues that affect your life. This website offers a small collection of organizations within the community that may help you with your problem. Use it on your own or with friends and family to start you on your way to getting help."

As Vargas (2005) argues, libraries should also help teens evaluate health websites. Teens are even less likely than adults to pay attention to items such as authority and currency, and a quick, cursory look at the homepage of a website, or reliance on the URL domain, is not sufficient. Vargas recommends that libraries point users to the following two resources:

Evaluating Health Information, on MedlinePlus (www.nlm.nih.gov/ medlineplus/evaluatinghealthinformation.html), a sixteen-minute tutorial that teaches consumers how to evaluate health information on the Web.

10 Things to Know about Evaluating Medical Resources on the Web, on the National Center for Complementary and Alternative Medicine's website (http://nccam.nih.gov/health/webresources/), including who runs and pays for the site, how the site chooses links to other sites, and what information about a user the site collects and why.

MOVING BEYOND THE YOUNG ADULT WEBSITE

The National Network of Libraries of Medicine (http://nnlm.gov/outreach/ consumer/htthlit.html) suggests that libraries do more than just provide technological access to consumer health information. One project that does this is the Health Information Project at the Mid-Hudson Library System (http://hip.midhudson.org). Each summer, teen interns between the ages of 14 and 19 are hired to review DVDs/videos, websites, and books for inclusion in the system's six substance abuse/health information center libraries. The teens receive training in media literacy and website evaluation. In the fall following their internship, the teens make presentations at local schools and organizations. Through this project the teens learn to work independently and to evaluate health-related information. They also gain knowledge about health issues facing today's teens and recognize the importance of talking to friends, family, or peers about topics of concern. As Clapp and Lindsley (2005) explain, parts of the project can be implemented in any library with members of teen advisory councils, teen volunteers, or teen staff members.

Here are a few more initiatives to consider, drawn from Lukenbill and Immroth (2007) and the National Network of Libraries of Medicine:

Developing partnerships with school librarians, health teachers, and school nurses to share information and support health-related tasks in the K–12 curriculum, such as evaluating online health information and credibility of online sources.

Partnering with community-based organizations, such as the Boys & Girls Clubs, to develop outreach programs to discuss health information topics.

Asking physicians and other health care workers to select topics and formats that should be included in the collection, suggest local health resources and events the library should advertise, and develop columns for the library's newsletter.

Providing health information classes at the public library to teach health-related topics.

Working with consumer advocate organizations on outreach programs to vulnerable teen populations.

Participating in and lobbying for research on teen health literacy topics.

CONCLUSIONS

Improving the Health of Adolescents and Young Adults: A Guide for States and Communities (CDC 2004) outlines a community-based approach to promoting the health and well-being of America's teens. Recognizing that societal institutions have a significant influence on adolescent health, the publication argues that health promotion and prevention strategies should not be implemented in isolation but should be a collaborative effort across multiple organizations. As this chapter's study shows, libraries, as members of the broader community, can support the health information needs of urban teenagers and, by doing so, can assist these teens in making sound decisions about their health—decisions that can affect the rest of their lives.

CHAPTER 9

SPACING OUT WITH YOUNG ADULTS
Translating YA Space Concepts into Practice

ANTHONY BERNIER

THEY ARE "a disruptive force that interrupts the study of serious readers." Constantly "talking and giggling." Always eating in the library. Stealing library materials. Preening and strutting. They are interested only in "trivial things" and creating "chaos" in the library. When contemporary librarians hear this passage, they guiltily recognize it as an everyday screed against young people. So they laugh nervously when it is revealed that these complaints were actually made in the nineteenth century by male librarians in the United States against middle-class white women (Van Slyck 1996).

Female library users not only were accused of disrupting proper library order but were thought to be threatening the very social fabric of respectable society itself. Exasperation at these outrageous behaviors reached a head in the 1880s. In response to all these pesky women, public libraries attempted to minimize their impact on "serious" library users and began, grudgingly, to give "ladies" a room of their own as it were, their own space. In this "room of their own" they could talk and giggle, preen and strut, and pursue their "trivial" little interests without disturbing "serious and scholarly" gentlemen.

The point here is that women were gradually accepted as entitled agents in the public world. And libraries made space for them. Later, as women gained an increasing share of professional status and authority as librarians, those women made space for children. A half-century later in U.S. history, and under various racially segregated schemas, libraries incorporated nonwhite patrons and later still fully incorporated nonwhite citizens in nonsegregated libraries. Libraries gradually made space for non-English-speaking populations and supplied materials in their respective languages. They made space for handicapped patron access. They made space for computers. Indeed, libraries are constantly changing the concept of who "counts" and what activities "matter."

Although young adults are widely recognized as constituting nearly 25 percent of all library users in the United States, the vast majority of libraries devote more space and design attention to bathrooms than to young people's spatial needs. Worse, there is no scholarly research connecting young adults to the civic space of libraries. There are no metrics, no evaluation standards, and no best or comparative practices. This chapter inaugurates such a scholarly exploration.

Library buildings, like all urban public spaces, represent and manifest ideals about who counts and what activities matter in a community. Public library buildings certainly trumpet values about being open and democratic spaces. At the heart of this chapter, however, is the realization that urban young people have yet to be considered part of that community or civic ideal.

U.S. libraries have historically been ambivalent about urban youth. Since the turn of the nineteenth century, even as they increasingly needed to attract youth populations to justify their public purpose, librarians openly expressed hostility toward youth, considering them "on probation" from the moment they walked in the door (Garrison 2003; Van Slyck 1995). And libraries continue to be challenged by them. Immigrant youth frequently come from homes where traditions of public library service remain remote from parental experience and expectations. Further, together with youth coming from urban intergenerational poverty, many young people share relatively small living spaces. Historically this has placed more utilitarian value on urban public spaces. Under these circumstances, for instance, it is not unusual for parents to send their offspring into public places together—entrusting younger children to the custody of their teenaged youth. The spatial implications here reveal that a library design not considering this common scenario risks placing youth in role conflict with building design based on a cliché about how all teenagers desire as much distance from children's space as possible. Even many of today's marquee YA spaces are guilty of this design concept flaw.[1]

These same urban youth benefit disproportionately from the library's function as intergenerational public space as well. Separating these young adults from the general population for much of the day in age-segregated school environments, public libraries offer them a unique intergenerational social experience. They are at least nominally treated as legitimate library users. They observe, interact with, and are served by information professionals; they gain access to the full array of library materials; they share the library with children and adults alike, as well as being afforded a noncommercial space in which to establish and build social competence with other youth. Indeed, in public libraries less materially well-off urban youth gain the opportunity to observe up close the workings of middle-class concepts of publicity as well as professional public services being delivered immediately and tangibly more on their own terms than those dictated in other adult-centered public spaces. For many urban youth the public library serves as a "gateway institution" not simply to information but to the larger civic world, where these goals might bed.[2] It is simply not enough, though, to rely on virtual spaces when imagining age-appropriate young adult public space (Crawford 2007; Hodkinson and Lincoln 2008; Hughes-Hassell et al. 2008).

The remedy, of course, is for libraries to express this civic value in their public space. To get there, libraries must address the central question of how they can deliver developmentally appropriate library space for young people.

Probably because of long-prevailing institutional preoccupation with collections, library standards have largely conflated the concept of *young adult space* with the mere shelving of printed materials for young adults. They commonly rely on a meager allocation of shelf space within, or adjacent to, children's sections or on repurposed paperback racks. Sometimes a YA magazine collection appears in the children's section; sometimes it is interfiled with adult magazines. For all of our professional claims to making materials consistently accessible, such ad hoc practices have existed in libraries for decades and illustrate how we have systematically marginalized the young adult experience. Historically, libraries have considered young adults entitled to neither space for their needs nor an equitable share of the library's common environments (Chelton 2002; Kelly 2007). Classic Carnegie buildings, for instance, only bifurcate into "sides" for children and adults. New buildings frequently do little more. Adults then widely interpret the consequent underutilized library resources and youths' negative perceptions of libraries as antipathy and apathy. Service barriers for young people can further be seen in the physical features of generations of new and refurbished library buildings, policies, and procedures and in the ways in which young people socially experience libraries, "as aristocratic, authoritarian, unfriendly and unresponsive" (Rubin 2004; see also Marston 2001).[3]

On the other hand, there is growing awareness of this decades-long inequity as libraries begin to see how they can add public value by providing young people with developmentally appropriate spaces. Inspired by the Los Angeles Public Library's purpose-built landmark Teen'Scape project (Bernier 2000a) and aided mightily by the subsequent introduction of "YA Spaces of Your Dreams"—a column in every issue of *Voice of Youth Advocates* (VOYA)—as well as the appearance in 2002 of a guide to redecorating YA areas (Taney 2002), libraries are learning that YA spaces deserve a place within the broader context of the public spaces that libraries offer their communities.[4] The most recognized YA services advocate, Patrick Jones, noted that the emergence of YA-specific spaces ranked among the most exciting innovations in the field. "Libraries," he said, "are saying this service is important, and they want to profile it. This is a huge change" (Gorman 2006).

The first "post-occupancy study" of YA space in library literature appeared in the November–December 2006 issue of *Public Libraries* (Cranz and Cha 2006). An architecture professor at the University of California at Berkeley conducted a two-phase ethnographic study examining the degree of young adult customer satisfaction achieved in a new branch facility. This is probably the first branch library ever to offer a purpose-built YA space in a new library building. Not only were young people central in the design and décor of this space, but local youth were the study's primary subjects.

In the Teen'Scape project in Los Angeles, the dedicated VOYA column, the published guide, and expanding expert recognition we see evidence that libraries are becoming increasingly aware of a historic inequity. Nevertheless, these are only very qualified advances. The regular *VOYA* column reproduces brief anecdotal and simple narrative descriptions. And even under the best circumstances, with some libraries attempting to advance the more recent service paradigm of "youth development," the results are seldom distinguishable from conventional library designs (Jones 2002). Libraries may ask architects or designers, librarians, and even young people to come together as a team to create a spatial solution, but a kind of "triangle of half-knowledge" then develops. Architects frequently know little about the functioning of libraries or young people. Librarians generally do not possess architectural backgrounds and do not know a great deal about how young people enact spaces of their own. And young people usually know little about the functioning of libraries or architecture. The resulting "triangle" is destined, even with the best intentions, to produce mediocrity.

So, although these early efforts are important, no systematic evidence-based research, guidelines, methods, or metrics exist to facilitate developmentally appropriate YA spaces. The lack of empirical research on young adults extends beyond YA space, of course, as Jenkins's (2000) seminal historical review of youth services research observed. Furthermore, libraries, informed by predominant and erroneous media representations, a seemingly endless flow of moral panic about youth behavior, and the routinely exaggerated and inaccurate claims found in adult nonfiction literature, news media, and public policy—even, tellingly, in library bond campaign literature linking reduced crime with library services—institutionally convey a belief that young people present more problems than they are worth.[5] Therefore it should come as no surprise that libraries perpetually underfund YA services, underdevelop professional capacity, and undertheorize a YA services research agenda, as well as manifesting a rather uninformed vision of youths' space needs. Libraries need and deserve research on how to serve young adults better.

The fledgling efforts made to date have been done without data or history, without systematic evaluation of best practices, skill capacities, institutional infrastructure, evaluation, or theoretical grounding. For the profession, this lack of systematic spatial knowledge yields a raft of challenging questions (Chelton 2001; Kelly 2007):

- What data should be collected, and how?
- How do youth conceive of and enact public space?
- What do library leaders need to know to effect successful YA spaces?
- To what degree do age-appropriate YA spaces add design value to libraries?
- How can libraries better identify and incorporate youths' spatial preferences?
- What age-appropriate aesthetic overlaps exist between what is enticing for young adults and what is acceptable to libraries?
- What attitudes and concerns do professionals (including architects) and adult patrons exhibit about YA spaces?

- How does the presence/absence of a separate YA space influence recruitment or retention of professional YA staff or service capacity?
- What are the most important factors that can improve library space (e.g., seating options, access to technology, allowing food)?
- How can young people's needs to develop social capital in space be balanced with the space libraries need for materials and services?
- How can libraries improve current spaces or policies based on information about youth behavior?
- What are the best techniques for involving young people in space design, and how can young people best be included in the community design review process?
- What are the best evaluation metrics for current and new spaces?
- What is spatial equity for young adults?
- To what degree do libraries "design out" young people because they suffer under the same misconceptions about contemporary youth behavior as does the larger society?

Further, without more systematic knowledge and research, introductory YA courses in library schools, focused as they are on YA literature, do not meaningfully engage the complex topic of space or its connections to services, programs, or developing relationships with young adults.

Libraries design and implement spaces in ways that contradict or conflict with nearly every aspect of normal and developmentally appropriate young adult public behavior. The consequence of these institutional deficits is that libraries, inadvertently or not, create what I have elsewhere described as a "geography of no" (Bernier 1998, 2000b, 2003). Youth are told "no" for doing or wanting things entirely appropriate for young people, such as sitting convivially in small groups. Instead, libraries enforce one-to-a-chair policies.

THE APPLICABILITY TO PRACTICE

The ultimate goal of this chapter is to advocate the administration of equitable library services for youth and increase their profile in the library's service portfolio. The assumption is that spatial equity often brings with it other dimensions of service equity.[6] But although we do have some anecdotal evidence, the field has yet to produce empirical evidence or guidelines to establish or substantiate best practices. Therefore the short-term objective here is to develop a conceptual framework in which to apply some preliminary standards to achieve developmentally appropriate YA spaces informed by an accurate portrait of today's youth. Such findings will help library professionals assess, imagine, and evaluate current spaces and involve young people in future redesigns.[7]

This chapter exploits my experience as a YA specialist librarian since the mid-1990s, my role as a scholar of public space, and preliminary findings I have developed as a design team member and consultant to five library architecture firms. I present a language of youth-specific experience in library spaces, menus of adaptable ideas, and preliminary evaluative criteria within the context of three rubrics or levels for offering YA library space. For each of the three levels, I discuss the *what*, the *how*, and the *impacts* anticipated in developing purpose-built YA spaces. Each level builds on the previous, so that the third level includes almost everything introduced up to that point (see figure 9.1).

LEVEL ONE: DECORATIVE PRACTICES

The first level of treating library space amounts to applying some basic decorative practices. The point is to improve dramatically the visual experience young people encounter with even modest spaces and collections.

The *what* of this treatment requires increasing the shelf space that already exists by aggressively and strategically weeding current collections. Conventional definitions of YA space are limited to linear shelf feet, and most libraries today at least segregate some specific "YA literature." Unfortunately this commonly means only the fiction material. Once the shelves have been weeded and pruned, the staff should study and enact visual merchandising (face-outs, posters, and a host of related techniques). Furthermore, libraries should make a concerted effort to incorporate graphic representation of local youth art, experience, and culture into any new space project in a variety of ways, ranging from buying commercially available popular cultural images, to posting local high school achievement, to rotating curated youth-produced artwork, writing, and photography regularly.

The *how* of achieving decoration-level treatments involves upgrading and cultivating professional and paraprofessional shelving techniques. It requires that staff create and employ a variety of shelf decoration techniques and that they share and develop these techniques with all appropriate coworkers. Staff should study the preferences of local youth and borrow from those preferences and practices. The best option is to involve young people in both identifying these things and enacting them.

The *impacts* on the library of decoration-level treatment require that YA materials continually undergo aggressive weeding and that shelf merchandising be maintained by both professional and paraprofessional

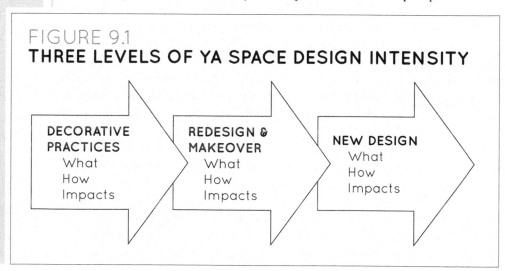

FIGURE 9.1
THREE LEVELS OF YA SPACE DESIGN INTENSITY

DECORATIVE PRACTICES
What
How
Impacts

REDESIGN & MAKEOVER
What
How
Impacts

NEW DESIGN
What
How
Impacts

staff. Underperforming materials can be interfiled with other collections, reassigned, or discarded. This requires staff training or retraining and maintaining a tight focus on collection and shelf maintenance. Staff will also be broadening conventional definitions of youth participation, including young people not simply in the selection but also in the merchandising of the collection. These measures do not require any supplemental funding, and staff members are not asked to make major accommodations in the library's overall spatial operation. Still, the impact on circulation will be immediate and very positive.

LEVEL TWO: MAKEOVER

If there is more than mere shelf space to work with, the YA makeover level adds furniture and fixtures to the decoration-level treatment discussed above. Among the most important elements in a makeover, however, is that young people's own developmental needs are inscribed into the new space, most notably through the inversion of the library's traditional privileging of materials for a heightened accommodation of young people's social experience.

Unlike library audiences of adults and children, young people are not primarily attracted to the library for its holdings (Gross 2001).[8] If libraries wish to deepen their connections with young people, they must enact the aesthetic and developmental preferences of that age group spatially, just as they do for adults and children. Implementing a makeover without incorporating young people's developmental needs may ultimately offer only heightened spatial competition with other, more powerful library user groups such as adults. A makeover that fails to take into account these considerations runs the very real risk of raising expectations only to disappoint them, because young people lose the competitive struggle between the spatial enactments that are sanctioned and those that continue to be marginalized.

The *what* of the makeover-level treatment seeks to establish a distinct footprint in an existing building, a separate spatial identity or *portal*, to use an architectural term. Portals can be porous to varying degrees, from soft partitions like curtains or screens to harder partitions like bookshelves, doors, and walls. The function of a portal is to delineate a YA space from the other service areas in the library.

A prevailing and erroneous cultural assumption persists about the location of a specific YA space in a public library. The assumption that teenagers want to be as far from the children's section as possible requires some revision. Although it is true that young adults do want and deserve their share of distinct library space, they do not require three floors of separation. This is particularly true, for example, with respect to communities containing large populations of immigrant families. Parents often send their offspring to the library together and place the children under the control of their teenagers. Thus, locating the children's department on the first floor and the YA space on the third places these young people in an unnecessary quandary: do they stay with the children on the first floor or drag them into the YA area with older youth? A better solution for a makeover-level treatment is to ensure that the YA space footprint establishes its own identity even if it is located adjacent to the children's room, where young adults can utilize library resources without conflict or disobeying their parents.

A separate YA space makeover usually includes freshly painted walls and perhaps ceilings. It may include new windows or new window dressings, new carpeting, and the addition of accent lighting. A makeover might also include a "signature shelving unit" or other technique for uniquely inscribing a perimeter, or what architects call an *implied barrier*, to help define the YA space.

Above all, however, a makeover should include new thinking about seating. The best approach is not simply to order new seating elements but consciously to avoid standard institutional "table and chair solutions." Here the emphasis should be on a *variety* of seating options. Consideration should be given to the kinds of seating and postures assumed by young people when they are most comfortable. This would include the introduction of ottomans, stools, and carpet-covered seating platforms and even facilitation of floor seating.

The *how* of the makeover-level treatment includes at least six different dimensions identified so far: staff issues, greater youth participation, and the introduction of YA-specific technology, collection issues, staff space, and administrative support.

Developing and deploying staff capacities for planning, selecting, and scheduling the necessary design activities are an obvious and critical dimension of a makeover. Library staff may not have much experience working with facilities management personnel and their various requirements. Involving non-YA staff is also important to ensure the success of a makeover. They should be involved in, prepared for, and kept informed of coming changes. This is particularly true when the makeover is the first move a library is making toward spatial equity for young people. It is common for non-YA staff to misunderstand or express varying degrees of trepidation about the prospect of devoting valuable library resources to an otherwise marginalized patron group. Being involved in and apprised of the steps and stages of the project helps all staff make the necessary adjustments. It is also a good idea to show non-YA staff other successful YA space projects.

A second dimension of the *how* of the makeover includes a much greater infusion of youth participation in the drafting and revising of a space's plans. Staff members should devote time to cultivating youth input on choices of furniture as well as floor and wall coverings, colors, and other fixtures. They should first prepare a list of acceptable options and then ask young people to discuss and decide on the final choices. This can occur informally or more formally through surveys (both print and digital) and well-run focus groups.

A third dimension is the introduction of YA space-specific technology. This includes an increasingly wide range of options. At the lower end, installing a simple music system helps provide a more youth-centered atmosphere, particularly when the library does not own a large music collection, because young people can be invited to bring their own music into the library via their PDA devices. At the higher end of the technology spectrum, libraries can install multiple computer stations capable of accommodating shared experiences (rather than one person per station) and video screens for watching movies, playing games, and learning research skills, among other options.

The introduction of YA-specific technology also offers the library an opportunity to accommodate various learning styles better. Offering access to textual and graphic materials through a variety of technical modes allows youth with learning-dominant audio, visual, or kinesthetic styles to utilize library resources better (Dunn et al. 1989; Silver et al. 2000).

A fourth dimension of the makeover suggests a different function for the library's YA materials collection. Conventionally, libraries shelve YA and curricular materials together, irrespective of their circulation performance or potential. This is another manifestation of a library-centric practice of privileging collections over a more youth-centric vision of this public space. Instead, the collection should reflect highly desirable YA materials and the poorer performing materials should be relocated, perhaps interfiled with adult collections. Thus the YA space becomes more of a showcase for very popular materials as well as something of a "launchpad" librarians can use to connect young people to the deeper library collections throughout the facility.

A fifth dimension treats an articulated space for professional staff more seriously than can a merely decoration-level treatment. Although not necessarily requiring a reference or service "desk," YA professionals should be allotted sufficient space for basic work tools, resources, and materials.

The final necessary dimension of the makeover is substantial administrative support. Makeovers can have a significant fiscal impact, so library administration should be cultivated and focused from the start of the project. Not only is administrative support required to help develop and allocate the funding sources for the makeover project, but administration is also key in keeping non-YA staff and the community informed of progress. Administrators might, for instance, invite YA staff to make presentations at the library's Friends group or write a column in the library's annual report.

The *impacts* of the makeover-level treatment are considerable. Unlike the decoration-level treatment, the makeover commonly requires a year or longer. In many cases architectural drawings or sophisticated design skills are helpful, though not mandatory. Also, depending on the degree of change instituted, fiscal impacts can range widely. Buying a few new ottomans, for instance, hardly requires a major capital outlay. Staff impacts can be challenging, however, as staff adjust to a more spatially inclusive service model.

One commonly reported impact on service may well be the need for a more active YA volunteer program. As young people develop connections with their space and relationships with staff, the desire to participate in the shaping of the library's service as a volunteer may result. Staff development in volunteer administration is a good idea as a new space opens.

The innovations from the decoration-level treatment that are integrated into the makeover also continue to affect the library. Greater involvement of young people, the continued use of collection merchandising techniques, and the attempt to create a separate spatial identity ensure a much higher profile for the YA space.

LEVEL THREE: NEW DESIGN AND THE COMING OF "4DSPACE"

A purpose-built YA space designed as part of a brand-new library facility is still extremely rare. Indeed, none of the current marquee or "model" YA spaces fit that description. So far they have been redesigned into existing library structures.[9] Thus much of the following remains theoretical. Nevertheless, we can draw some important conclusions from what we already know. Finally, libraries can take one step further by introducing young people to the increasingly pervasive "fourth dimension": digital-technology-enhanced spaces certain to appear during their lives.

The *what* of a YA space at the new design level includes developmentally appropriate YA library spaces containing all of the decoration and makeover-level treatments. These elements include privileging young people's social experience over materials and shelving units in addition to establishing a clear edge/perimeter/identity and a high profile for the graphic representation of local youth art, experience, and culture.

Beyond these basic elements, a new design should derive from a comprehensive and professionally rendered new building process and program.[10] Conceptual design and building programs at this level require deep and iterative collaboration with architects and design professionals. Furthermore, because few design professionals have significant experience working directly on public spaces designed for or with young people, it is incumbent on library staff to both support young people and serve as intermediaries to ensure that their participation and contributions to the building's planning and program process address youths' developmental needs and maximize their preferences.

Furnishing a YA space, as with any new building, must be addressed systematically and thoughtfully. Young people should be prominent decision makers on major options and selections, including seating options, implementation of new information and communications technology, and the degree of incorporation of young people's aesthetic values and amenities of value to them such as vending machines, storage space for their backpacks, and other appropriate creature comforts.

New design-level treatments should also consider the broad teaching roles that thoughtful spaces can assume in the lives of young people. For example, working closely with design professionals, libraries can deliver enticing spaces appealing to young people no matter what their dominant learning mode.

Furthermore, YA spaces, because of their arguably greater freedom from design conventions and common expectations of what libraries "should be," can more easily incorporate newer "green" spatial solutions.[11] Recycled rubberized floor treatments, for instance, have already emerged as a preferred choice of young people. This practice can also demonstrate these options to other, perhaps more reluctant, library user groups.

Finally, the increase in pervasive technological and immersive communications, particularly in the lives of young people, suggests that libraries can help pioneer the interactive hybrid architecture called "4dspace" (fourth-dimension space) (*Architectural Design* 2005; Bullivant 2005). Fourth-dimension space interprets digital and communications media in physical form and promises to blur conventional separations between work and play spaces, between the retrieval of information and its uses, and between reading and producing literature. In approaching this spatial digital turn, we can experiment with new immersive and gestural interface media such as Wii gaming and Second Life, exploiting higher degrees of interactions between information, young people, and imagined spaces. But we can also enlist the creative intelligence and energies of architects and designers to enrich physical spaces with higher degrees of this interactivity.

The *how* of a new design-level YA space requires a substantial (and still rare) institutional commitment. Administrative support must be evident from the start. Top administrative oversight regarding the degree and quality of youth participation is essential. A library executive would ideally ensure that youth participate even in the selection, or at least the evaluation process, of the project's architect. Furthermore, administrators should ensure that the architect includes young people in each step of the major phases of design and construction (reviews of original proposals, conceptual designs, construction documents, etc.). Administrators should also make sure that staff, community support groups, and other concerned agencies (e.g., city facilities department personnel) are informed about and welcome young people's participation. Finally, the administration should effect appropriate staff skill-capacity building to incorporate a YA service profile fully from the start of the project.

Library staff should also anticipate a higher degree of exposure to a variety of new skills. The YA staff should become and remain familiar with the planning and scheduling of the project's major phases. They should facilitate meaningful discussions among young people, the design professionals, facilities staff, and library administration. Contemporary YA professional competencies, for instance, now call for the incorporation of young people in envisioning and executing a YA service profile (YALSA 2003). But given that few YA professionals possess substantial experience working closely on new building projects or serving as effective youth advocates during the design and construction of a new building, YA staff will also gain valuable professional exposure to a wider range of experience.

The *impacts* of a new design-level treatment require much more substantial roles than the previous two levels. The design of a purpose-built, developmentally appropriate YA library space does not necessarily require different factors or considerations per se than the makeover-level treatment. However, the degree of implementation and heavy youth participation do require more time, skill, and professional collaboration than either of the first two levels.

Not surprisingly, designing a new building requires years of preparation and hard work on the part of many people both inside and outside of the library. The years of community and staff meetings should include a changing cast of young people at every major stage. The young people may not be involved to the extent, degree, or frequency that the professionals are involved. But exposing them to the developing community resource of a new library at various strategic junctures, negotiated from the start with the architect and design professionals, should be a serious consideration. Representative young people should be trained to read and discuss conceptual and design drawings as well as to assess and advance their own ideas.

Funding, of course, is also a consideration, but it does not necessarily add astronomical expense to the overall project, particularly if the space is conceptualized from the beginning and approached like any other part of a new facility. Some elements are YA space–specific, such as furniture or shelving units or a higher degree of technological sophistication. But every department, region, or zone of a new library has its own specific requirements. The important consideration here is that the youth-specific needs are articulated and considered from the beginning.

Among the more complex impacts on a new design-level treatment, for several reasons, is the introduction of significant youth participation. Neither libraries nor design professionals are necessarily wired to involve young adults as partners or constituents. Participatory youth innovations in professional YA specialist librarianship still present a rather new paradigm in contrast to decades of either considering youth "at risk" or not at all. Understandably, non-YA professionals are even further behind in these considerations. And architects and other design professionals frequently involve clients as little as possible, to say nothing of considering young adults as clients and partners.

But involving young people, from the selection of the architecture firm, through the construction phases, and even through post-occupancy evaluation, is essential to producing a developmentally appropriate YA library space. Staff may require special training to attract, facilitate, and sustain youth participation during the years a new building design requires. Various approaches to youth participation may be indicated; various modes of communication and input are needed. And there are differing intensities of participation as well, ranging from tightly facilitated focus groups through more loosely orchestrated and virtual participation.

As in other levels of YA space design, non-YA staff should be included in a new design-level treatment. Once again, introducing the concept that young people deserve status as partners along with other constituencies can require a cultural shift for many library professionals. That partner status entitles them to an equitable share of the library's public space can challenge even the preconceptions of young people themselves. Thus it is incumbent on the library's administration, YA staff, and design team to model, demonstrate, and perhaps even defend the proportional time and fiscal resources required to involve young people in YA space design meaningfully.

An even more challenging and progressive posture on young adult participation in the new design is participation across the entire new building project, not simply the YA space. Indeed, young people, if they are well prepared, have proved they are capable of contributing meaningful insights into many phases of a new building design. One such project is under way currently in Berkeley, California. Eight young adults were selected on a competitive basis, were trained, and are now being supported by their local YMCA board to work as the entire new building project's primary clientele.[12] If adopted by libraries, such a vision of youth participation promises to yield multiple and complex benefits for youth development as well as raising the profile of young people in the library and in the community at large.

CONCLUSIONS

Considering our own young people as fully entitled citizens is something long overdue. That we are only now developing a youth-inclusive language for a public space so proud of its aspirational creed, "free to all," is both shameful and optimistic. But we are indeed at a new beginning. Though urban libraries have been slow to take into account the service opportunities inherent in providing youth with spatial equity, the landscape of YA information services is changing rapidly. Increasing numbers of young people gravitate to the more adaptable "spaces" of virtual and immersive worlds as well as to ever-cheaper, ever-smaller, ever-more-versatile communication devices. Consequently libraries face keen competition, as well as new opportunities, in attracting the attentions of youth in currently conceived physical public spaces. Further, the rapid increase in nontraditional school environments in the United States also will impact library services. The alternative, continuation, and small-school site movements, combined with the nation's growing population of homeschooled youth, offer additional new ways for libraries to attract young people.

To return to my first concern, how libraries can deliver developmentally appropriate space for young people, the answer depends to a large degree on particular circumstances. But all libraries can do *something* to improve their appeal to young people and entice them with a more positive regard for the materials and services we work so hard to offer them. Libraries can do this even if the effort is only paying more attention to decorating modest existing spaces. And many libraries can do more than "something" to manifest a higher regard for youth in library space by recapturing a piece of library real estate and giving it a makeover. I call on libraries to experiment with and conduct research on what spatial practices, methods, and techniques will best incorporate these otherwise marginalized library users.

Notes

1. This early pattern of establishing renovated or new YA spaces at some remove from children's departments can be seen at the main libraries in Los Angeles, Phoenix, and Seattle, among others.
2. This notion of an intergenerational public space is similar to the notion of the commons argued by Kathleen de la Peña McCook (2004, 221).

3. For other studies on decades-old young adult attitudes and libraries, see Cook et al. (2005). See also Benton Foundation (1996) and Wallace Foundation (1999).

4. *VOYA* is published bimonthly by Scarecrow Press. The column features examples of library space redecoration projects submitted by practicing YA librarians.

5. For a sampling of the more popular books consistent with this claim, see Garbarino (1999), Hardy and Laszloffy (2005), Pipher (1995), Prothrow-Stith and Spivak (2006), Simmons (2002), and Twenge (2006). For recent discussion on moral panics about youth behavior, see Hajdu (2008) and Osgerby (2004).

6. The dedication of specific space for library service to children prefigures the young adult circumstance. In the instance of the development of the central library of the St. Louis Public Library system in 1912, the hiring of the first children's specialist librarians was preceded by "space dedicated specifically for children" (Kimball 2007).

7. More broadly, because the concept of space brings together issues of culture, history, power, and policy, the implications for dissemination of this research promise to inform (if not inaugurate) discussions in architecture, urban planning and design, education, justice studies, and public administration as well as youth-related domains of public policy. Finally, because youth space in general is a new arena for systematic study, this research has the possibility of teaching other design professionals how to think better about young people in public space. And in this scenario, libraries do not follow, they actually lead. As argued by several scholars, the concept of *youth space* per se has been perpetually ignored by the design and spatial arts. From among many examples, see Aitken (2001), Childress (2000), Sibley (1995), and White (1990).

8. Furthermore, although libraries have been discussing a flagging interest in books for some time, there is now an increasing recognition that libraries need more than books to attract today's young people as well. See Swope (2008).

9. The most notable YA spaces remain the Teen'Scape department of the Los Angeles Public Library and Teen Central at the Phoenix Public Library. Both of these model spaces resulted from redesign projects in existing buildings.

10. The term *program* is used here in the architectural sense as a description of the actual floor plan of the space with all its detail.

11. Architects, for instance, are increasingly familiar with the Leadership in Energy and Environmental Design (LEED) certification system. Developed in 1998 by the U.S. Green Building Council, LEED provides a suite of standards for environmentally sustainable construction. See Sullivan (2007).

12. The Teen Task Force reviewed, scrutinized, interviewed, and selected the architectural firm (Noll and Tam in Berkeley, California) from proposals submitted by sixteen original firms.

PART III
FOCUS ON BEST PRACTICE: MODEL PROGRAMS FROM U.S. PUBLIC LIBRARIES

CHAPTER 10
YOUTH DEVELOPMENT AND EVALUATION
Lessons from "Public Libraries as Partners in Youth Development"

ELAINE MEYERS

IN 1998 I LEFT the security of Phoenix Public Library, where I served as the coordinator of Children's and Teen Services, for an undefined tenure with the Urban Libraries Council and the Wallace Foundation's "Public Libraries as Partners in Youth Development" (PLPYD) initiative. The siren call that lured me was the promise of professional evaluation combined with an unfamiliar discipline called "youth development." Unlike many who have heeded a siren call, I was not disappointed by my adventure. Indeed, the experience has reshaped my thinking about service to urban teens using youth development as an essential lens and has confirmed my belief that our programs are best designed, refined, and justified on the basis of solid evaluation that is outcome based.

Evaluation often comes with a stiff price tag, and the Wallace Foundation invested in a five-year PLPYD evaluation for an expenditure of over a million dollars. In this chapter, I review the learning from the four evaluation documents produced as part of the project, discuss the core elements of youth development, review a best practice case study in the Tucson Pima Public Library, and conclude with principles from the initiative that shaped service at the Phoenix Public Library during my late tenure there. The learning from PLPYD offers insights not only for urban libraries but for any library that wants to join its community in providing a web of support for teens — one based on solid evaluation and youth development.

WALLACE FOUNDATION'S EVALUATION PHASE ONE: DOCUMENTING NEED

In 1999, ALA and the Wallace Foundation released *Programs for School-Age Youth in Public Libraries* (ALA 1999) at the ALA midwinter meeting.

The release was the precursor to the announcement of a significant investment in documenting and encouraging the role of public libraries in the well-being of youth in their communities. The research was conducted in February 1998, with questionnaires sent to 1,500 public libraries in the United States. These 1,500 libraries included all 461 libraries serving populations of 100,000 or more as well as a sampling of libraries serving 5,000–100,000.

By May 1998, 83 percent of recipients had returned surveys with information about their current public library programs for youth. Wallace was particularly interested in information about six common types of library programs: reading programs, cultural programs, community service/leadership programs, computer classes/workshops, homework assistance, and career development. Respondents who offered these programs were then asked the same set of questions about each type of program. Libraries were also queried about their service to low-income youth and the nature of community partnerships created to support youth.

This original research produced several key findings relevant to urban teens and served to shape the goals of PLPYD. Key findings are captured in the publication's executive summary. The first finding was that public libraries did offer the six common types of afterschool programs defined by the research design. These programs clustered by age of the youth being served, with reading programs common for primary (90.7 percent) and middle school (72.2 percent) students, and cultural and homework assistance programs generally also aimed at primary school students. Middle school youth were the primary target for computer classes and workshops (72.6 percent) and community service/leadership (82.6 percent). High school youth were the primary target of the career development programs (81.9 percent) (ALA 1999, 1–3).

The survey also determined that, of the many roles possible for youth to take in planning and implementing library programs, they were most commonly used for recruitment and cleanup. Youth were not integral to program planning or implementation. Program schedules and frequency varied from homework and community service programs being offered once a week or more to computer and career programs offered two to eleven times a year. The public libraries' top program objectives were promoting reading for pleasure (64.7 percent) and helping youth become better users of the library (45.9 percent). Public libraries collaborated on programs most often with schools (70.8 percent) and park districts or recreation centers (37.5 percent) (ALA 1999, 1–3).

A second and complementary Wallace publication was released later in 1999: *Challenges and Opportunities: Public Libraries as Partners in Youth Development* (DeWitt Wallace–Reader's Digest Fund 1999). Wallace challenged public libraries to serve youth more effectively. Citing the survey findings, Wallace wondered why only one out of three of the 1,248 libraries returning surveys provided computer classes or workshops. It noted that fewer than 25 percent of public libraries offered homework assistance or career programs. Although reading and cultural programs were the most prevalent in libraries, they overwhelmingly served elementary school students, with far fewer programs targeting high school students. Even though low-income communities were the most frequently targeted population, very few libraries designed programs to reach youth in low-income communities.

The document concluded with a profile of ten libraries (see table 10.1) that had received planning grants to develop multiyear proposals to respond to low-income communities' needs and to design programs that addressed technology, cultural and service programs for older teens, and new service models that would more fully engage teens beyond recruiting and cleaning up for programs.

The Urban Libraries Council was chosen to administer the PLPYD grant and to provide technical assistance to nine of the ten original libraries taking part in the program. The Council's core belief that urban libraries are urban assets and its leadership in forecasting and spotting trends in

TABLE 10.1
PARTICIPANTS IN PLPYD PLANNING GRANT

LIBRARY	POPULATION SERVED IN 2000	NUMBER OF BRANCHES
Brooklyn Public Library Brooklyn, New York	2.5 million	60 and Central Library
Enoch Pratt Public Library Baltimore, Maryland	650,000	21 and Central Library and bookmobile
Fort Bend County Libraries Richmond, Texas	350,000	8 and Central Library
Free Library of Philadelphia Philadelphia, Pennsylvania	1.5 million	54 and Main Library
King County Library System Seattle, Washington	1.7 million	47
Oakland Public Library Oakland, California	375,000	15 and Main Library
Public Library of Charlotte and Mecklenburg County Charlotte, North Carolina	695,000	23 and Main Library
San Antonio Public Library San Antonio, Texas	1.1 million	23 and Central Library and Bookmobile
Tucson–Pima Public Library Tucson, Arizona	817,000	26 and Main Library and Bookmobile
Washoe County Library System Reno, Nevada	340,000	15

public library service aligned with Wallace's passion for principles of youth development and innovation. I was selected as the national director for the initiative at the end of 1998.

CORE ELEMENTS OF YOUTH DEVELOPMENT

Over the course of the PLPYD initiative, a variety of youth development philosophies, languages, and frameworks were discussed and reviewed. The most prominent included Karen Pittman's Forum for Youth Investment (www.forumforyouthinvestment.org), Peter Benson's 40 Developmental Assets (www.search-institute.org/assets/forty.htm), and, in Washington, D.C., the National Training Institute for Community Youth Work (www.nti.aed.org). Libraries were encouraged to use their local youth development framework (if one existed) as the most likely model to assure communication among partners and civic bodies. Among PLPYD initiative sites, Tucson, Arizona, and Fort Bend, Texas, adopted the 40 Developmental Assets because of its community relevance. Again, finding the language that best resonates with one's own community is a necessary first step in program planning based on principles of youth development.

For the sake of discussion and training, I developed a simplified youth development model and used this framework in *Teens and Libraries: Getting It Right* (Walter and Meyers 2003). The acronym POP!!! summarizes the key elements inherent in any youth development plan—*program, outcomes,* and *participation.*

A developmental way to conceptualize *program* begins with a belief that for impact programs must have duration and intensity. Program design includes a variety of services, supports, and opportunities defined in the following manner:

Services: provision of resources, knowledge or goods *to* young people

Supports: things done *with* young people—interpersonal relationships addressed by expectation, guidance, and boundaries

Opportunities: activities, roles, and responsibilities taken on and done *by* young people—chances to explore, express, earn, belong, and influence

A single event is not a program but a single service. We need to think holistically and consider a full range of services, supports, and opportunities in planning teen programs. These programs need to be outcome based.

Outcomes remain a growth area for many libraries, and teen services reflect the reluctance to provide meaningful outcome measures that shape both program content and evaluation. Outcomes most commonly cited for teens include these:

- Youth contribute to their community.
- Youth feel safe in their environment.
- Youth have meaningful relationships with adults and peers.

- Youth achieve educational success.
- Youth have marketable skills.
- Youth develop personal and social skills.

Outcomes reflect a change in knowledge, skill, attitude, behavior, or condition and are the true test of our value in the community. Outcomes qualify the library impact in the lives of teens. We must be intentional in selecting outcomes and testing our effectiveness in program models that result in positive changes resulting from our interventions.

Participation promises that teens will be engaged in the development of services for their peers. This premise was captured in the "for teens by teens" motto of Phoenix Public Library's "Teen Central" space and services and is reflected in countless best practices where teen councils or teen advisory groups help libraries with a range of programs, collections, and volunteer and community service programs. The Youth Council of Northern Ireland has documented a participation scale that enables libraries to gauge the level of participation for teens. It also suggests that teen librarians would do well to set realistic goals for teen participation with the ultimate realization that some teens should attain self-mastery as a result of working with the library. The participation scale includes the following (from National Training Institute 2000):

None. Library staff has unchallenged and complete authority.

Tokenism. Library staff set agendas and make decisions. One or two young people may be consulted, with or without the staff necessarily taking heed of their views.

Consultation. Library staff consult youth, but parameters are set by staff.

Representation. A select number of young people are put forward as representing their peers, usually via a committee system but with varying degrees of accountability.

Participation. Youth set agenda, decide on issues and activities, and have joint accountability with library staff.

Self-managing. Youth manage their group with little or no adult guidance.

FORUM FOR YOUTH DEVELOPMENT PROVIDES STRUCTURE AND INSIGHT

In 2003, the Forum for Youth Development published *Public Libraries as Partners in Youth Development: Lessons and Voices from the Field* (Yohalem and Pittman 2003). In this document, the authors captured the key elements of each of the nine PLPYD projects:

Brooklyn Public Library: A variety of programs have the Teen Advisory Group as a key partner, including Book Buddy, Teen Explorers, and Teen Time.

Enoch Pratt Free Library: Youth Internship Program has teens using community service for homework and program assistance.

Fort Bend County Libraries: Low-income Tech Teens provide technology assistance and programs in libraries.

Free Library of Philadelphia: Teen Leadership Assistants work in existing afterschool enrichment programs.

King County Library System: Techno Teen program promotes high-level tech training for teens and introduces a wide range of library work to promote library careers.

Oakland Public Library: Teen tutors in the PASS! (Partners in Achieving School Success) program receive a wide range of career and interpersonal skill training as well as tutoring skills.

Public Library of Charlotte and Mecklenburg County: Teens Succeed! enables teens to set up their own copy center in a branch library serving low-income families.

Tucson–Pima Public Library: Teen spaces and teen employment opportunities as well as new library advocacy roles are created.

Washoe County Library System: Teen employment programs include creating a Spanish Dial-a-Story team, promotional video, and technology wizards to assist the public.

Yohalem and Pittman (2003) created an invaluable tool for libraries that want to scan their teen services in the light of the Forum for Youth Investment's basic and universally accepted youth development framework. Their checklist "Libraries as Positive Developmental Settings" (table 10.2) is an essential filter for programs, policies, and strategic planning.

CHAPIN HALL CENTER FOR CHILDREN'S NATIONAL EVALUATION OF THE PROGRAM

New on the Shelf: Teens in the Library (Spielberger et al. 2004) is a summary of key findings from the evaluation of the PLPYD initiative. When PLPYD was launched in 1999, the Chapin Hall Center for Children at the University of Chicago was contracted to conduct a four-year study of the initiative. The purpose of the Chapin evaluation was not to assess individual sites but to derive lessons that were relevant to the library field as a whole. The evaluation focused on identifying which types of youth programs and implementation strategies were effective in engaging youth and furthering the goals of PLPYD, a cost analysis, and the identification of sources for future financing and the benefits to youth, libraries, and communities realized by the initiative. Evaluation data included interviews and surveys of youth, library staff, and community informants; program observations; and administrative records at all sites.

In the introduction to the report, Chapin Hall highlighted three key findings (Spielberger et al. 2004, iv):

TABLE 10.2
LIBRARIES AS POSITIVE DEVELOPMENTAL SETTINGS

BENEFITS ZONE	FEATURES	DANGER ZONE
Physical space is safe; youth feel comfortable and welcome; building is open weekends and evenings.	Physical and psychological safety	Physical hazards are present; youth feel unwelcome; building hours are inconsistent.
Some spaces and activities are designed with teens' needs in mind; managed consistently with mutual respect for youth and adults.	Appropriate structure	Spaces and activities are too restrictive (e.g., not allowing groups to meet, talk); activities are inconsistent, unclear, or change unexpectedly.
Designated areas are available for youth to interact with peers; youth feel supported by staff.	Supportive relationships	Youth do not have opportunities to interact with peers; youth feel ignored or not supported by staff.
Youth are encouraged to join groups and activities, and materials reflect youth interests.	Opportunities to belong	Youth are excluded from activities; programs, activities, and materials do not reflect youth interests.
Library staff have high expectations of youth and encourage and model positive behaviors.	Positive social norms	Library staff allow negative behaviors to go unaddressed or make some teens feel unwelcome, rather than helping them conform to expectations.
Youth-focused programs and activities are challenging and based on youth input; youth are encouraged to take active roles in the overall functioning of the library.	Support for efficacy and mattering	Youth input is not considered; activities are not challenging.
Staff help youth identify interests and opportunities to develop and practice skills in the library and in the community.	Opportunities for skill building	Youth do not have opportunities to develop and practice skills in the areas of interest.

(cont.)

TABLE 10.2 (cont.)

BENEFITS ZONE	FEATURES	DANGER ZONE
Library offers opportunities for families; homework help is available; provides space for youth and community meetings and activities; works with schools.	Integration of family, school, library, and community efforts	Library does not offer opportunities for family activities; homework help is not available; no partnerships with schools and community organizations.
Library offers information on health and social service resources, helps assess options, may make referrals; transportation, snacks, small stipends available for special programs.	Basic care and services	Library is not equipped to make social service referrals; snacks, transportation never available.

Source: Yohalem and Pittman 2003, 12. Reproduced with permission.

Public libraries have the potential to design youth programs that provide developmentally-enriching experiences to teens and have a positive effect both on youth services and on the library more broadly.

Implementing and sustaining these projects is complicated, time-consuming, and expensive.

The success or failure of particular programs depends on the library's resources and the degree to which these programs are an integral part of the institutional mission and goals of the library.

In short, high-quality programs are attainable with adequate staff, resources, and alignment with the library mission. The evaluation found that all nine programs met outcomes, and that teens developed a wide range of technical and social skills, contributed to their communities, developed positive relationships with peers and adults, and impacted the quality and relevance of the library program in the community.

STRATEGIES FOR SUCCESS AND SUSTAINABILITY: TUCSON CASE STUDY

Chapin Hall's final finding that the success or failure of a project depends on its integration with the core mission and goals of its institution seems obvious to us. Yet how many of our efforts in teen services begin with vetting our system's core mission and values? Frequently we do not think of programs holistically—as integrated services, supports, and opportunities—but as a random series of events and activities based on current fads or funding opportunities. Best practices in the PLPYD initiative were rooted in the core mission of their institutions. A review of one PLPYD site, the Pima County Public Library (PCPL), illuminates the holistic approach of any best practice and shows how sustainability is built into programs with mission alignment, teen-identified needs, and strategic partnerships for sustaining new programs.

MISSION ALIGNMENT

The City of Tucson was already invested in youth development and had an established Tucson program evaluation and grants office when PCPL began its planning grant year. The city had an active Metropolitan Education Commission and hundred-member Youth Advisory Council/Tucson Teen Congress to assist in Tucson's PLPYD planning phase—to name two among a variety of city partnerships that supported youth. The teens of Tucson and Pima County worked with city and library staff to create a unique vision statement for youth: "To create a partnership of advocacy among youth, the library, and the community which will inspire youth creativity, strengthen youth leadership, and support self determination to secure a successful future in a safe, fun, educational, and enjoyable space" (Teens and TPPT 1999). This vision statement complemented the library's mission and clarified the work planned in the PLPYD years.

FOCUS ON TEEN-IDENTIFIED NEEDS

As the PLPYD project unfolded, conversations with teens all over the country validated Tucson's plan to create unique space for teens. Whereas PLPYD centered on program development, the teens in every conversation in the initiative cities mentioned the need for a space just for teens. One of the most innovative products of the planning year was a concept for a youth space designed by the teens. Tucson library staff worked with numerous local teen advisory groups and a specific group from Cholla High School that had created an illustration of an ideal youth career/recreation center.

Creating a place just for teens was an excellent investment, especially relevant in the current economic times. The description of their space captures the wisdom of both library staff and Tucson teen partners:

> We've learned that young people have their own definition of what is a welcoming and safe environment. The library must train staff to be more knowledgeable about adolescent developmental stages, more responsive to teens' needs and interests. Library buildings need to be modified and made more youth friendly. Young adult services librarians need to reevaluate the ways information for teens is organized and delivered. It is important to provide print, non-print, and electronic resources. (Teens and TPPL 1999, 9)

Since the end of the Wallace grant, all PCPL branches have teen spaces. (See chapter 9 for continued discussion of the importance of unique library spaces for urban teens.)

STRATEGIC PARTNERSHIPS
FOR SUSTAINABILITY

Many sites developed teen employment programs and created unique job descriptions and opportunities, but Tucson was unique in working with the city's human resources department. Staff knew that sustainability would require modifications to the civil service library page job description to accommodate younger teens and that younger teens would need staff support to succeed in new jobs. They were able to change the age of employment to teens younger than 18 years (16- and 17-year-olds for part-time work and 14- to 17-year-olds for five-week summer internships) and to provide training for adult staff who would be supervising teen pages and summer interns.

This approach created a culture of youth employment that remains today. In fact, when the city and county libraries merged, the library was again faced with a civil service system that would not hire pages younger than 18 years. The library culture of teen employment motivated library staff to work with city and county One Stop Career Centers to broker employment for younger teens. Currently teens can find out about jobs on the library web page and then work with One Stop Career Centers, which provide the library with assistance in teen recruitment, intake, testing, and process paperwork and time cards for all teen employees. The mission of service to teens, commitment to teen space, and teen employment is alive and well today—five years after Wallace Foundation funding.

PLPYD PRACTICES IN 2008:
PHOENIX CASE STUDY

The lessons from PLPYD provide insight on managing teen services for library systems today as they did during the four years of PLPYD practice. When I returned to the Phoenix Public Library in 2003, teen services had changed dramatically. A state-of-the-art "Teen Central" space had opened, and teen councils and teen services were flourishing. Teens appeared as library advocates at budget hearings to thank city council members and city staff for the improved services and spaces. Teen spaces were being planned or were under construction in all Phoenix branches, and frequent visitors came from around the country to consult on teen spaces. The Phoenix Public Library 2002 Strategic Plan began with a statement of guiding principles that included "make service to children and teens a priority." A new grant for techno-teens provided employment for teens who reported increases in a variety of skills based on their employment. Library teens had started a new "Read What You Want Book Club" in Teen Central and participated in a countywide readers' advisory training sponsored by the Arizona State Library. There were no changes or stresses to bring PLPYD learning into focus until the central library began a process to renew and reinvent services under the leadership of a new central library deputy in 2007.

"Renewing Phoenix" was a citywide challenge from the Phoenix city manager that began in 2007 when the manager asked city agencies to "provide an inventory of core services and programs to include costs and performance measurements. Departments were asked to relate services to department goals, objectives and mission statements" (http://phoenix.gov/MGRREPT/index.html). This renewal resulted in recommendations for change at the Burton Barr Central Library, including the development of a technology program for teens and a reorganization of existing services for teens and children into a Youth Services unit that included the new teen technology center.

A team was assembled to create a Library Services and Technology Act (LSTA) planning grant to develop a service plan for the teen technology center. Initial conversations on the center recalled PLPYD principles, and the ensuing search for a local outcome-based structure produced the "Framework for 21st Century Learning." This framework was created by the Partnership for 21st Century Skills—a national professional development program to strengthen education in the United States. Arizona's K–12 Center was one of eleven inaugural organizations to receive training in the skills. The 21st Century Skills framework met the criteria for local outcomes and meshed perfectly with the library's goal of lifelong learning and a key principle to "promote creativity and reward innovation to maximize Library resources, programs and services."

The Framework for 21st Century Learning identified student outcomes (represented by the arches of the rainbow in figure 10.1) and support systems (represented by the pools at the bottom).[1] This model allowed the Phoenix team to see the library as a "learning environment" support system and to identify the "life and career skills" as the outcomes for the new technology center. Life and career skills are flexibility and adaptability, initiative and self-direction, social and cross-cultural skills, productivity and accountability, and leadership and responsibility. Another possible skill set for this project was "learning and innovation skills"—creativity and innovation, critical thinking and problem solving, and communication and collaboration.

The Center was named 21st Century Learning Center for the purpose of the planning grant, and it was selected as a 2008 Arizona LSTA Award recipient. In the course of the planning grant, teens were interviewed in focus groups, program models were tested, and a national youth development expert and member of the Arizona K–12 committee from Arizona University's Family Studies and Human Development Division, Lynne Borden, consulted with library staff on refining program outcomes that would be used in the final service plan.

While staff worked on the innovative new teen technology center, another series of events tested the library's commitment to youth development. The local high school district implemented an early-release Wednesday that ended the school day at 11:30 a.m. This coincided with an early-release day at the local middle school, resulting in over 1,200 students arriving at the Burton Barr Central Library between the hours of noon and two on the first Wednesday of early release for the high school.

The teens were at the library to socialize, use computers, complete homework, and "just hang out." These are tasks that the library usually managed successfully on a daily basis, but the surge of teens created a chaotic and unsafe environment for all. The need to restore safety necessitated moving staff to different positions within the library. For the first time in library history, Teen Central was closed because room capacity was exceeded, and the local police were called because of fighting in the parking lot. The crowd was managed for the day, and subsequent events resulted in the library spearheading a change in school policy, serving as a case study for PLPYD principles.

The day after the "teen surge," a series of meetings with library and community partners began. The head of the Phoenix Youth and Education office opened a dialog with key school personnel at both the high school and middle school. The city librarian spoke directly with the chief of police and superintendent of the high school district. Police officers, school resource officers from local high school and middle schools, and school administrators attended meetings at the library to discuss solutions to the overcrowding and resulting unsafe conditions. Library staff wrote a letter to parents of local high school students telling them of the pride the library took in serving teens and enlisting their help in making sure

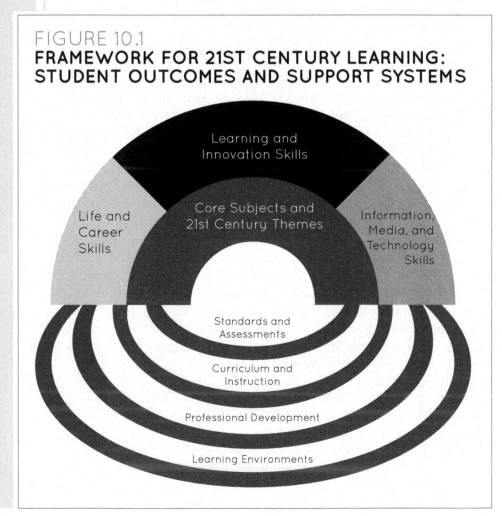

FIGURE 10.1

FRAMEWORK FOR 21ST CENTURY LEARNING: STUDENT OUTCOMES AND SUPPORT SYSTEMS

their teens adhered to principles of safety and conduct when visiting the library. School personnel and police officers were assigned to the library to assist with safety on early-release days. All unassigned library staff were enlisted to help maintain service and safety throughout the building on early-release days as crowds continued to come to the library. The high school district began to discuss other options for teacher training and the timing of early-release days.

The library met the needs of staff stressed by the events with a new training program, "Safe @ the Library: Working with Teens That Don't Follow Our Rules." The training was created by a branch manager, who had experienced similar conditions, and me. The core messages included the following:

- Youth development provides insights for effective responses to teens.
- Our code of conduct and policies on reporting incidents are aids to maintaining safe environments.
- We have community partners with expertise who share our goals and can help.
- There are effective ways to communicate with teens with role-playing examples.
- What are your questions and concerns?

The prereading for this training included Karen Pittman's "Library as a Positive Developmental Setting" from the Forum for Youth Investment (www.forumforyouthinvestment.org). The training was appreciated by staff, who used the information not only on early-release days but daily as they served teen customers. The end to this story was a solution by the high school district to change the time for teacher in-service training to the morning. Teens came to school two hours late and were released at their regular dismissal time—an elegant solution that let teens sleep a little later and maintained afterschool routines.

HOW DOES PLPYD APPLY TODAY?

In the process of writing this chapter, I remembered a comment from a colleague who responded to our "new" information at a conference early in the PLPYD initiative. After hearing about youth development, she said, "You know this really isn't new stuff." At first I was taken aback by her comment, but on reflection I realized the truth in her statement. Effective teen programs have always engaged teens as leaders, used their skills and talents, and provided them opportunities to develop new skills and avenues to serve their communities. We have worked to freshen and clarify past practices in our discussions of youth development and in the many best practices and partnerships begun and still implemented by PLPYD. The value of well-planned teen spaces began at the Los Angeles Public Library before PLPYD began. Teen spaces will be even more important as libraries reinvent their roles in the community as places for conversations and meet expectations to provide informal educational support imposed by dynamic technologies and their myriad applications. We work best using the most current insights provided by program evaluations and customer feedback. The ideal test for any program is meeting outcome goals set for our internal and external customers.

I conclude with a quote from creativity guru Roger von Oech in his twenty-fifth anniversary edition of *A Whack on the Side of the Head*. Von Oech has developed a principle he calls the "Thuban Phenomenon," which refers to the changing of the star that directs us to true north. Over a 26,000-year cycle our current "north star," Polaris, will no longer assist us in finding true north because of Earth's wobbling on its axis. Polaris will be replaced by the star Thuban—the former north star that guided us from roughly 4000 to 1800 B.C. Von Oech states: "The right idea can become the wrong idea, but under certain circumstances it can become the right idea once again" (2008, 84). I believe that regardless of what we call the principles of youth development, or whatever system we use to describe feedback, they are the right ideas for serving urban teens effectively. We can hope that they will be ideas that return and resurface, leading to excellence in programs and service for urban teens.

Note

1. Detailed discussion of the Framework for 21st Century Learning, along with this graphic image, are available at www.21stcenturyskills .org/index.php?Itemid=120&id=254&option=com_ content&task=view.

CHAPTER 11
THE LOFT AT IMAGINON
A New-Generation Library for Urban Teens

MICHELE GORMAN, AMY WYCKOFF, AND REBECCA L. BUCK

LOCATED IN THE HEART of the city's urban cultural district, Imagin-On: The Joe and Joan Martin Center is an award-winning library for young people in Charlotte, North Carolina. Unique in the country, this joint-use facility is a collaborative venture between the Public Library of Charlotte and Mecklenburg County (PLCMC) and the Children's Theatre of Charlotte. The 100,000-square-foot facility houses a library for children; a teen library that includes an animation, film, and music production studio; a technology education area; interactive exhibits; a fully equipped, state-of-the-art computer lab; classrooms; rehearsal spaces; and two professional theaters that seat 570 and 250. ImaginOn's goal is to provide excellent and developmentally appropriate programs, collections, and spaces for young people from birth through age 18. Together, the library and the children's theater share a programmatic mission at ImaginOn: to bring stories to life through extraordinary experiences that challenge, inspire, and excite young minds.

ImaginOn's teen library, commonly referred to as the Loft at Imagin-On, is now one of the premiere library spaces for teens in the United States. Located on the second floor of ImaginOn, the 4,000-square-foot space includes comfortable chairs, café tables and stools, booth seating, other lounge space, and a bank of desktop computers. The entire Loft is Wi-Fi accessible, and laptop computers are available for in-house use with a library card. Adjacent to the Loft is "Studio i," a 1,225-square-foot film and music studio where teens create original live action and animated films and music compositions.

HISTORY

ImaginOn opened to the public in October 2005, but planning began almost a decade earlier. In 1997, Bob Cannon, executive director of PLCMC, and Bruce LaRowe, executive director of the Children's Theatre of Charlotte, were both running out of space in their buildings. They began to explore the notion of a shared facility for young people that would serve both organizations. As planning proceeded, it became clear that these two partners engage youth in complementary ways. They realized they could share both a building and a mission, and ImaginOn was born. Holzman Moss Architecture, together with Gantt Huberman Architects, designed a fully integrated facility that captivates the minds and imaginations of children and teens.

AUDIENCE AND VISION

The largest city in North Carolina, Charlotte has a population of a little less than 700,000. PLCMC serves not only Charlotte but the surrounding county, for a total service population of approximately 903,000. According to the Charlotte Chamber of Commerce, the racial composition of the city is approximately 55.1 percent white, 32.7 percent black, 7.4 percent Hispanic, and 3.6 percent other. The estimated median household income in 2008 was $46,163.

Although ImaginOn does serve a cross-population of users as both a tourist destination and a popular location for fieldtrips for middle and high school students from throughout the county, the city center location makes it a hub for urban teens who live or go to school in the downtown area looking for something to do in the afternoon, on weekday evenings, and throughout the weekend. In fact, a majority of the Loft's collections, programs, special events, and services are developed specifically to meet the needs of urban teens. One of the Loft's regular teens described it as "a place without too many rules where you guys realize I'm growing up and need a place to hang out, relax, make music, check my MySpace page, and talk to friends." Another teen mentioned that he felt the Loft was a haven because "home wasn't too great" and he needed "a place to hang out where there was no yelling or anger." At the same time, a local home-schooled teen described the Loft as his "second home" and a place where he could meet other people his age.

These teens are living proof that the Loft's goal of being a refuge for young people in the community who want a place to hang out, recreate, and be comfortable without prejudice is possible. In keeping with the YALSA vision, the staff of the Loft understand and respect the unique needs of teens and always strive to provide them with equal access to information and up-to-date and innovative services, programs, and collections. They also attempt to include teens in the decision-making process for everything from planning programs and developing the collection to hiring teen-serving staff members and evaluating events and services. Loft staff also make it a point to collaborate with local youth-serving agencies to meet the needs of teens throughout the county.

As a direct result of this vision, the Loft staff strictly enforce a teens-only policy with all visitors, allowing only teens between the ages of 12 and 18 to stay in the Loft for extended periods. The policy is not anti-adult, but it is pro-teen. The staff work hard to create a welcoming and friendly environment for teens that is both safe and developmentally appropriate, and the teens-only policy allows staff to assure parents and other adult caregivers that their teenagers are as safe as possible in this library space. Loft staff ask visitors under 12 or over 18 to limit their visits to this "teen-only" space to browsing the collection, dropping off or picking up a teen, or taking a first-time tour through the space.

ImaginOn as a whole is intended to serve youth. In keeping with this goal, the building does not provide public computer access for anyone over the age of 18. The Main Library, less than two blocks away, has a computer lab open to adults. In response to requests from parents, ImaginOn provides free wireless Internet access, and visitors of any age may use their personal laptops to get online. There is also a parent lounge where adults can use their laptops or read while they are waiting for teens using the Loft or finishing an activity at ImaginOn.

SPACE

The Loft was designed with input from a teen advisory council made up of teens who described the ways they wanted to use the library. Their vision for this library was very different from libraries they had experienced in the past, which contained rows of shelves and quiet study spaces where teens were expected to come in, get a book, maybe do some homework, and leave. Instead, the advisory council wanted the Loft to be a place where teens felt comfortable spending time, engaging staff and other teens in conversations, and asking for help when they needed it. In other words, they envisioned a new-generation library that offers teens all the benefits of a public library (free materials, engaging programs, homework help, readers' advisory, etc.) without the shushing, laundry list of rules, or space overrun with grown-ups and younger children. Was this vision realized? Based on teen feedback, usage statistics, and staff observations, the answer is undoubtedly yes. One of the Loft's regular teens summed up this fulfillment of the initial council members' vision for the Loft when he told a staff member, "You guys aren't a real library. I mean, you are, but you let us do what we want, and you're awesome, and it's a fun place to be."

In keeping with the teens' initial vision of creating an inviting space where teens will want to hang out, all the furniture in the Loft is comfortable yet durable. Booth seating (resembling old-school seating from a classic diner, with a modern twist) is ideal for teens working on group projects, playing one of the Loft's board games, or just hanging out and talking. Windowed walls between the booths provide privacy for teens working or socializing but still allow staff an unfettered view of the Loft as a whole. Teens can use window markers to write and draw on the windows in the dividers between booths, and several of the bookshelf ends are fully functional chalkboards. These customizable aspects of the Loft allow teens to express themselves and to claim the space visually. They also serve as a legitimate outlet for graffiti art, a problem many urban libraries experience.

Overall, the Loft is an active space on most afternoons and weekends. There are quiet pockets where teens can read, do homework, or just reflect, but unlike traditional library spaces neither staff nor rules mandate quiet. Instead, the space is intended to be a place where teens can interact with their peers, talk among themselves, and generally have a good time. All staff members at the Loft are hired based on a demonstrated dedication to working with teens and improving their lives through library services. To create an environment where all teens feel comfortable, the Loft has a set of rules that are simple but essential to all that takes place in the space: "Respect Yourself. Respect Others. Respect the Space." These rules are enforced at all times in the Loft. Not surprisingly, the rules have taken on a life of their own, with teens self-regulating and letting staff know when someone in "their" space is disrespecting another teen, a staff member, or the library itself.

A bank of computers adjacent to the reference desk is one of the most popular spots in the Loft. Here teens are often seen helping each other with homework assignments, playing games online, and checking or updating their Facebook and MySpace pages. All computers are equipped with Internet access, the Microsoft Office Suite, and advanced graphic design and multimedia software including Photoshop, Dreamweaver, and Flash. Wi-Fi access and in-house laptops allow teens to get online wherever they feel most comfortable. Teens can also move furniture to accommodate their needs, including impromptu study sessions, group meetings, or large groups of friends looking for a place to hang out. This makes the Loft a more functional space, but it also gives teens ownership by allowing them to adapt the environment as they see fit.

In Studio i, teens take advantage of a wide range of visual and audio techniques, including blue screen technology, stop-motion animation, paper cutout animation, Claymation, shadow puppet animation, and digital music production. Studio i also includes a foam-walled sound booth that allows teen movie-makers and musicians alike to record without interference from other sounds in the room. All computers in Studio i are equipped with professional-grade graphic design, music composition, animation, and editing software, including Stop Motion Pro, Pinnacle Studio 9, Acid Music Studio, Garage Band, and Photoshop Elements. On any given day, teens working alone or in groups spend hours in the studio creating videos, laying down tracks, and ultimately producing original works of self-expressive multimedia.

COLLECTION

Loft staff maintain a collection that is not only visually appealing but diverse enough to satisfy a wide range of interests. The Loft's collection includes fiction and nonfiction for teens, classic literature, study guides, a script library selected in partnership with staff from the Children's Theatre of Charlotte, the latest movie releases on DVD, books on CD and MP3, music CDs, graphic novels, manga, comic books, and teen magazines. The Loft staff encourage teens to submit suggestions for purchase, and these recommendations help staff tailor the collection to the changing needs and interests of local teens. The Loft's YA fiction collection includes predominantly teen books but also adult titles of interest to teens, including Alex Award winners, best-selling authors and titles, adult titles that are often selected for book clubs by mainstream media, popular adult genre fiction (e.g., James Patterson, Stephen King, Patricia Cornwell, Terry Pratchett), and adult classics.

The Loft's nonfiction collection includes a large number of adult titles in addition to nonfiction books specifically created for a teen audience to ensure that teens find a wide variety of information and sources about various topics. Weeding is frequent to ensure that the collection is current and that the books within the collection are still of interest to teens. The Loft's reference collection is up to date with the latest college, scholarship, and test prep books, and Loft staff members make every effort to assist teens with print reference materials as well as the electronic databases available through the PLCMC website.

YOUTH PARTICIPATION

In addition to developmentally appropriate spaces and a well-developed and diverse collection, meaningful teen participation is encouraged in all areas of the Loft's library services to teens, from developing and renovating the space, to weeding and adding to the collection, to developing new and exciting programs. It is this meaningful involvement, coupled with age-appropriate programming, spaces, and materials, that allows the Loft staff to help meet the developmental needs of teens, including the Search Institute's 40 Developmental Assets—"concrete, common sense, positive experiences and qualities essential to raising successful young people" (Search Institute 2007). Staff use these assets as cornerstones on which to build, continually developing and evaluating their library services and programs to help teen library patrons as they move from adolescence into adulthood.

Meaningful participation in the Loft takes on many forms, with teens actively engaged in creating and presenting programs, performing during special events, and selecting new movies and graphic novels for the collection from vendor catalogs. Teens also help with everyday upkeep of the physical and virtual space, including creating innovative displays, developing original content for the teen website, contributing content to the Loft's MySpace or Facebook page, keeping track of which volumes are missing in a manga series, and stapling comic books that have been ripped. High school students have the opportunity to intern in Studio i year-round, gaining not only technical skills but also experience working with and teaching the public. In addition, teens have opportunities to get involved in more passive ways, including suggesting titles for purchase, answering surveys about library services for teens, or voting songs onto the Loft's weekly top ten playlist on MySpace. One of the most popular opportunities for teens to get involved in a meaningful way is our annual teen summer volunteer program, in which they can log hours for school credit or simply volunteer as a way to pass the time, get involved in the community, and feel useful.

PROGRAMMING

Programming for teens lies at the heart of the Loft's services. Loft staff members know that not all teens are interested in books or reading, and many will never visit the library if reading is the only option for spending time there. To create nontraditional library programs that are responsive to teens in the community, the Loft staff encourage teens to share feedback and ideas for future programs. A suggestion box is also available so that teens can submit their ideas anonymously. Programs begin with a proposal prepared by Loft staff members outlining costs, marketing, time line, potential community partners, and developmental rationale. This process ensures that all programs are well thought out, offer a wide range of experiences, are appropriate for teens, and are true to the mission of ImaginOn and the library as a whole.

The majority of programs at the Loft are designed to help urban teens grow, learn, develop a positive identity, and express themselves. For example, "Rock the MIC!" a monthly "open mic" competition where teens perform in front of their peers, helps teens build self-esteem by providing a safe and nurturing forum to express their feelings and share their work. Several dozen teens show up each month to hear their peers and to vote on the winner of the competition. Similarly, the Loft's "Explosive" Step Team provides teenage girls from Charlotte an opportunity to develop dance skills, build their confidence, and perform. Participating team members visit the Loft weekly to practice their routines and prepare for future performances across the city. A culinary program called "Delicious Dish" teaches basic cooking skills and allows teens to practice these skills in a setting where they are encouraged to take risks and try something new. The library is a safe environment for teens to begin to develop their talents and to make decisions about their personal goals for the future.

One of the Loft's most popular programs—and national winner of *Voice of Youth Advocates'* Most Valuable Program of 2008 award—is the "6R Movement" (Gorman 2008). Inspired by ImaginOn's silver LEED certification and status as the first county-owned green building in Charlotte, programs in the 6R Movement emphasize reducing, reusing, reclaiming, redesigning, recycling, and renewal. The goal of the Movement is to keep these six "Rs" in mind with everything teens do—from waste disposal and repurposing of old materials to finding imaginative ways to extend the life of existing items. A 13-year-old 6R program participant explained, "I want to be involved in the 6R Movement because it's fun! I also want to help the environment because I don't want the ozone layer to completely disappear because that's a harsh living environment." Teens not only learn the importance of recycling but also have opportunities to display their creativity, work with their peers to complete projects, and create products that they can take home and show off to their family and friends. Participants have created chairs out of old phonebooks; a corkboard out of bottle corks; a table surface from broken CDs; wallets out of cassette tapes, playing cards, and half-gallon drink containers; jewelry and key chains from old computer hardware; lamps from plastic CD spindles; bookmarks out of computer motherboards; and clocks out of old vinyl records.

Programs in the Loft also focus on literacy, creating lifelong learners, and planning for the future. The Guys Read Book Club encourages reluctant readers to think about reading in a new way. These club meetings, held at local middle schools in Charlotte, focus on building literacy skills and allowing teen males to bond with each other and with the discussion leader, who demonstrates his own passion for reading. Loft staff members also work closely with ImaginOn's technology education department to plan programs that build technological competencies. The goals for these programs are to provide teens with opportunities to learn new things, build skills, and play and experiment with emerging technologies. Some of these shared initiatives and special events include ongoing teen DJ classes with a professional DJ as well as classes that address graphic and multimedia design, video game design, robotics, digital photography and editing, cloud computing, digital storyboarding, and more. Teens can also participate in programs that directly impact their futures, including college and career fairs and informational sessions about finding alternatives to college, getting into college, filling out FAFSA forms, and securing other financial aid for school.

The Loft staff embrace teens' interest in video games and frequently host gaming tournaments as well as impromptu gaming free play. The Loft offers Dance Dance Revolution, Guitar Hero, Rock Band, and Little Big Planet and hosts a monthly session of the dice-based tabletop role-playing game Dungeons and Dragons. Teens at ImaginOn also have the opportunity to participate in library-sponsored, online video game tournaments several times a year, competing with teens from other libraries throughout the country.

The Loft's presence on Teen Second Life (TSL, http://teen.secondlife .com) is another example of how PLCMC is providing a new generation of library services to teens. TSL allows libraries to reach teens online, where they are already spending a great deal of their time, and it helps libraries stay relevant. Library-sponsored programs in TSL allow teens to use their creativity and technological skills to construct their own surroundings and to interact with each other in a safe online environment.

Other civic engagement programs explore current local, national, and world events. Each year Loft staff encourage teens to participate in the annual budgeting process with the county by attending information sessions and holding up signs of support for the library. In October 2008, the Loft hosted "Participate in '08," a nonpartisan teen rally to encourage voter participation and civic engagement. The rally featured several teen civic groups, each with the goal of informing the greater public that teenagers do have opinions on politics and care about how adults' decisions today impact people of all ages tomorrow. Groups such as the Junior Statesmen of America, Kids Voting, Generation Engage, and Mecklenburg Youth Voice each presented their message of youth involvement. The partnership with the local chapter of the Junior Statesmen of America (JSA, a nationwide, nonprofit, nonpartisan political organization for high school students) was so successful that the teens in the group decided to make the Loft at ImaginOn their official home—meeting every other Wednesday in the back corner of the Loft. In fact, Charlotte's JSA is the only chapter in the entire country to meet in a public library.

Like the Loft's collaboration with the JSA, many of the library's teen programs are enhanced by partnering with other local youth-serving organizations. Partnerships not only bring new patrons to the Loft but also enable the Loft staff to offer programs that feature information or skills that are outside the in-house knowledge or resource base. Annually, the Loft hosts "Prom Project," a program born out of a partnership with Girl Talk Foundation. Since the program's debut at ImaginOn in 2005, more than two thousand teen girls have attended special etiquette, hair, and makeup sessions and then "shopped" for new or gently used dresses, shoes, bags, and accessories—all at no cost to the teens. All dresses and other materials are donated by the community, shining a spotlight on how it is possible to get the community engaged and contributing to the overall health and well-being of teens.

The Loft also partners with Teen Health Connection (THC), a local organization that provides a safe, family-centered environment where teens can receive medical and mental health services and health education, for "Hot Movies, Hot Topics!" Each summer this weekly program focuses on hot new movies that address issues of interest to teens, such as teen pregnancy, making choices, domestic abuse, race relations, friendship, suicide, death, and depression. After each film screening, one of the THC health educators facilitates a talk-back session on relevant issues.

Finally, a few of the Loft's programs are simply about creating a fun and inviting space where teens know they are welcome. Each year PLCMC's Teen Read Week Party brings thousands of teens to ImaginOn for an after-hours bash that features a live DJ, local radio personalities, teen performances, free food and drinks, video games, a dance contest, prizes, and for many a first-time introduction to the library as a place where teens are understood, welcomed, and valued.

CONCLUSION

The Loft at ImaginOn is PLCMC's flagship program. It provides nontraditional library services to the urban teen population of Charlotte, North Carolina. A developmentally appropriate space, a well-developed and diverse collection of print and electronic resources, and a focus on programs that appeal to the population of users served by the Loft allow staff to provide a continually new generation of library services to a new generation of library users. Meaningful teen participation is encouraged in all areas of the Loft's library services to teens.

The response to the Loft space has been immensely positive since ImaginOn opened its doors in 2005. It is a place where teens can hang out during their free time and feel safe—physically safe, and also safe to try new things and express themselves without judgment. Programs facilitate positive interaction in an effort to create bonds between community members and to promote cultural competence through an understanding of other individuals.

As an example of the impact the Loft has on the lives of teens in Charlotte, here is an interaction between two teens overheard by a staff member during a 6R program:

Teen 1: Do you two go to school together?

Teen 2: No.

Teen 1: So how do you know each other?

Teen 2: I just met her at ImaginOn . . . like how I meet everyone.

This conversation is not unusual. Teens from all of Charlotte's neighborhoods come uptown to use the Loft at ImaginOn, as do teens involved in Children's Theatre productions and classes. The shared space brings together teenagers from different neighborhoods and backgrounds to meet and befriend one another on this unique common ground.

WANT TO FIND OUT MORE?

The Loft's MySpace Page: www.myspace.com/libraryloft

The Loft's Facebook Page: www.facebook.com/pages/Charlotte-NC/The-Loft-at-ImaginOn/53823725107

ImaginOn: www.imaginon.org

PLCMC: www.plcmc.org

PLCMC's Teen Services Flickr Photo Stream: www.flickr.com/photos/libraryloft/

PLCMC's Teen Services YouTube Video Site: www.youtube.com/ImaginOnTeens/

PLCMC Teen Services: www.libraryloft.org

CHAPTER 12

BEFORE IT'S READING, IT'S WRITING
Urban Teens as Authors in the Public Library

AUTUMN WINTERS AND ELIZABETH J. GREGG

Here in This Place
Here in this place, we are no less than wonderful young
People
This is the space where we express what we feel in our
Soul
and the thoughts that run through our mind.
This is our chance to confess what simply lies on our
chest.
Here in this place, we can rest from all the stress that life
Brings us.
Week after week we impress each other with our
creativity.
For it is our responsibility to show our community that
Young people can be amazing, because we are no less
than that.
Here, we are like one family and together we have fun.
Here, behind closed doors we are the teenagers of Write On!

Mahogany Woods, from *Behind Closed Doors*

IN 2006, DURHAM COUNTY Library partnered with the University of North Carolina at Chapel Hill (UNC-CH) Writing Center to start Write On!—a writing workshop for teenagers. Write On! teaches young people to redefine their relationship with the written word by turning them into writers as well as readers. This commitment to teen literacy through writing has created a life-altering experience for two dozen teens and twenty tutors at the Durham County Library that has lasted for more than three years. Here's our story.

WRITING INSTRUCTION AS COMMUNITY SERVICE: WRITE ON! IS CONCEIVED

Write On! is the creation of Kim Abels, former director of the UNC Writing Center and current assistant director for Education, Outreach and Administration at the Kenan Institute for Ethics at Duke University; Julie Wilson, currently the Writing Center coordinator at Warren Wilson

College and a doctoral student in the UNC-CH School of Education at the time of Write On!'s inception; and Kristal Moore, also a doctoral student in the UNC-CH School of Education. Abels, Wilson, and Moore were interested in the idea of writing instruction as community service. They were influenced by the work of two other academic writing center/public library partnerships: the Salt Lake Community College Community Writing Center (www.slcc.edu/cwc/) and the University of Wisconsin–Madison Community Writing Assistance program (www.wisc .edu/writing/AboutUs/SerPlaces.html).[1]

Wilson was also influenced by the 826 Valencia model of drop-in writing workshop created by author Dave Eggers (www.826valencia.org). 826 programs offer free project-based workshops on creative topics not usually covered in school curriculums—comics, college admissions essays, journalism and zines—as well as drop-in homework help. According to its website, the 826 mission "is based on the understanding that great leaps in learning can happen with one-on-one attention, and that strong writing skills are fundamental to future success." Wilson was particularly inspired by the emphasis 826 placed on writing outside of the typical school curriculum. She explained:

> I sat in one afternoon during their afterschool program and was impressed that students could choose to do homework or some other kind of activity, or they were just as welcome to hang out, eat snacks, talk with friends, chill, etc. We tried to have this kind of atmosphere at the library, where students could choose to write. 826 also reinforced our sense that seeing their pieces in print, in published volumes, is motivating to writers.

And Abels added:

> We had a sense that the pedagogy that we were using with the UNC-CH undergrads would work in other areas. At the Writing Center, we taught writing as a collaborative point of view. We used the idea of meeting somebody where they are in their process. We were very comfortable with the idea of figuring out what might engage a particular group of students.

PHILOSOPHY OF WRITE ON!

"In school I never get writing back with anything positive written on it."

First and foremost, Write On! is not school. According to Abels, "In school, you write to avoid. You think 'I gotta write something!' and you turn it in and hope. We wanted to show that what you write can matter." Write On! accomplishes this task by providing a loose structure based on feedback and revision. Tutors are referred to as "coaches" and create a supportive, trusting atmosphere like that in a college-level writing workshop. Peer feedback trumps adult evaluation. Students are expected to share their writing with the group and to provide constructive feedback for their peers. Kristal Moore instituted a practice of "passing the mic" to formalize respectful behavior within the group. One person "has the mic" at a time, so the attention of the entire group is directed toward that person. When critiquing a fellow writer's work, students are expected to keep their comments specific and to offer praise along with criticism. The feedback sheet shown in figure 12.1 is used to guide the critique and discussion.

Within this loose structure, students are given a great deal of freedom. They can respond to prompts however they like, even with art. More than anything, they are expected to take ownership of their ideas and to expand on them. Coaches provide prompts for each session; typically one coach is responsible for a week's activities and pulls ideas from library or personal resources to implement in the workshop. For example, a coach may collect various photography books from the library's collection and ask writers to choose an image to reflect on. The prompts serve as jumping-off points for writers and can be adapted to the previous week's activities or to a topic that writers wish to address. Again, this flexibility allows writers to control the direction and scope of the workshop's content.

Coaches are explicit in discussing and modeling the type of behavior they expect from the group. Ground rules are created as a group exercise, written down, discussed, and then followed consistently. The coaches complete writing exercises and share their work with the students, modeling the kinds of work and feedback they expect. Student writers who have previously participated in Write On! sessions also help introduce new participants to the workshop approach. Often they remind others of rules and make sure to support new writers' work. In this sense they become even more involved in the structure of the workshop and understand their positions as behavior models for new participants, owning and legitimizing the practice.

FIGURE 12.1
SAMPLE FEEDBACK SHEET

1. What impression or idea does the piece leave you with?

2. What is working well in the piece?

3. What do you think about the first sentence? Does it grab your attention?

4. What do you think of the last sentence? Does it leave a strong impression?

5. What are the most memorable words in the piece?

6. Are there any vague words that you think the author could replace with more descriptive ones?

7. Does the piece leave you with any questions that you would like the author to answer? Anything you want to hear more about?

Despite what parents may think when they sign their teens up for the free program, Write On! never uses grammar skills and drills or sentence structure exercises. Abels explains that the coaches instead emphasize that "the reason to care about your commas is to be able to get someone else to understand your idea." This focus on meaning dovetails with the importance of peer feedback. Abels adds, "Reading and revision is the only way you can really improve your writing. If a teen writer shares a piece and realizes, 'Oh, I was trying to say this and they didn't hear that,' it helps them clarify their writing. It's the way that real writers work."

WRITE ON! AT THE DURHAM COUNTY LIBRARY

Durham County Library (DCL) consists of a main library, seven branch libraries, and a bookmobile. We are moving toward a model that focuses on regional libraries, with two regional libraries currently in service and two more under construction. The main library is located in downtown Durham, an area currently being revived after a long period of suburban growth. It was built in 1980 and is scheduled to undergo renovation in 2012.

DCL serves a population of over 240,000 within the county. Our patron base is 51 percent white and 40 percent African American within the county; within the Durham city limits, the population of African Americans and whites is nearly equal. We also have a rapidly expanding Hispanic population in Durham. More than 17,000 students attend public high schools in Durham County. Forty-seven percent of students under age 18 are eligible for free or reduced lunch. According to an August 2008 study of disconnected youth in the Research Triangle, 28.5 percent of youth in Durham live in poverty, the highest rate in the Triangle region and 9 percent higher than the national average (MCD Incorporated 2008).

DCL employs one full-time YA librarian and two YA/reference librarians as well as a youth services division manager who oversees the services for children and teens. In 2008 we held 822 YA programs system-wide, with a total attendance of 12,700. Programs held at the three largest branch libraries include Wii gaming sessions, anime clubs, teen advisory boards, and teen craft programs. Write On! currently runs only at the main library.

INITIAL PLANNING FOR WRITE ON!

Wilson and Moore performed an initial community assessment, funded by the UNC-CH Center of Teaching and Learning, in 2005 to find out what literacy-based community services were already available in the area surrounding UNC-CH. They discovered that organizations such as the Durham Literacy Center and the Orange County Literacy Council were doing a great deal of work with low-literacy adults. One unfilled niche seemed to be everyday literacy programs for adults, much like the University of Wisconsin community writing help model (www.wisc.edu/writing/

AboutUs/SerPlaces.html). Under this model, tutors assist adults with cover letters, job applications, eulogies, community newsletters, and any other type of writing.

For one semester, Wilson and Moore tried out a few partnerships in the Chapel Hill area. Both were variations of afterschool writing assistance for a preestablished group of teens. Given that they were working with teens, they tried both homework help and creative writing activities. Neither partnership lasted, so they began looking for another home.

Again drawing on the University of Wisconsin model, Wilson and Moore decided to contact DCL to find out if our adult patrons could use writing assistance. Fortunately that initial call was routed to Karlene Fyffe, Youth Service division manager. Fyffe had recently hired Autumn Winters as the system's first full-time YA librarian. Fyffe and Winters were struggling to connect with teens who were not frequent library users. One thing that was succeeding for teens on a micro-level was poetry programming, so Fyffe was receptive to Wilson's idea for a writing workshop. When Winters, a former English major and veteran of college-level writing workshops, found out about the idea, she was equally enthusiastic. She was already focused on the idea of the library as an avenue for self-directed teen learning and was delighted by the prospect of a noncurricular writing workshop.

Planning for Write On! at the main library began in August 2005. Wilson and Winters met a few times during the fall to discuss the program. Wilson attended formal training with 826 Valencia in hopes of establishing 826 Durham, which would be funded and supported by the 826 Valencia Foundation. Winters began working with teen advisory board member Stephanie Humphreys on planning for the program.

THE FIRST SEMESTER

Write On! activities began at DCL in January 2006. The first Write On! activity was a one-shot workshop specifically directed toward writing college application essays. Wilson and Moore recruited Writing Center tutor and UNC-CH English department doctoral student Bond Thompson to round out the coaching staff for this event. The workshop was fairly well attended. We hoped to use the application essay workshop as a recruitment tool for teens who might be interested in attending weekly writing events.

Finally, all the elements were in place to begin holding workshops regularly on Tuesday nights. DCL had marketed Write On! using fliers, news releases, and coverage in a programming calendar distributed to all students in Durham public schools. Despite our efforts, no students showed up for the first three Tuesday nights.

Wilson persevered, however, and Winters tried to keep in mind that DCL's weak track record with teen programming meant that it would take a while for word to get out. On February 12, 2006, DCL learned that a reporter from the local newspaper wanted to write a story about Write On! We eagerly invited Dawn Vaughan from the Durham *Herald Sun* to attend the Tuesday evening class, with hope that the *idea* of Write On! would be interesting even if the event itself was still a bit theoretical.

Then, it happened: "Wilson sat at the head of the table, waiting patiently for young writers. A few minutes past the starting time . . . two teenage girls walked into the third floor conference room. Homeschoolers and sisters Angelica and Precious Powell were interested in improving their writing skills" (Vaughan 2006). Angelica worked on a book report about *Great Expectations*. Precious asked about an upcoming assignment on Amelia Earhart. Vaughn's story about Write On! appeared with a beautiful photograph on the front page of the Durham *Herald Sun*, and the calls started coming in. Write On! was off.

Classes continued on Tuesday nights through April 25 of that year. Sixteen middle school and thirteen high school students attended, with an average nightly attendance of eleven. Students came from all over Durham County and from public, private, and home schools. By April 4 a core group of eleven students had been formed, and they remained in the program to publish in Write On!'s first publication, *Unbreakable*, and to perform their work at the first public reading in May. Five of these students remained with the program for the next three years: Dominique, Malcolm, Clarence, Aria, and Mahogany.

THE FIRST PUBLICATION

Unbreakable features poetry, prose, and artwork from the core group of eleven students who came together in Write On!'s first semester. Wilson, Moore, and Thompson designed the book and printed two hundred copies at UNC-CH. A potluck celebration and reading was held during the first week in May. The room that was so empty at the beginning of January was now packed with an appreciative audience, proud students, and tons of delicious food. Young authors shared their work with increasing confidence. Several students bravely addressed personal trauma in their work, ranging from body image issues to the death of a parent. Others chose to take an uplifting tack on the theme, encouraging peers to "always stay true and faithful to yourself."

The Gift in Me

When God put the dancer in me,
He knew what I was born to be
It expresses my joy, my pain,
And my determination to break free

When life seems to get me down,
My doubts, my tears, my weary mind
The dancer begins to rise,
Dries the tear drops from my eyes

I can see a brighter day,
I can hear my heart say,
Dance! Until your joy is back
Dance! Until your tears subside
Dance! For the world to see
The dancer . . . the gift in me

Aria Ross, in *Unbreakable*

Unbreakable was distributed for free to the general public at all DCL branch libraries. The first print run was gone by the end of the summer. By then, it was time to start another wonderful semester of Write On!

Many lessons were learned as we produced *Unbreakable*. First and foremost was the level of staff involvement in the nuts and bolts of putting a publication together. Staff and coaches spent about twenty hours typing the work, formatting it for publication, and getting the copies made. Second was the importance of the authors' role in choosing a theme, aiding in the overall concept and layout of the document, and providing images and author briefs (at the closing of each issue). During the first semester, Wilson and Winters attempted to come up with a theme on their own, but that idea was quickly scrapped when teenagers got involved, thus validating the importance of writer ownership of the content and structure of the books.

WRITE ON! TODAY: THE STRUCTURE OF THE PROGRAM

Class meetings are held on Tuesday evenings at the downtown library facility, either in an auditorium that seats one hundred or a smaller conference room that holds twenty. The number of classes within the semester varies from as few as four to as many as thirteen.

The writing form is loosely broken down by semester. Spring semester classes focus on creative writing, fall semester on personal narratives, essay writing, and memoir. Of course, the individual student ultimately defines the form of writing. No one who wants to write poetry in the fall is discouraged.

A typical evening includes a warm-up game and an activity focused on a particular writing skill, writing time to allow teens to work on a topic suggested by coaches, and a feedback session for teens to present their work to the group, sharing praise and constructive criticism. The workshop ends with a wrap-up. Coaches complete the writing exercise along with the students. Coaches often have a wealth of experience with writing in their own lives and also bring with them the knowledge and perspectives of the field in which they specialize. Former coaches have backgrounds in education, compositional literature, library and information science, and communication.

Before fall and spring each session, a meeting is held to discuss scheduling of lead coaches and goals for the workshop. Lead coaches (two per week) create a warm-up activity and a main writing activity for the class every week, and additional coaches (ranging from two to four total) act as support staff by greeting students and circulating during the free write. Often a coach is assigned the task of taking minutes as a record of the students there, how participation went, success of writing exercises, and so forth as an aid to planning for the next week's workshop.

WRITE ON!'S PUBLIC PEDAGOGY STATEMENT

To communicate the philosophy of Write On! to DCL's board, potential participants and their parents, and the general public, we developed a pedagogy statement, shown in figure 12.2. The statement contains three main principles: fund, freedom, and focus. This statement is available on the Write On! website, and parts of it are used in documentation given to new coaches.

STUDENT RESPONSE TO WRITE ON!

To document the benefits of Write On! we asked students to complete self-assessments at the end of the spring 2006 semester. Each student who responded felt that his or her writing had improved: "I feel that my best writing has come out in Write On! I never knew I could write poetry before I started this program." "I feel good about the writing I've done. I often needed help to express a certain feeling, but now I'm able to do that better." One student especially appreciated the participation requirement: "Definitely continue to require a piece from everyone and for them to share their progress. This obviously increases participation, but my reason is because EVERYONE has something to say."

In 2008, Write On! coach and UNC-CH School of Information and Library Science student Elizabeth Gregg completed her master's paper on the topic of Write On! Gregg interviewed eight students, including three from the core group that began participating in 2005. The interviewee ages ranged from 15 to 18, with five males and three females. The overwhelming majority of the students reported never having participated in library programming in the past, with only one reporting an experience with tutoring programs. All reported having been told about Write On! by a family member who had seen publicity about the program in local newspapers. None had experience in writing programs outside of school.

FIGURE 12.2
PUBLIC PEDAGOGY STATEMENT

WRITE ON!

Fun: Too often, people think of writing as an ordeal, something they can't do, boring. We view writing as exploration, trying out new forms, ideas, and words. While this exploration can be playful or serious, we keep in mind the enjoyable aspects of writing.

Freedom: Good writers make choices, such as what to write about, how to start, and what particular words to use. We encourage teens to make many choices themselves, allowing them time to decide when they are ready to write and what they want to say.

Focus: While some pieces of writing get balled up and thrown away, other pieces get rewritten, proofread, and printed. Our best written work needs readers. We teach teens to give each other feedback on their writing, revise, and share the work they're proudest of.

The goal of Write On! is to encourage teens to explore their intellectual and creative abilities in the company of other teens and with the guidance of writing coaches. We offer writing support in a casual atmosphere where teens can explore ideas and make their own choices about writing.

Gregg asked the students to explain what experience in Write On! most affected them. Responses (figure 12.3) ranged from working as a group to create a poem to learning from individual coaches.

Gregg also asked the students about the specific skills they had learned and the personal impact of the program. As figure 12.4 shows, though the benefits included academic improvements for the students, self-expression, confidence, and a sense of community were also important.

Use of the library before participation in Write On! was reported to be minimal by those interviewed. After joining the program, their use increased. As one student pointed out, "Now I come [here] every Tuesday!" Another student expressed an increased awareness of library programs, and still others noted a better understanding of what services libraries actually provide. Another simply stated that the library was not what she had expected, that it had more resources of interest than she had realized. All of these examples show how programs like Write On! not only change student attitudes about the library but also provide valuable information that can be used to guide decisions related to library services, programming, collection development, and marketing.

THE FUTURE OF WRITE ON! AT DCL

In summer 2008, Julie Wilson and Kim Abels accepted positions outside UNC-CH. Kristal Moore was deeply involved in finishing her doctoral thesis as well as working with a Children's Defense Fund Freedom School project. Three of the five core students who had been with the program for five semesters left to attend college. And several experienced coaches also accepted positions at distant schools. How could the program continue?

No one involved with Write On! wanted to lose the momentum we had gained or disappoint the remaining students. How could we keep DCL's most successful teen program afloat?

Fortunately, coach Liz Gregg, freshly armed with her M.L.S. from the UNC-CH School of Information and Library Science, agreed to host four workshops in October 2008, with a focus on persuasive writing and current events. Thankfully, the UNC-CH Writing Center kept the program in

FIGURE 12.3
WRITE ON! EXPERIENCES THAT MOST AFFECTED STUDENTS

1. Group work, like the "I am" poem
2. Free-writing exercises and warm-up activities
3. Performing written pieces
4. Performance of self-expression that is common in other areas of life
5. Becoming more confident in writing and voice
6. Exposure to a new atmosphere/community
7. Meeting other writers
8. Learning from individual coaches

mind. Full-time ESL specialist Nigel Caplan has Write On! service in his job description, and he began coaching in February 2009. Julia Osman joined Write On! as a coach in October 2008. Gregg, who drove 70 miles on Tuesday nights from her new job in Rocky Mount, North Carolina, to coach in October 2008, is now spreading the Write On! spirit to urban teens at her own library. Her dedication to the program is not unusual within the Write On! community and is testament to the value both coaches and writers place on participation.

WRITE ON! AT YOUR LIBRARY: WHAT WE HAVE LEARNED

Building teen literacy through writing is something you can and should pursue in your library. Libraries are one of the best places to teach teens that their writing matters. As noncurricular institutions of learning, libraries allow teens to explore ideas they find interesting. And because teen librarians are not teachers, they are prepared to listen and connect with young people in a way that demonstrates that their lives, dreams, and hopes matter. Turning teens into published authors subverts the typical relationship among librarians, books, and kids. Instead of distributing the wisdom of the ages to the young, try revitalizing your services by sharing the insights of youth with the old.

Additionally, programs like Write On! promote an array of the developmental assets identified by the Search Institute that adolescents need to be successful, including developing healthy relationships with adults other than parents or teachers, a sense of empowerment and belief that the community values these writer-individuals, and positive identities through increased self-esteem.

FIGURE 12.4
REPORTED BENEFITS OF THE PROGRAM

REPORTED SKILLS	REPORTED IMPACT
Self-expression	Articulation of feelings
How to communicate with adults	Confidence
How to interact socially with a variety of people	Sense of community
Better writing skills	Journal keeping
More artistic	"I write what I feel."
Increased understanding poetry/creative writing	
Improved schoolwork	

PARTNERSHIP IS POWERFUL

Without the UNC-CH Writing Center, DCL would not have been able to host high-level writing classes consistently for as many as twenty-nine students a semester. Without the DCL, the UNC-CH Writing Center would not have been able to gather a diverse community of young people who truly needed their help. If you wish to hold teen writing workshops in your library, look for partners in local college and university education programs, English departments, and community outreach centers. They are the experts.

BUILD A FIRM FINANCIAL FOOTING

Once your partnership is in place, be sure to support it financially. Look for funding to provide stipends or honorariums to volunteers. Work within your own library and within the partner organization to find stable funding for the program. Apply for outside grants, but have a backup plan for when they inevitably run out.

DCL's Write On! project runs on a tight budget. DCL provides free meeting space, pays about $200 a year for book production offsite, purchases snacks for each meeting, and buys some food and supplies for the book party. The UNC-CH tutors work on a strictly voluntary basis. UNC-CH provides writing supplies including notebooks, pens, scissors, and glue. Members of the Write On! team have pursued various forms of outside funding. In fall 2006, for example, Winters was able to secure $3,300 in funding for two laptops for the program from an annual in-house grant funded by the DCL Friends of the Library. In December 2008, DCL used *Behind Closed Doors*, the most recent publication to result from the program, as a fundraising gift for donors who gave at least $50 to the library foundation. We distributed nearly 150 copies to our library family during the promotion, along with a letter highlighting the achievements of the program.

What's in That Bag?

Off the wall a crazy thought
wondering what that lady bought
Driving in a purple Jag
still wondering why she hid the bag
It's stuck on my brain . . . it won't let me be
Wanna snatch the bag and say "LET ME SEE!!"
not knowing what she might have had
this mystery really makes me mad.
It could be bread, a ring, a case full of water
some candy, a bra, or a gift for her daughter.
Xbox, pound cake or PS3, money or
An iPod would be cool to see.
Maybe she's crazy and loves some fun
Some liquor, high heels, or even a gun,
Maybe a . . . Ohhh!!! She dropped the bag

So I ran and got the bag. So so hype
I dropped the bag. Picked it up and looked inside
My jaw dropped and my eyes got wide....................
Dominque Allen, in Behind Closed Doors

BE CONSISTENT

Once you set a time and date for your program, stick with it. Students often refer to Write On! as "Tuesday night." If you hope that overscheduled teens and busy parents continue in your program for years, make it easy for them to keep it on the calendar.

MARKET THE PROGRAM

As noted earlier, the initial success of Write On! was entirely due to a front-page newspaper article in our local paper. A second article in the same paper in fall 2006 brought new students and volunteers, including Stan Chambers, the reporter who wrote the story.

DCL is fortunate to have a separate marketing department that produces a quarterly events calendar, press releases, and fliers. We use all of these tools to market Write On! For us, it has been most important to market to the parents of potential Write On! participants rather than directly to teens. Parents are more likely to see the value of a writing workshop and to make the necessary scheduling and transportation arrangements. Winters is careful to stay in touch with potential attendees and their parents. After the second newspaper article appeared, for example, she received calls from parents for months afterward. Some families heard of the program too late to join in fall 2006, but Winters was sure to contact them personally once dates were set for the spring 2007 session. She also keeps an updated phone list with each potential attendee's name, parent or guardian's contact information, age, school, grade, and e-mail address.

Additionally, we use the Internet to promote the program. In the early days, DCL did not do much program promotion on our website, but as times have changed so have we. Photos from the 2008 book party were featured on our teen MySpace page (www.myspace.com/durhamcounty library). Tutor Liz Gregg formed a Facebook group in order to connect tutors and students, even those who have aged out of the program (www .facebook.com/group.php?gid=12496941052).

ADVICE FOR CREATING YOUR OWN LITERARY MAGAZINE
ALLOW STUDENTS TO DETERMINE THE THEME AND TITLE

Write On! students have the freedom to determine the theme and title of their publication. Occasionally this has led to a spirited discussion of the merits of an avant-garde title like "Deez Chips are Uncensored (to my Pencil)." The process of coming up with a title and theme creates a sense of ownership within the group along with emphasizing problem-solving skills, communication, and overall group cohesiveness.

MAKE THE WORK AVAILABLE IN MULTIPLE FORMATS

Write On! work is presented and preserved in several different formats: as the hard-copy literary magazine, on a website hosted by the UNC-CH Writing Center, and as a live performance piece. Kristal Moore was even able to get the Behind Closed Doors group into the recording studio to make a spoken word CD, through a partnership with the North Carolina Central University Hip-Hop Initiative. Although initially students were shy about hearing their voices out loud, they were also proud to hand a CD to a friend, relative, or parent. Using multiple formats keeps the students interested and invested in the process by demonstrating that words have life on and off the printed page.

KEEP IT SIMPLE

The Write On! books are laid out simply. We used the UNC in-house copy shop for the first book but switched to a chain copy shop for the next two. The folks at the copy shop were glad to give us a good deal on a bulk order for an established account, especially once they saw that we were doing it to benefit kids. We have managed to keep the cost of printing to one dollar a copy, even though the books have ranged from thirty-seven to fifty pages in length.

Our first two covers were designed by coaches in the year-end layout process, but our latest and best cover comes from a collaboration between a student and a coach. In the spring 2006 session the writers came up with the title for the book: *Word*. *Word* is the resulting collaboration, and the front cover image was drawn by one of our seniors, Dominique (see figure 12.5).

MAKE IT PERSONAL

Photos and a personal statement from each author are included in the back of each book. This yearbook-style feature celebrates the identity of the group and the individuals who form it. Kids and parents who pick up a copy of the book at their local library can easily recognize authors they know. And students feel like stars when they pose for their portraits. The personal statements are as wide ranging as any yearbook quote. Sometimes they are short and to the point, like Chelsea McQueen's "I'm currently in the process of finding out about myself, so when I figure everything out, I'll let you know."

Sometimes students use the personal statement as the opportunity for another poem, as in this entry from Clarence (CJ) Hargett from 2008:

> Look at me,
> What do you see?

I see C,
But you look right through me.
People say all he is good for is sports,
Not thinking.
But I am getting an education and playing sports.
While you blinking
I rising to the top
Kid—you still sinking.
Yeah, I cross you up
But I am going for the number one goal.
No more sitting back on Sunday
Looking at the Super Bowl
But studying and dribbling at the same time.

Students often choose to make a comprehensive public list of things that are important to them, like Brittany Coleman in 2007:

Age: 12
Favorite foods: Pepperoni pizza
Favorite books: Twilight, New Moon
My inspiration: My mom

FIGURE 12.5
FRONT COVER ART FROM *WORD*, SPRING 2007

Art by Dominique Allen

My hopes, goals, dreams: I want to get a good education to get a job
    as a vet or a chef.
Favorite subject: Math
What I play: Alto saxophone
What grade I'm in: 7th
Phrases/words that describe me: Funny, silly, quiet, always there to
    lend a helping hand.
Favorite drinks: Dr. Pepper, Orange Soda, Pepsi
Favorite music: Rap, R&B

No matter how the students choose to express their identities, this element of the publication allows them to develop self-esteem, to express a positive view of their personal future, and to exercise building a positive identity as defined within the Search Institute's 40 Developmental Assets.

GET IT ON THE SHELF

Our cataloger, Jean Amelang, created original cataloging for each Write On! publication. We hold copies of each book and the spoken word CD in our local history archive. The students were quite proud (and somewhat dumbfounded) to see their names in WorldCat. Cataloging the work lends legitimacy to the whole affair and offers something beyond the typical high school literary magazine experience.

HOLD A CELEBRATION

The book party was an essential element in our spring writing sessions. Writers would spend the last few meetings making last-minute revisions and practicing their pieces aloud. Many were shy about reading their work, but when book party day came they raised their voices with pride. As one coach noted, "Poetry should be spoken!" This also reinforced the emphasis Write On! gave to the participants' ideas and opinions, giving them relevance when often teens' opinions are overlooked. Having the opportunity to do this no doubt contributed greatly to their confidence along with giving them an opportunity to speak aloud in front of a room full of adults, family, peers, and coaches. From the electricity in the air on the first day of the workshop, to the candid discussions and feedback sessions, to the pride in holding a published copy their work, Write On! gives teens a stronger sense of themselves and their communities.

Note
1. Our review of the development of Write On! was aided by interviews with Kim Abels and Julie Wilson, from which we quote.

CHAPTER 13

FOLLOWING AND LEADING TEENS ONLINE
Using Digital Library Services to Reach Urban Teens

KARA REUTER, SARAH COFER, ANN PECHACEK, AND MANDY R. SIMON

IN THIS CHAPTER, WE offer a few principles of effective digital service to teens for those who may be just beginning to bring their library into the digital realm. For those who may be expanding their existing digital services, we offer some best practices tailored to a variety of services, including ideas for reaching teens through your library's website, blogs, social networking sites, social media sites, and podcasts; we also identify some potential pitfalls to watch out for. Finally, we explore what may be next in digital library service for teens.

WHY OFFER DIGITAL SERVICES AT YOUR LIBRARY?

Young people's predilection for technology, and especially for online social media, is by now legendary and well documented. Countless articles, studies, and reports have explored the behaviors and habits of today's teens, sometimes dubbed the "net gen," "digital natives," or "screenagers." Since 2000, reports from the Pew Internet and American Life Project have tracked young people's technology and media use. A recent report focusing on teens finds that virtually all of those ages 12–17 use the Internet, and that more than half use social networking sites such as MySpace or Facebook and social media sites such as YouTube (Lenhart et al. 2007). Over the years, the Pew studies have found that teens are among the most avid users of digital services such as online gaming, video sharing, photo sharing, blogging, text messaging, instant messaging, social networking, and podcasts—and their use of all of these technologies and media has risen steadily.

Although such results would seem to indicate that technology pervades all aspects of teen life, many have expressed concerns that some teens are being left out or left behind because of lack of access to computers and the Internet or inadequate technological skills and abilities. Many teens from low-income families have reported substantially lower levels of Internet use and instant messaging and text messaging activity than teens from families with higher incomes (Lenhart et al. 2005). One study found that teens lacked the patience, reading skills, and research strategies necessary to complete a variety of online tasks at a level comparable to adults (Nielsen Norman Group 2005). However, a new study suggests that the situation may be improving on both fronts (Greenhow and Robelia 2009). Teens from low-income families are increasingly finding ways to be connected technologically. Moreover, this study finds that online social networking activities offer teens valuable educational benefits, including not just technological skills but also opportunities to practice their communication skills, express themselves creatively, and network with their larger communities.

Where do libraries fit into this picture? Studies have shown that public library use is highest among the youngest generation (Estabrook et al. 2007) and that young people are more likely to be library card holders than those older than 25 (OCLC 2005). Still, library usage lags far behind use of technology. Only 21 percent of young people say they seek information from the public library compared with 76 percent who turn to the Internet as a source of information (Estabrook et al. 2007).

An international survey of people of all ages conducted by OCLC had similar results (OCLC 2007). More than 80 percent of respondents used a search engine in the previous year compared with fewer than 20 percent who searched a library website. When compared with results from an earlier OCLC survey, the use of digital services such as e-mail, search engines, blogs, and online bookstores increased sharply in eighteen months, while use of library websites declined. Given these trends, it comes as no surprise that teens who do use the library report the highest rates of computer and Internet use at the library of any age group (OCLC 2005). At the same time, teens also lead the way in using the library to socialize with friends and even in borrowing print books and researching with reference books (OCLC 2005). Though teens may be turning increasingly to technology, the library is still important in their lives, especially when it comes to reading, research, and leisure.

Against this backdrop, digital services offer an opportunity to expand the reach of your library and to extend your library's resources and social experience to the interactive, online environment many teens today take for granted. At the same time, digital library services can offer teens, especially those in urban areas or from low-income families, exposure to and experience with the online environment so that they can develop the skills and abilities they need for school, work, and their personal lives. Finally, digital services can revitalize the library for a new generation, offering new opportunities to provide and promote access to library resources and services.

WORTHINGTON LIBRARIES

At Worthington Libraries, we are embracing new technologies to serve the current and future needs of the young people in our community, but we are also rooted strongly to our past. When it was founded in 1803 by the original settlers who came from New England to the central Ohio region, our library was the first in the county and only the third in the state. More than two centuries later, *Library Journal* named Worthington Libraries the 2007 national Library of the Year and rated us as a 5-Star Library for 2009.

Located in a first-ring suburb north of Columbus and serving a community of approximately 60,000, Worthington Libraries is one of the busiest library systems in Ohio, ranked only behind the state's eight metropolitan libraries in terms of use, with circulation of over 3.2 million in 2008. Historically an affluent, upper-middle-class community, Worthington has seen distinct changes in its population in the past decade. Since 2000, data from the state indicate steady growth in the number of students eligible for free or reduced meals as well as increases in ethnic diversity among students in Worthington's schools (Ohio Department of Education 2003, 2008a, 2008b); our local schools estimate that thirty different native languages are spoken by students (Worthington City Schools 2009).

In our increasingly diverse community, each of our three locations caters to different segments of our population. Our main location, Old Worthington Library, sits just off the Village Green, the historical center of Worthington, reminiscent of the town's New England heritage. Old Worthington serves a large population of affluent empty nesters but also sees high traffic from teens due to its location adjacent to a middle school and within walking distance of a high school. Our second location, Northwest Library, was opened in 1996 as a joint operation with the Columbus Metropolitan Library and serves younger, upwardly mobile families, including a sizable immigrant population. More recently, in 2008 we opened Worthington Park Library. Situated in a storefront, Worthington Park serves the most densely populated portion of our district, consisting of a large proportion of young families living in rental housing.

Each of our three library locations houses a teen librarian who oversees a dedicated collection and space for teens. We offer several services especially for teens, including the Homework Help Center and a wide variety of events such as crafts, gaming, and movies. Our teen librarians and technology staff also work together to offer the teens in our community a variety of digital services, many of which are among the most popular and heavily trafficked of all our online services. Among our digital offerings, we provide a blog for teens authored by our teen librarians, podcasts recorded by librarians and by teens, videos released on YouTube, photos posted on Flickr, and social networking profiles at MySpace and Facebook. Our library's website (www.worthingtonlibraries.org) acts as the clearinghouse for all our online efforts.

PRINCIPLES OF EFFECTIVE DIGITAL SERVICE TO TEENS
MEET TEENS WHERE THEY ARE . . .

Given reports like those cited above, many librarians worry that libraries are no longer relevant in the digital age, especially to teens. In an effort to increase library relevance, commentators have advocated a new model of library service called Library 2.0, with principles such as "the library is everywhere" and "the library has no barriers" (Stephens 2005). The first principle of digital service has been popularly conceived of as "meet people where they are." Considering the vast numbers of teens who are online today, this can mean maintaining a library blog, creating profiles for your library at social networking sites, sharing library photos on Flickr and library videos on YouTube, or maybe all of the above. If teens are visiting MySpace on a daily basis, this principle says you should find a way to get the library there, too.

. . . Show Teens Where They Can Go

But we cannot reach teens effectively just by *following* them to their online hangouts. We should also strive to use our expertise as librarians to *lead* teens to useful technologies and resources they might not know about or show them how to use technologies and resources they may not be adept at using. If teens are turning to libraries to borrow books and use reference materials, we can introduce them to resources such as our e-book collections and our online databases. If teens are coming to the library to socialize with friends, we can offer online spaces for them to interact with one another. Although we may start the process of reaching teens with digital services by following them online to gain insight into their habits and needs, the ultimate goal should be to show teens where else they might go to meet their information and entertainment needs.

KNOW YOUR AUDIENCE . . .

If we aim to meet teens where they are, we must know where to find them first. Are the teens in your community on MySpace or Facebook? What about Xanga, Bebo, Ning, or some other emerging social networking site? Next, we should find out how teens access their online hangouts, an especially important issue in the urban environment. Do they have adequate access to computers and the Internet at home or at school or do they rely on your library to stay connected? Finally, once you know where the teens are and how they get there, we must find out what they are doing. Are they using chat or instant messaging? Do they subscribe to RSS feeds? Do they browse others' blogs, photos, and videos? Are they blogging or sharing their own photos and videos? The answers to these kinds of questions should guide your efforts to reach teens online—and you cannot know the answers until you ask. As part of a major redesign of our library's website and online presence through 2007 and 2008, we conducted focus groups, card sorts, usability testing, and an online survey. We included teens in each part of the process. As in the other studies cited above, the 12- to 17-year-olds who took our survey reported some of the highest levels of a variety of online activities of any age group, including use of search engines, blogs, online question services, instant messaging, online gaming, social networking, and video sharing.

Although teens in our community were among the most avid users of digital services, we learned that the 18- to 24-year-olds almost always exceeded their use. Middle-school- and high-school-age teens may not have as much access to the Internet as their older counterparts, perhaps because their use is mediated through home and school. In fact, in our survey teens reported the least amount of time using technology compared with other age groups. Two out of three 12- to 17-year-olds reported that they use computers and the Internet for fewer than ten hours per week.

The one area in which the teens exceed the young adults is use of the library online. Although use of the library website lags behind other online services, the teens in our community reported higher levels than other age groups when it comes to using the library website to look up information, seek book recommendations, and find out about library programs. In contrast, the 18- to 24-year-olds reported the lowest levels. This young adult age group includes many college students, who have likely turned to their academic libraries. In contrast, the teens in our community still appear to rely on the public library to meet their information and entertainment needs, and teens may represent the first wave of library patrons for your digital services.

. . . Be Proactive, Not Just Reactive

As you get to know your audience, it is relatively easy to find out what they are doing online and what they say they want, but do not forget to assess what they might be missing and what they need. Though more than 80 percent of teens who took our survey reported browsing videos online at sites such as YouTube, fewer than 20 percent have created their own videos to post online. When it comes to the library, three out of every four teens reported using our library's website in the past year, but only about one in four reported using our subscription research databases. Reading between the lines can help you identify gaps in teens' online activities and experiences and lead you to opportunities to introduce teens to new technologies and resources, such as library research databases, and to help them acquire new skills and abilities, such as video creation.

KNOW YOUR TECHNOLOGY . . .

Different technologies offer different affordances, and different online communities have different rules. Podcasts might be a great way for librarians to deliver engaging book talks, but they do not offer any way for teens to talk back to you. YouTube offers many ways for teens to interact with you—through ratings, comments, and even video responses—but the community is not well moderated and the atmosphere is often uncivilized. Before offering a new digital service through your library, it is crucial that you sign up for your own personal account and spend some time figuring out what the service might offer teens and getting a sense of the "vibe" of the community. Find other libraries and monitor their activities for inspiration. (Be sure to look out for ways you might improve on what they are doing.) Better yet, try to find teens from your community to see what they are up to and how you might join them online.

. . . Find Out What Your Audience Values about the Technology

Keep in mind, however, that teens may not want to find the library in their online spaces. Teens have dozens of options for online activities that your digital services will be vying with. To reach teens effectively, your digital services must be targeted to your audience as well as the environment. For instance, dozens of academic libraries and a few public libraries have developed widget-style applications for Facebook that allow people to search their library's catalog directly from the social networking site. When we asked some of the teens in our community what they thought of this idea, they said they used Facebook as a way to keep in touch with friends and have fun and would not think to look there for the library catalog to do research. OCLC's international survey (2007) backs this up. The vast majority of teens (80 percent) use social networking sites because their friends do, half of teens (49 percent) because social networking is fun, only 26 percent because they are useful. Given these results, a more effective use of Facebook—and other social networking sites—could be to promote fun library events and to create a gathering place for library teens.

USE YOUR PERSONALITY . . .

Teens are accustomed to putting themselves "out there" through social media and generally do not share our adult concerns about privacy. OCLC's international survey (2007) found that teens are less likely than other age groups to feel that online activities are private and are more comfortable sharing their "true personalities" online than other age groups. As a result, personality is powerful in reaching teens online. Following our own second principle (Know your technology), we initially signed up for Facebook accounts to try out the social networking site. Our teen librarians did not solicit any teens in our community to connect, but within a matter of a few months the teens found them. In fact, more teens have friended our librarians through their personal Facebook profiles than have become fans of the library itself on our official Facebook page. Those who have become fans have often found the library page through our librarians. Using your profile to post cute photos of your dog or a review of the latest movie you have seen does not reveal too much about your personal life, but it gives a glimpse into who you are, which, in turn, invites teens to connect with you. By using your personality on social networking sites, you can play the role of library ambassador.

. . . Don't Try Too Hard

Though you should be yourself and share your hobbies, do not try to adopt teen lingo or embrace teen trends. It is helpful to be aware of some slang terms so you can understand teens, but trying to speak their language only makes you sound desperate. Chances are, if *you* are aware of the slang or the trend, it probably ceased to be cool to teens months (or even years) ago, and your results will be the opposite of those you intended. Although we work hard to be friendly with teens, we know we are not their friends.

We believe that using natural, adult language will give you more credibility with teens in the long run.

PLAY TO YOUR STRENGTHS . . .

Are you always snapping photos on vacation or at special events? Have you kept a journal for years and years? Posting photos from your library in a Flickr account or starting a library blog may be a natural fit for you. But if you have no specialized skills to translate to the digital realm, don't force it. Instead, take advantage of the inherently social nature of digital services today. Think about where you might find hidden talent elsewhere on your library's staff. Maybe someone has experience recording audio or shooting video (from former days in a band or as an amateur wedding videographer) and can work with you to get a podcasting or video-logging service off the ground. Better yet, why not recruit teens themselves? For your next library program, invite one or two teens to "cover" the event by blogging the event or taking photos to post online.

. . . Learn as You Go

When it comes to learning how to use these new technologies, take a lesson from the teens. They were not born knowing how to blog, but teens don't hesitate to jump in and try new things. The array of tools currently available to the everyday person is astonishing. Nowadays your cell phone may have a camera, and most digital cameras shoot decent video. Powerful software is available for free that you can use to edit photos and video. Though you might start out by playing to your strengths, spend some time experimenting with all the new tools and resources you probably already have available to you, and you just might acquire new strengths.

ACT AS A GATEWAY TO OTHER LIBRARY SERVICES . . .

Digital services are fun and cool and offer many benefits to teens in and of themselves, but don't lose sight of promoting the library and its resources. Talking about a great movie or a cool new band on MySpace? Link to a DVD or CD in your library's catalog. Itching to blog about a hot topic in the news? Weave in a reference to one of your library's research databases as a resource to learn more. Is it a hot new teen title available as an e-book? Post an announcement on your blog or Facebook page. Have a big teen program coming up? Create a video teaser to generate buzz. Although teens may be using your library website, they may not be aware of the range of resources your library has to offer.

. . . Remember the Gateway Goes Both Ways

In-person library services and programs can also drum up traffic to your digital services. One way we raise awareness of our digital services is by handing out "calling cards" for our podcasting site to attendees of our library programs. We have also found that teens in our community routinely post comments to our blog before and after library programs. Dozens of teens participated in our most recent Read-a-Thon. In the days following, a few teens checked in on the blog to say how much they enjoyed themselves, and others expressed disappointment that they could not attend. For the teens in our community, digital services appear to be a natural extension of our in-person library programs and services, continuing the library experience outside the walls of the library.

DON'T BE AFRAID TO FAIL . . .

For many public libraries, the social Web is uncharted territory. Nearly anything you decide to try is going to be new—for your library, your staff, and your patrons—and not everything you do is going to work. Although we have had many successes with our digital services, we have had our fair share of missteps, too. But we never let our mistakes keep us from trying new things. We simply use what we learn to refine our efforts in another venue or for another time. Fear of failure is not an excuse not to try.

. . . Give Yourself a Chance to Succeed

At the same time, don't be afraid to succeed. You may have the instinct to underplay your efforts, quietly introducing a new service and waiting to see what happens. We know, however, that many people, including teens, have outdated ideas about libraries and library services. As a result, teens may not expect to find the library on MySpace or YouTube, so you have to get the word out. If you are going to take the time to develop new digital services, you must promote them.

BEST PRACTICES IN DIGITAL SERVICE TO TEENS

In this section we share some best practices for a variety of digital services. We offer service ideas we have tried and some ideas from other libraries. We also share some possible pitfalls of each digital service, including barriers and issues we have faced that you may want to be prepared for.

INTERNET ACCESS

Perhaps the number-one digital service your library can provide for teens—particularly in the urban setting—is Internet access. Without a means to go online, how can teens access your digital services? As we found in our survey, the teens in our community have limited access to computers, spending the least amount of time online compared to other age groups. Teens without computers at home likely rely on the library for their access to the Internet. Latchkey teens, who spend their afterschool hours in the library, also turn to library computers to pass the time, complete homework, or socialize. With this in mind, when we undertook renovation of the teen areas at each of our locations, we increased the number of computers available. In each of our libraries, teens now have access to a "computer bar" with multiple stools at each station so that they can gather around together to use library resources, post comments on our teen blog, watch library videos, listen to library podcasts, and use all our other digital services (*Voice of Youth Advocates* 2009).

WEBSITES

Although library websites are de rigueur today, just ten years ago they were the cutting-edge digital service. We launched our library website in 1998, offering little more than our address, phone numbers, and hours. In the decade since then, our website has been through several incarnations in terms of visual design and content offerings. Most recently, we undertook a major redesign using Drupal, an open-source content management system that helps us offer our patrons more interactive features.

Service Ideas

Digital clearinghouse. Our redesigned library website acts as a clearinghouse for all our online services, with a dedicated section linking to the library's Facebook page, MySpace profile, YouTube channel, Flickr site, and other interactive content. We also offer a dedicated section on our site just for teens that highlights our digital services. Since we introduced these high-profile links to our social media efforts on our website, we have added an average of one fan each day at Facebook. Your library's website can help attract teens to all your online efforts.

Teen section. At the same time we were redesigning our website, we were also renovating our library locations. The renovations made it possible to create dedicated teen areas in each of our locations with bright colors, funky furniture, and modern, industrial touches. One of the goals of our website redesign was to connect our online presence to our physical spaces, so for the teen section (www.worthingtonlibraries.org/teens/) we picked up the color schemes and patterns from the teen areas in our buildings to create a teen-friendly space on the Web.

Teen events calendar. Since teens continue to value libraries as places to socialize with their friends, in-library events are important. The teens who took our technology survey reported the highest levels of use of our library website to find library programs and events: about one in three teens. Library calendars are often so jam-packed with storytimes and other children's programs that it may be difficult for teens to spot the programs and events meant for them. If your library website includes a calendar of library programs, find a way to isolate the events meant for teens or to highlight popular game or movie nights aimed at teens.

Homework help. Does your library subscribe to research databases targeted at middle or high school students? Does your library offer after-school tutoring services? Does your library offer telephone, e-mail, or even chat reference services? Create a "homework help" section on your library website to pull together all of your resources targeted at students in one easy-to-access place.

Possible Pitfalls

Teens vs. kids. Whatever else you do on your library website, do not lump teens in with "kids." According to the Nielsen Norman Group (2005), the word *kid* is "teen repellant" and teens dislike anything they perceive as childish. If you create a separate section on your website for teens, aim for a distinctly more mature mood than in the children's section.

Off the beaten path. Compared with other digital media, websites are static and out of the way. Teens (and other visitors) have to make a special trip to visit your website. Sure, they can bookmark it or even set it as their homepage, but they have to make a point of checking it to see what's new. One way to get your content "out there" is with RSS feeds.[1] You can set up your RSS feeds so that teens (and other visitors) can subscribe to receive updates whenever a new post appears on your blog, a new event is added to the calendar, or any content is updated on your website. Even better, you can also use RSS feeds to post your content automatically on social networking sites.

Although requiring more advanced technical skills, widgets are another way to push library content beyond your library website.[2] The New York Public Library has a widget you can add to your iGoogle page to keep up to date with upcoming library programs. The Waikato University Library in New Zealand has a widget for iGoogle that allows you to browse items recently added to their collection. Dozens of libraries have created widgets that allow you to embed a search of their library catalog in iGoogle, My Yahoo! and Facebook. These techniques offer ways to put your online content and services in the path of teens where they may be more likely to encounter it.

BLOGS

Blogs—a contraction of "web logs"—are a kind of online diary and have been around in some fashion since the Web emerged. The term *blog* was coined in 1999 and popularized through the use of the free online blogging software Blogger. The use of blogs by teens has increased steadily in recent years. In 2004, 19 percent had created their own blogs; in 2007 the number rose to 28 percent (Lenhart et al. 2007). Teens in our community reported slightly higher rates of blogging in our survey: approximately one in three reported that they created their own blogs. In the midst of this growth, we launched our teen library blog—called *Worthingteens* (www2 .worthingtonlibraries.org/teen/blog/)—in summer 2006.

Service Ideas

Summer reading integration. As noted above, our 2008 summer reading program rewarded teens not just for reading books but also for posting comments on our teen blog. Throughout the summer months, our blog posts routinely received dozens of comments from teens eager to earn their prizes. Teens could also get points for accessing research databases and e-mailing librarians to ask for book recommendations, which they did in much higher numbers than usual.

Book discussions. Hoping to extend the success of our summer reading program integration, in fall 2008 our teen librarians introduced "Book Chat," a monthly online book discussion on the blog. We announced three titles in advance—placing books on hold at our libraries for teens to pick up—and posted questions on the blog to foster a "conversation" in the comments.

Stunts. When we initially launched our teen blog in summer 2006, one of our teen librarians challenged her local teens to enroll in the summer reading program. She vowed that, if more than 220 teens enrolled and completed the program, she would dye her hair and they could vote on the color. The teens responded, and at the end of the summer reading program we had a purple-haired teen librarian. Of course we documented the stunt on the teen blog with photographic evidence. More than two years later, teens continue to ask our librarian to dye her hair again.

Possible Pitfalls

Lack of participation. Although teens often report high levels of use of social media, the extent of their participation in social environments can be quite low. For instance, when it comes to the use of blogs by teens in our community, we found that about 40 percent of them reported reading blogs, but only about 25 percent reported commenting on blogs and about 20 percent reported posting content to their own blogs in the past year. We experienced the consequences of this phenomenon firsthand with our Book Chat service, outlined above. Although a few teens commented on the first title in the first month, we received no comments from teens on the following two titles. Although we knew that it was a struggle to get teens to participate, we were hopeful after the success of our summer reading program integration. So what happened? The teens' participation during the summer was driven by a specific incentive, namely, points toward the summer reading program prize. And though teens can be a captive audience in the summer months, in the fall when they are back to school, they have many more demands on their attention. With this knowledge, we plan to introduce book discussions again during our next summer reading program.

Keeping it up to date. If you want teens to visit your blog regularly (let alone participate), they have to see that you update it regularly. Before committing to a blog, you must be prepared to devote significant time to preparing posts and facilitating feedback. Our teen librarians sometimes struggle to find time in their busy schedules to write blog entries. One way they found to cope with the pressure of regular blog posting is to write several entries in one sitting, scheduling them to be published on a specific date in the future. Collaboration among our three teen librarians also helps spread the responsibility.

Keeping it fresh. Pressure can also mount to keep your blog posts fresh and interesting to teens. Collaboration can help in this respect as well, by introducing different voices and perspectives. Over time, our teen librarians have developed their own styles, favorite topics, and unique voices, which brings variety to the blog. Keeping up with the news—especially local news from the schools in your community, like the upcoming school play or basketball game—and writing related blog entries also help ensure timely, relevant content.

Moderation. Sometimes success can create problems. The flip side to the increased traffic to our blog during our summer reading program is that we had some bad behavior from teens commenting on the blog. Early in the summer, a few insulting and borderline abusive comments appeared on our teen blog. Because our teen librarians and technology staff—five individuals in all—receive e-mail notification each time a comment is posted to the blog, we were able to moderate the inappropriate comments quickly. Be prepared to monitor the blog—including evenings, weekends, and holidays—so that you can expunge inappropriate comments as soon as possible. Consider drafting a policy of mutual respect—ours is an extension of our library's board-approved Acceptable Use of the Internet Policy we call the "Rules o' the Blog"—and linking to it prominently on the blog. Such a policy helps teens understand the ground rules from the start, but should inappropriate behavior arise it also can guide you in taking appropriate action.

Acceptable use violations. So, aside from deleting inappropriate comments, what do you do when someone violates the rules? In the case of inappropriate comments posted on our blog during the summer reading program, we had the opportunity to find out. Because the e-mail notifications that our teen librarians and technology staff receive whenever a comment is posted to the blog include the IP addresses where the comments originate, we were able to determine that the inappropriate comments were coming from inside the library. Our technology staff was able to identify the particular computers involved, and the teen librarian in that library was able to confirm that the comments were coming from teen volunteers who were helping with summer reading program registration.

Together, our teen librarians and technology staff decided that the inappropriate comments were a violation of our Acceptable Use of the Internet Policy as well as our volunteer agreement. The teen librarian on site approached the teen volunteers and alerted them that we were aware of their activities. She spoke to them in private and helped them understand that their comments were hurtful and abusive to the other teens commenting on the blog and were, in fact, in violation of library policies. Upset and remorseful, one of the teens posted an apology on the teen blog for the undesirable behavior, which immediately ceased. After the dust settled, we also posted a message on the blog restating the "Rules o' the Blog" and received dozens of comments from teens in support of the rules as a way to maintain order. Although it was a difficult experience for all of us, we believe the teens—both the perpetrators and the targets—learned a valuable lesson about online etiquette.

SOCIAL NETWORKING SITES

According to a definition from OCLC (2007), social networking sites are websites "primarily designed to facilitate interaction between users who share interests, attitudes, and activities." For teens, social networking sites like MySpace and Facebook function as online hangouts where they can create their own profiles and view the profiles of their friends. According to Pew, in 2006 about half of teens (55 percent) had a profile on a social networking site. Among the teens in our community, social networking use is substantially higher; three out of four of the teens who responded to our survey reported using social networking sites. We created our Worthingteens MySpace profile (www.myspace.com/worthingteens) in spring

2007. We created our Worthingteens Facebook page (www.facebook.com/pages/Worthingteens/6493617723) in fall 2007, shortly after Facebook allowed groups and organizations to create pages.

Service Ideas

Connecting friends and family. Social networking sites exist to connect people to one another. We learned that one of our teen patrons found herself in our district after she and her brothers and sisters were placed in foster homes across the state and the country. Staying in touch via telephone was impractical—not to mention expensive—so we helped her set up a MySpace profile to communicate online with her fractured family. For teens in immigrant or transient families, social networking sites can provide an inexpensive way to remain connected to family members and friends left behind.

Hands-on training. As a way to offer technology training to teens who may not have ready access to computers and the Internet or who may not be as technologically savvy as some of their peers, we offer regular "Teen Tech Fun Nights" as a drop-in program. Teens can stop by for basic instruction on various topics such as starting a blog, editing MySpace pages using HTML, or editing digital photos with free web-based software. If teens do not have time to try out the software at the library, we also offer instructional pamphlets they can take away with them to try out the programs at home.

Online clubs. Does your library have a teen volunteer program or advisory board? Consider using Facebook to set up a group space for you to communicate with teens and for teens to communicate with each other. Since teens today are moving away from e-mail as a form of communication (Lenhart et al. 2007), you may be able to reach your volunteers or advisory board more effectively on Facebook. Since teens focus on the social aspects of sites such as Facebook, other teen clubs in place at your library might also translate to a Facebook group.

RSS feeds. If teens are not coming to the library website, make your Facebook page or MySpace profile your digital clearinghouse. With RSS feeds, social networking sites can be automatically updated when you update your blog or website. By cross-linking all of your online efforts, you create a more vital web of online content and experience.

Social networking. Although it may seem obvious, do not forget to use social networking sites to create a social network for teens. On MySpace, we are very choosy about who we friend. We connect exclusively with teens in our community and teen-oriented individuals and groups, such as authors (like John Green and Laurie Halse Anderson), publications (like *Teen Ink Magazine* and *HarperTeen*), other libraries, and bands, especially those with literary appeal (like Harry and the Potters and The Remus Lupins). This way our friend list functions as "recommended reading" for the teens of our community, helping them discover, connect, and network with individuals and groups they might be interested in. In this way, social networking can serve to expand the horizons of teens in an urban environment, offering them a way to discover opportunities outside their existing social sphere.

Possible Pitfalls

Indiscriminate friending. If your MySpace friend list represents "recommended reading," who you reject is as important as who you add. If someone adds you as a friend, before you accept, review his or her profile carefully. Consider how the parents of the teens in your community would react if they saw their child accessing that profile. And then consider how they would react if they found out they got there through the library. The same goes for groups and other organizations that submit friend requests. We believe that public libraries should maintain a neutral and unbiased position, and friending a religious or political group could come off as promoting a certain perspective. To maintain a safe online environment for teens, we regularly reject MySpace friend requests from anyone who is not a teen or a group related to teens or teen media in some way. Although you probably do not need to develop a full-blown library policy on MySpace friending, a little advance thought about the criteria to use when deciding what kinds of friends to accept online may help guide you in a tough decision somewhere down the road.

Spreading yourself too thin. As with blogs, keeping your profiles at social networking sites up to date is a necessity. You can use RSS feeds as noted above to add content to your social networking with minimal effort, but spreading yourself too thin is a real danger. If you sign up for library accounts on every social networking site out there without ensuring that you update all of them regularly, you may be inadvertently creating online "ghost towns" in your library's name, thereby giving the impression that your library is not a vital place. Find out which social networking sites reach the largest numbers of your teens and limit yourself to those. But do keep your ear to the ground for emerging sites in case teens end up migrating elsewhere.

SOCIAL MEDIA SITES

As an extension of social networking sites, social media sites, according to OCLC (2007), are "Web sites that allow individuals to share content they have created. . . . While interaction occurs on social media sites, the primary purpose of the site is to publish and share content." Social media sites offer teens the opportunity to share videos on sites like YouTube or photos on sites like Flickr. Nationally, just over half of teens (57 percent) say that they watch videos on YouTube (Lenhart et. 2007). In our community, virtually all teens (98 percent) report using social media sites like YouTube. To reach this audience, we created our Flickr account (www.flickr.com/photos/coollibrary/) in spring 2006 and started our YouTube channel (www.youtube.com/worthingtonlibraries/) in fall 2007.

Service Ideas

Author interviews. Have an author visit coming up? Why not ask your author to sit down in front of a video camera and answer some questions? Our most viewed video on YouTube is an interview with author John Green. We solicited questions from teens in the library and on our blog and printed them up on note cards. Before Green's scheduled program, we gave him the questions to review and then set our video camera up on a tripod and filmed his answers. Our own teens got to see a renowned author answer *their* questions. And thanks to Green's online notoriety from his own video-blogging project on YouTube, teens from all around the world flocked to the video, leaving comments, rating it, and subscribing to our channel.

Video contests. Other libraries, including Denver Public Library and Skokie Public Library, have recently run successful teen video contests. In each case, teens were asked to create videos around a theme, such as "How I have fun at the Library" (Denver) or "I love reading!" (Skokie). Teens submitted their entries via YouTube, where judges viewed them. After the winners' entries were decided, the videos were embedded in blogs or library websites. During and after the contest, other teens could rate and comment on the contest videos. As the top prize, Denver Public Library offered an MP3 player and Skokie Public Library offered a video camera.

Photo galleries. If teens in your community have their own Flickr accounts, try setting up a Flickr group to allow teens to upload their own photos and add them to a group. Flickr accounts are free (with some limitations), and straightforward privacy options at Flickr make it possible to limit outside access to the content to address privacy concerns. Teens could document library programs and share photos online. You could try running a photo contest, perhaps with a tie-in to a library program on digital photography.

Program promotion. Photos and video of library events can be posted on your library's website or teen blog to promote future programs. In advance of our 2008 summer reading program—themed "Just Read It"—we filmed a spoof of Michael Jackson's "Beat It" video, complete with costumes and a closing dance sequence featuring sixteen librarians and library staff members. Because the teens did not always have a point of reference for the 1982 Jackson video, they did not necessarily "get it," but a post on the blog pointing to the video did generate dozens of comments, and we certainly got to show off our personalities.

Possible Pitfalls

Participation. Inspired by the libraries in Denver and Skokie, in fall 2007 we tried to do our own teen video contest on YouTube, but we did not receive a single submission. As we noted above with regard to blogging, the extent of participation in social media sites can be quite limited. For instance, when it comes to the use of YouTube by teens in our community, we found that nearly 90 percent of them reported viewing videos, but only about 40 percent reported commenting on or rating videos and less than 20 percent reported creating and posting their own videos. Although we seem to have an audience of eager consumers of videos, we do not yet have a critical mass of video creators to participate in a video contest.

Equipment and expertise. When it comes to creating online content like photos and especially videos, teens face a variety of barriers to entry. Teens may not have access to the camera equipment or software or may lack the specialized skills required to capture and edit video footage. Supplying teens with equipment, including cameras and video-editing software, and hands-on training in a series of library programs might have helped drum up a greater response to our video contest.

Moderation. As noted above in our section on blogs, the interactive nature of social media can be a blessing and a curse. We have found that different communities are more prone to abuse than others. We have never had an issue with inappropriate comments in Flickr, but we routinely find ourselves deleting ugly and downright disgusting comments at YouTube. What's the difference? Flickr employs a "Director of Community," and individual accounts are reviewed by Flickr staff and rated as safe, moderate, or unsafe. If you come across inappropriate content or behavior, you can flag it for review. Overall, Flickr maintains a civilized atmosphere. In comparison to Flickr, YouTube is more like the Wild West. YouTube allows you to flag videos as inappropriate and mark comments as spam, but that is about where their community management ends. Thankfully, when you post a video YouTube gives you the choice of permitting comments and video responses to be posted automatically or of requiring your approval. With YouTube, we strongly recommend the latter.

PODCASTS

Podcasting—a play on the words *iPod* and *broadcasting*—is the distribution of audio or video content online, usually in a syndicated fashion for people to download automatically and listen to on portable devices. Unlike other digital services, podcasting has not seen particularly high levels of adoption. Only about one in five teens (19 percent) has downloaded a podcast (Lenhart et al. 2007). We started "Programs to Go," our podcasting site (www.worthingtonlibraries.org/interact/programs2go/) in summer 2007.

Service Ideas

Writing contest. Every year since 2002 at Worthington Libraries, we have conducted a teen poetry and short story writing competition. Middle school and high school students submit their writings, and a panel of judges select winners. In 2008 we invited the first-, second-, and third-place winners in each category to record their winning entries for release on our website. The winners were enthusiastic about participating and being able to share their work with their families and friends. We plan to continue recording contest winners in 2009.

Book talks. Worthington Libraries is currently collaborating with a regional organization that offers professional development opportunities for K–12 educators. As part of the "Literature Lounge" initiative, our librarians introduce and review noteworthy books for K–12 students in hour-long book talks. These book talks are broadcast to educators in our local school districts in an interactive video-conferencing environment and will also be made available as downloadable content for teens.

Possible Pitfalls

Equipment and expertise. Compared to videos, audio-only podcasts are a cinch. But some specialized equipment and software are required to record and edit your audio. We use free, downloadable software called

Audacity (http://audacity.sourceforge.net) and an inexpensive USB head-set microphone. Our setup works well for recording one person at a time, but to record conversations or interviews would require additional equipment. Quiet office space—sometimes very hard to come by—is also a good idea to ensure good sound quality.

Permission. We require signed releases for anyone not on staff whose content we intend to publish. For anyone under the age of 18, we also require parental permission. Such releases are an important way for us to acknowledge the contribution teens are making to the library and also a way for contributors and parents to be informed about their rights. Our releases grant us nonexclusive rights to distribute the content online in perpetuity. In practice, however, we would almost certainly remove content at the contributor's request.

You may encounter parents who raise concerns about releasing identifying information about their children. In the case of our podcasts from the writing contest, the content was audio only and did not include any likenesses of the teens, so parents were less concerned. Nevertheless, although the recordings do open with the teens introducing themselves with their first and last names, we specifically chose not to include their ages or the schools they attend to provide some additional measure of privacy.

WHAT'S NEXT IN DIGITAL LIBRARY SERVICE TO TEENS?

To keep up with the always cutting-edge teen audience, our technology staff and librarians monitor new digital services. We are exploring ways to use social reading sites. You can find our teen librarians at Goodreads (www.goodreads.com) and our library locations at LibraryThing (www.librarything.com). We have just launched a new instant-messaging reference service and, in conjunction, are exploring text-messaging reference. On the basis of our survey results, we expect both services to have high interest among our teens. We are also considering how we might use the "micro-blogging" service Twitter (www.twitter.com) to broadcast news and announcements and to promote services and events.

Because the technology evolves so quickly and teens are so quick to adopt new technology, it is impossible to predict what we will be doing with digital services next year or next month at Worthington Libraries. Even as we worked together to write this chapter, we came up with new ideas we hope to pursue. Although we may not know what's next, we will continue to follow our principles of effective digital service, especially "Know your audience" and "Know your technology." That way, we do not have to wait and see what's next. We can lead the way in digital library service for teens.

Find out what's next in digital library service to teens at Worthington Libraries by visiting our website (www.worthingtonlibraries.org). Look for Worthington Libraries and for Kara, Sarah, Ann, and Mandy on Flickr, YouTube, MySpace, Facebook, Goodreads, and LibraryThing. Tell us about your digital library service ideas, too.

Notes

1. RSS feeds are a method of publishing frequently updated content such as blog entries or news headlines. Subscribers to RSS feeds receive alerts of new content automatically through their web browser, e-mail program, or other specialized software, sometimes called a feed reader or an aggregator. RSS feeds allow people to keep up to date with a variety of websites in one place.

2. A widget (also referred to as a *gadget* by Google) is a small program, usually developed by a third party, that can be embedded in a web page to import content from other websites (e.g., the latest photos from Flickr or videos from YouTube) or provide functionality from other websites (e.g., a library catalog search or chat interface). Widgets can be embedded on websites and blogs and at web portals such as My Yahoo! iGoogle, and MSN.com.

WORKS CITED

Abbas, June, Melanie Kimball, Kay Bishop, and George D'Elia. 2008. Youth, public libraries, and the Internet: Part four: Why youth do not use the public library. *Public Libraries* 47, no. 1 (January/February): 80–84.

ABC-CLIO. 1998. *Encyclopedia of urban America: The cities and suburbs.* Santa Barbara, CA: ABC-CLIO.

Agosto, Denise E. 2002. Bounded rationality and satisficing in young people's web-based decision making. *Journal of the American Society for Information Science and Technology* 53, no. 1 (January): 16–27.

———. 2007. Why do teens use libraries? Results of a public library use survey. *Public Libraries* 46, no. 3 (May): 55–62.

Agosto, Denise E., and Sandra Hughes-Hassell. 2005. People, places, and questions: An investigation of the everyday life information-seeking behaviors of urban young adults. *Library and Information Science Research* 27, no. 2 (Spring): 141–163.

———. 2007. Language, culture, and the school library. In *School reform and the school library media specialist,* ed. Sandra Hughes-Hassell and Violet Harada, 145–157. Westport, CT: Libraries Unlimited.

Agosto, Denise E., Kimberly L. Paone, and Gretchen S. Ipock. 2007. The female-friendly public library: Gender differences in adolescents' uses and perceptions of U.S. public libraries. *Library Trends* 56, no. 2 (Fall): 387–401.

Aitken, Stuart C. 2001. Geographies of young people: The morally contested spaces of identity. New York: Routledge.

ALA American Library Association, Office for Research and Statistics. 1999. *Programs for school-age youth in public libraries.* Chicago: American Library Association.

Alessio, Amy J., ed. 2008. *Excellence in library service to young adults.* Chicago: Young Adult Library Services Association.

Allington, Richard L., and Anne McGill-Franzen. 2003. The impact of summer setback on the reading achievement gap. *Phi Delta Kappan* 85, no. 1 (September): 68–75.

Alvermann, Donna E. 2001. *Effective literacy instruction for adolescents.* Chicago: National Reading Conference.

APSL Association of Philadelphia School Librarians. 2008. SDP highly qualified (certified) librarians, selected years 1987–2005. www.apsllive.org/APSLqualgraphA87-06.pdf.

Architectural Design. 2005. Vol. 75, no. 1 (January/February).

Au, Katherine H. 1993. *Literacy instruction in multicultural settings.* Fort Worth, TX: Harcourt Brace Jovanovich.

Banks, James A. 1999. *An introduction to multicultural education.* 2nd ed. Boston: Allyn and Bacon.

Barack, Lauren, and Brian Kenney. 2006. Libraries losing teens. *School Library Journal* 52, no. 1 (January): 18.

Barak, Azy, and William A. Fisher. 2001. Toward an Internet-driven theoretically-based, innovative approach to sex education. *Journal of Sex Research* 38, no. 4 (November): 324–332.

Barton, David, Mary Hamilton, and Roz Ivanic. 2000. *Situated literacies: Reading and writing in context.* London: Routledge.

Beers, G. Kylene. 1996. No time, no interest, no way: The 3 voices of aliteracy, part I. *School Library Journal* 42, no. 2 (February): 30–33.

Benton Foundation. 1996. *Buildings, books, and bytes.* Washington, DC: Benton Foundation.

Bernier, Anthony. 1998. On my mind: Young adult spaces. *American Libraries* 29, no. 9 (October): 52.

———. 2000a. Los Angeles Public Library's TeenS'cape takes on the "new callousness." *Voice of Youth Advocates* 23, no. 3 (August): 180–181.

———. 2000b. Young adults, rituals, and library space. *Voice of Youth Advocates* 22, no. 6 (February): 391.

———. 2003. A library teen services director speaks out: The case against libraries as "safe places." *Voice of Youth Advocates* 26, no. 3 (August): 198–199.

Bilal, Dania, and Joe Kirby. 2002. Differences and similarities in information seeking: Children and adults as web users. *Information Processing and Management* 38, no. 5 (September): 649–670.

Bishaw, Alemayehu, and Jessica Semega. 2008. Income, earnings, and poverty data from the 2007 American community survey. U.S. Census Bureau. www.census.gov/prod/2008pubs/acs-09.pdf.

Bishop, Kay, and Pat Bauer. 2002. Attracting young adults to public libraries. *Journal of Youth Services in Libraries* 15, no. 2 (Winter): 36–44.

Bleakley, Amy, Cheryl R. Merzel, Nancy L. VanDevanter, and Peter Messeri. 2004. Computer access and Internet use among urban youths. *American Journal of Public Health* 94, no. 5 (May): 744–746.

Block, Marylaine. 2001. Consumer health information on the net. *Library Journal* 126, no. 8 (May): 21–24.

Bogdan, Deanne. 1990. In and out of love with literature: Response and the aesthetics of total form. In *Beyond communication: Reading comprehension and criticism,* ed. Deanne Bogdan and Stanley Straw, 109–137. Portsmouth, NH: Heinemann.

Bolan, Kimberly, Meg Canada, and Rob Cullin. 2007. Web, library, and teen services 2.0. *Young Adult Library Services* 5, no. 2 (Winter): 40–43.

Borzekowski, Dina L., and Vaughn I. Rickert. 2001. Adolescent cybersurfing for health information: A new resource that crosses barriers. *Archive of Pediatric and Adolescent Medicine* 155, no. 7 (July): 813–817.

Boyd, Danah. 2007. *Why youth (heart) social network sites: The role of networked publics in teenage social life.* MacArthur Foundation Series on Digital Learning: Youth, identity, and digital media volume. (ed. David Buckingham). Cambridge, MA: MIT Press.

Brehm-Heeger, Paula. 2008. *Serving urban teens.* Westport, CT: Libraries Unlimited.

Britton, James. 1984. Viewpoints: The distinction between participant and spectator role language in research and practice. *Research in the Teaching of English* 18, no. 1 (February): 320–331.

Brooks, Wanda. 2006. Reading representation of themselves: Urban youth use culture and African American textual features to develop literary understandings. *Reading Research Quarterly* 41, no. 3 (July/August/September): 372–392.

Bullivant, Lucy. 2005. *4dspace: Interactive architecture.* London: Wiley-Academy.

Bumgarner, Brett A. 2007. You have been poked: Exploring the uses and gratifications of Facebook among emerging adults. *First Monday* 12, no. 11 (November).

Catsambis, Sophia. 1994. The path to math: Gender and racial-ethnic differences in mathematics participation from middle school to high school. *Sociology of Education* 67, no. 3 (July): 199–215.

CDC Centers for Disease Control and Prevention. 2006. Youth risk behavior surveillance—United States, 2005. MMWR 55, no. SS-5 (June 9, 2006), www.cdc .gov/mmwr/PDF/SS/SS5505.pdf.

CDC Centers for Disease Control and Prevention and National Center for Chronic Disease Prevention and Health Promotion. 2004. Improving the health of adolescents and young adults: A guide for states and communities. http://nahic.ucsf .edu//downloads/niiah/execsum.pdf.

Chambers, Stanley B. 2006. Library workshop gives students the write stuff. *Raleigh News and Observer*, September 30, A7.

Chance, Rosemary. 2000. SmartGirl.com reading survey: What are the messages for librarians? *Journal of Youth Services in Libraries* 13, no. 3 (Spring): 20–23.

Chandler, Kelly. 1999. Reading relationships: Parents, adolescents, and popular fiction by Stephen King. *Journal of Adolescent and Adult Literacy* 43, no. 3 (November): 228–239.

Chelton, Mary K. 2001. Young adults as problems: How the social construction of a marginalized user category occurs. *Journal of Education for Library and Information Science* 42, no. 1 (Winter): 4–11.

———. 2002. The "problem patron" public libraries created. *Reference Librarian* 36 (75/76): 23–32.

Childress, Herb. 2000. Landscapes of betrayal, landscapes of joy: Curtisville in the lives of its teenagers. Albany: State University of New York.

Chiles, Nick. 2006. Their eyes were reading smut. *New York Times.* www.nytimes .com/2006/01/04/opinion/04chiles.html.

Chu, Melanie, and Yvonne Nalani Meulemans. 2008. The problems and potential of MySpace and Facebook usage in academic libraries. *Internet Reference Services Quarterly* 13, no. 1 (Spring): 69–85.

Clapp, Barbara D., and Barbara N. Lindsley. 2005. The health information project: Involving teens in lifestyle issues in the library. *Voice of Youth Advocates* 28, no. 5 (December): 374–375.

Collins, Carol J. 1993. A tool for change: Young adult literature in the lives of young adult African Americans. *Library Trends* 41, no. 3 (Winter): 378–392.

Connaway, Lynn Silipigni, Marie L. Radford, Timothy J. Dickey, Jocelyn De Angelis Williams, and Patrick Confer. 2008. Sense-making and synchronicity: Information-seeking behaviors of Millennials and Baby Boomers. *Libri* 58, no. 2 (June): 123–135.

Cook, Sherry J., R. Stephen Parker, and Charles E. Pettijohn. 2005. The public library: An early teen's perspective. *Public Libraries* 44, no. 3 (May/June): 157–161.

Copenhaver, Jeane F. 2001. Listening to their voices connect literary and cultural understandings: Responses to small-group read-alouds of *Malcolm X: A Fire Burning Brightly. New Advocate* 14, no. 4 (June): 343–359.

Corwin, Miles. 2000. And still we rise: The trials and triumphs of twelve gifted inner-city high school students. New York: Morrow.

Cranz, Galen, and Eunah Cha. 2006. Body conscious design in a teen space: Post occupancy evaluation of an innovative public library. *Public Libraries* 45, no. 6 (November/December): 48–56.

Crawford, Walt. 2007. *Balanced libraries: Thoughts on continuity and change.* Mountain View, CA: Cites and Insights.

Cross, William E. 1991. *Shades of black: Diversity in African-American identity.* Philadelphia: Temple University Press.

Cullen, P. n.d. *Me read? No way. A practical guide to improving boys' literacy skills.* www.scribd.com/doc/3197997/Me-Read-No-Way.

Cunningham, Anne E., and Keith E. Stanovich. 1991. Tracking the unique effects of print exposure in children: Associations with vocabulary, general knowledge, and spelling. *Journal of Educational Psychology* 83, no. 2 (June): 264–274.

Davis, Sampson, George Jenkins, and Rameck Hunt. 2005. *We beat the street: How a friendship pact led to success.* New York: Dutton.

Day, Jenifer Cheeseman, Alex Janus, and Jessica Davis. 2005. Computer and Internet use in the United States: 2003. U. S. Census Bureau. www.census.gov/prod/2005pubs/p23-208.pdf.

de Anda, Diane. 1984. Informal support networks of Hispanic mothers: A comparison across age groups. *Journal of Social Service Research* 7, no. 3 (July): 89–105.

de la Peña McCook, Kathleen. 2004. *Introduction to public librarianship.* New York: Neal-Schuman.

Deutsch, Nancy L. 2008. *Pride in the projects: Teens building identities in urban contexts.* New York: New York University Press.

DeWitt Wallace–Reader's Digest Fund. 1999. *Challenges and opportunities: Public libraries as partners in youth development.* New York: DeWitt Wallace–Reader's Digest Fund.

Dickinson, Peter. 1976 [1970]. A defence of rubbish. In *Writers, critics and children,* ed. Geoff Fox et al., 73–76. London: Heinemann Educational Books.

Dixson, Adrienne D., and Celia K. Rousseau. 2006. And we are still not saved: Critical race theory in education ten years later. In *Critical race theory in education: All God's children got a song,* ed. Adrienne D. Dixson and Celia K. Rousseau, 31–54. New York: Routledge.

Drucker, Peter. 1993. *Post-capitalist society.* Boston: Butterworth-Heinemann.

Duke, Nell K. 2000. For the rich it's richer: Print experiences and environments offered to children in very low- and very high-socioeconomic status first-grade classrooms. *American Educational Research Journal* 37, no. 2 (Summer): 441–478.

Dunn, Rita, Jeffrey S. Beaudry, and Angela Klavas. 1989. Survey of research on learning styles. *Educational Leadership* 46, no. 6 (March): 50–58.

Durham County Planning Department. 2005. Population profile: Durham County and the City of Durham. www.durhamnc.gov/departments/planning/pdf/demographics.pdf.

Durham Public Schools. 2007. *Free and reduced lunch statistics.* www.dpsnc.net/about-dps/26/free-and-reduced-lunch.

Edwards, Susan, and Barbara Poston-Anderson. 1996. Information, future time perspectives, and young adolescent girls: Concerns about education and jobs. *Library and Information Science Research* 18, no. 3 (Summer): 207–223.

Eeds, Maryann, and Deborah Wells. 1989. Grand conversations: An exploration of meaning construction in literature study groups. *Research in the Teaching of English* 23, no. 1 (February): 4–29.

Erkut, Sumru, Jacqueline P. Fields, Rachel Sing, and Fern Marx. 1996. Diversity in girls' experiences: Feeling good about who you are. In *Urban girls: Resisting stereotypes and creating identities,* ed. Bonnie Ross Leadbeater and Niobe Way, 53–64. New York: New York University Press.

Esquith, Rafe. 2007. *Teach like your hair's on fire: The methods and madness inside room 56.* New York: Viking.

Estabrook, Leigh, Evans Witt, and Lee Rainie. 2007. Information searches that solve problems: How people use the Internet, libraries, and government agencies when they need help. Washington, DC: Pew Internet and American Life Project. www.pewinternet.org/~/media//Files/Reports/2007/Pew_UI_LibrariesReport.pdf.pdf.

Evans, Beth. 2006. Your space or MySpace. *LJ NetConnect* (Fall): 8–10, 12.

Ferguson, Ronald F. 2002. *What doesn't meet the eye: Understanding and addressing racial disparities in high-achieving suburban schools.* Naperville, IL: North Central Regional Educational Laboratory. www.ncrel.org/gap/ferg/index.html.

Fidel, Raya, Rachel Davies, Mary Douglass, Jane Holder, Carla Hopkins, and Elisabeth Kushner. 1999. A visit to the information mall: Web searching behavior of high school students. *Journal of the American Society for Information Science* 50, no. 1 (January): 24–37.

Fisher, Douglas. 2004. Setting the "opportunity to read" standard: Resuscitating the SSR program in an urban high school. *Journal of Adolescent and Adult Literacy* 48, no. 2 (October): 138–150.

Foley, Douglas. 1997. Deficit thinking models based on culture: The anthropological protest. In *The evolution of deficit thinking: Educational thought and practice*, ed. Richard R. Valencia, 113–131. London: Farmer.

Freedom Writers, with Erin Gruwell. 1999. *The freedom writer's diary.* New York: Broadway Books.

Garbarino, James. 1999. *Lost boys: Why our sons turn violent and how we can save them.* New York: Free Press.

Garrison, Dee. 2003. *Apostles of culture: The public librarian and American Society, 1876–1920.* Madison: University of Wisconsin Press.

Gates, Henry Louis, Jr. 1988. *The signifying monkey: A theory of African-American literary criticism.* New York: Oxford University Press.

Gillaspy, Mary L. 2005. Factors affecting the provision of consumer health information in public libraries: The last five years. *Library Trends* 53, no. 3 (Winter): 480–495.

Glaser, Barney G., and Anselm L. Strauss. 1967. *The discovery of grounded theory: Strategies for qualitative research.* Hawthorne, NY: Aldine de Gruyter.

González, Norma, Luis C. Moll, Martha Floyd-Tenery, Anna Rivera, Patricia Rendon, Raquel Gonzales, and Cathy Amanti. 1993. Teacher research on funds of knowledge: Learning from households. *Educational Practice Report 6.* National Center for Research on Cultural Diversity and Second Language Learning. www.eric.ed.gov/ERICDocs/data/ericdocs2sql/content_storage_01/0000019b/80/13/09/a3.pdf.

Gorman, Michele. 2006. "Mr. Inspiration": Patrick Jones on knockout teen services, mentoring, librarians, and yes, loving wrestling magazines. *School Library Journal* 52, no. 8 (August): 32–34.

———. 2008. The 6R movement: VOYA's MVP (Most Valuable Program) 2008. *Voice of Youth Advocates* 31, no. 4 (October): 304–307. http://pdfs.voya.com/Vo/yaT/The6RMovement200810.pdf.

Gray, Nicola J., Jonathan D. Klein, Peter R. Noyce, Tracy S. Sesselberg, and Judith A. Cantrill. 2005. Health information seeking behaviour in adolescence: The place of the Internet. *Social Science and Medicine* 60 (April): 1467–1478.

Greenhow, Christine, and Elizabeth Robelia. 2009. Old communication, new literacies: Social network sites as social learning resources. *Journal of Computer-Mediated Communication* 14, no. 4 (July): 1130–1161.

Gregg, Elizabeth J. 2008. Public library programming for youth: Creative writing as a tool for literacy and adolescent development. Masters Thesis, University of North Carolina at Chapel Hill, School of Information and Library Science.

Gross, Melissa. 2001. Imposed information seeking in public libraries and school library media centres: A common behavior? *Information Research* 6, no. 2 (January). http://informationr.net/ir/6-2/paper100.html.

Guild, Sandy L., and Sandra Hughes-Hassell. 2001. The urban minority young adult audience: Does young adult literature pass the reality test? *New Advocate* 14, no. 4 (Fall): 361–377.

Hafner, Lawrence, Barbara Palmer, and Stan Tullos. 1986. The differential reading interests of good and poor readers in the ninth grade. *Reading Improvement* 23, no. 1 (Spring): 39–42.

Hajdu, David. 2008. *The ten-cent plague: The great comic-book scare and how it changed America.* New York: Farrar, Straus and Giroux.

Harding, D. W. 1962. Psychological processes in the reading of fiction. *British Journal of Aesthetics* 2 (2): 133–147.

Hardy, Kenneth V., and Tracey A. Laszloffy. 2005. *Teens who hurt: Clinical interventions to break the cycle of adolescent violence.* New York: Guilford Press.

Harris, Christopher. 2006. MySpace can be our space: Let's turn the infamous networking site into a teachable moment. *School Library Journal* 52, no. 5 (May): 30.

Harris, Violet. 1993. *Teaching multicultural literature.* Norwood, MA: Christopher Gordon.

Harry, Beth, and Janette Klingner. 2007. Discarding the deficit model. *Educational Leadership* 64, no. 5 (February): 16–21.

Havighurst, Robert J. 1972. *Developmental tasks and education.* 3rd ed. New York: Longman.

Helfer, Andrew, and Randy DuBurke. 2007. *Malcolm X: A graphic biography.* New York: Hill and Wang.

Hennen. 2008. Hennen's American public library ratings 2008. *American Libraries,* October, 56–61. www.haplr-index.com/ratings.html.

Henry, Annette. 1998. "Speaking up" and "speaking out": Examining "voice" in a reading/writing program with adolescent African Caribbean girls. *Journal of Literacy Research* 30, no. 2 (June): 233–252.

Heyns, Barbara. 1978. *Summer learning and the effects of schooling.* New York: Academic Press.

Hinduja, Sameer, and Justin W. Patchin. 2008. Personal information of adolescents on the Internet: A quantitative analysis of MySpace. *Journal of Adolescence* 31, no. 1 (February): 125–146.

Hodkinson, Paul, and Sian Lincoln. 2008. Online journals as virtual bedrooms? Young people, identity and personal space. *Young* 16, no. 1 (January): 27–46.

Hughes-Hassell, Sandra. 2008. Urban teenagers talk about reading. In *Conference Proceedings, 37th Annual Conference of the International Association for School Librarianship,* Berkeley, CA, August 3–7.

Hughes-Hassell, Sandra, and Denise E. Agosto. 2007. Modeling the everyday life information needs of urban teens. In *Youth information-seeking behavior II,* ed. Mary K. Chelton and Colleen Cool, 27–61. New York: Scarecrow Press.

Hughes-Hassell, Sandra, Dana Hanson-Baldauf, and Jennifer E. Burke. 2008. Urban teenagers, health information, and public library websites. *Young Adult Library Services* 6, no. 4 (Summer): 3–42.

Hughes-Hassell, Sandra, and Christina Lutz. 2006. What do you want to tell us about reading? A survey of the habits and attitudes of urban middle school students toward leisure reading. *Young Adult Library Services* 4 (Winter): 39–45.

Hughes-Hassell, Sandra, and Ericka T. Miller. 2003. Public library websites for young adults: Meeting the needs of today's teens online. *Library and Information Science Research* 25, no. 2 (Summer): 143–156.

Hughes-Hassell, Sandra, and Pradnya Rodge. 2007. The leisure reading habits of urban adolescents. *Journal of Adolescent and Adult Literacy* 51 (1): 22–34.

Hynds, Susan. 1990. Reading as a social event: Comprehension and response in the text, classroom, and world. In *Beyond communication: Reading comprehension and criticism,* ed. D. Bogdan and S. B. Straw, 237–256. Portsmouth, NH: Boyton/Cook.

Iser, Wolfgang. 1978. *The act of reading: A theory of aesthetic response.* Baltimore: Johns Hopkins University Press.

Ito, Mizuko, et al. 2008. Living and learning with new media: Summary of findings from the digital youth project. Chicago: John D. and Catherine T. MacArthur Foundation.

Jenkins, Christine A. 2000. The history of youth services librarianship: A review of the research literature. *Libraries and Culture* 35, no. 1 (Winter): 103–140.

Jiménez, Robert T. 2001. "It's a difference that changes us": An alternative view of the language and literacy learning needs of Latina/o students. *Reading Teacher* 54, no. 8 (May): 736–742.

Jones, Patrick. 1997. A cyber-room of their own: How libraries use web pages to attract young adults. *School Library Journal* 43 (November): 34–37.

———. 2002. *New directions for library service to young adults.* Chicago: American Library Association.

Jones, Patrick, Michele Gorman, and Tricia Suellentrop. 2004. *Connecting young adults and libraries.* 3rd ed. New York: Neal Schuman.

Julien, Heidi E. 1999. Barriers to adolescents' information seeking for career decision making. *Journal of the American Society for Information Science* 50, no. 1 (January): 38–48.

Kaczmarek, Nancy, and Michelle Stachowiak. 2004. Independent reading is key to lifelong learning. *Momentum* 35, no. 1 (February/March): 54–58.

Kelly, Tina. 2007. Lock the library! Rowdy students are taking over. *New York Times,* January 2, 1.

Kim, Jimmy. 2004. Summer reading and the ethnic achievement gap. *Journal of Education for Students Placed at Risk* 9, no. 2 (April): 169–188.

Kimball, Melanie A. 2007. From refuge to risk: Public libraries and children in World War I. *Library Trends* 55, no. 3 (Winter): 455.

Kimball, Melanie, June Abbas, Kay Bishop, and George D'Elia. 2007. Youth, public libraries, and the Internet: Part three: Who visits the public library, and what do they do there? *Public Libraries* 46, no. 1 (November/December): 52–58.

Kotlowitz, Alex. 1991. *There are no children here.* New York: Anchor Books.

Krashen, Stephen. 1993. *The power of reading: Insights from the research.* Englewood, CO: Libraries Unlimited.

———. 2004. *The power of reading: Insights from the research.* 2nd ed. Englewood, CO: Libraries Unlimited.

Kuhlthau, Carol C. 1991. Inside the search process: Information seeking from the user's perspective. *Journal of the American society for Information Science* 42, no. 5 (June): 361–371.

———. 2003. *Seeking meaning: A process approach to library and information services.* Westport, CT: Libraries Unlimited.

Kupperman, Jeff, and Barry J. Fishman. 2002. Academic, social, and personal uses of the Internet: Cases of students from an urban Latino classroom. *Journal of Research on Technology in Education* 34, no. 2 (Winter): 189–215.

Laird, Roland Owen, Jr., and Taneshia Nash Laird. 1997. *Still I Rise: A Cartoon History of African Americans.* New York: Norton.

Lamb, Annette, and Larry Johnson. 2006. Want to be my "friend"? What you need to know about social technologies. *Teacher Librarian* 34, no. 1 (October): 55–57.

Latrobe, Kathy Howard, and W. Michael Havener. 1997. Information-seeking behavior of high school honors students: An exploratory study. *Journal of Youth Services in Libraries* 10, no. 2 (Winter): 188–200.

Leadbeater, Bonnie Ross, and Niobe Way, eds. 1996. *Urban girls: Resisting stereotypes and creating identities.* New York: New York University Press.

Lenhart, Amanda, and Mary Madden. 2007. Social networking websites and teens: An overview. Pew Research Center for the People and the Press. www.education.com/reference/article/Ref_Social_Websites/.

Lenhart, Amanda, Mary Madden, and Paul Hitlin. 2005. Teens and technology: Youth are leading the transition to a fully wired and mobile nation. www.pewinternet.org/PPF/r/162/report_display.aspx.

Lenhart, Amanda, Mary Madden, Alexandra Rankin Macgill, and Aaron Smith. 2007. Teens and social media: The use of social media gains a greater foothold in teen life as they embrace the conversational nature of interactive online media. www.pewinternet.org/PPF/r/230/report_display.aspx.

Lincoln, Yvonne, and Egon G. Guba. 1985. *Naturalistic inquiry.* Newbury Park, CA: Sage.

Lindberg, Claire, Carol Lewis-Spruill, and Rodney Crownover. 2006. Barriers to sexual and reproductive health care: Urban male adolescents speak out. *Issues in Comprehensive Pediatric Nursing* 29, no. 2 (April): 73–88.

Livingstone, Sonia. 2008. Taking risky opportunities in youthful content creation: Teenagers' use of social networking sites for intimacy, privacy, and self-expression. *New Media and Society* 10, no. 3 (June): 393–411.

Lukenbill, W. Bernard, and Barbara F. Immroth. 2007. *Health information for youth: The public library and school library media center role.* Westport, CT: Libraries Unlimited.

Lyons, David J., Joseph Hoffman, Joseph Krajcik, and Eliot Soloway. 1997. An Investigation of the use of the World Wide Web for online inquiry in a science classroom. Paper presented at the meeting of the National Association for Research in Science Teaching, Chicago, IL.

Marston, Judy. 2001. *Narrative summary report of teen focus groups for the young adult services program,* 8. Sacramento: California State Library.

Martin, Elmer P., and Joanne M. Martin. 1978. *The black extended family.* Chicago: University of Chicago Press.

Martin, Hillias J., and James R. Murdoch. 2007. *Serving lesbian, gay, bisexual, transgender and questioning teens: A how-to-do-it manual for librarians.* New York: Neal-Schuman.

Massey, Sheri Anita, Ann Carlson Weeks, and Teresa Y. Neely. 2005. Providing library services to urban children: Challenges and strategies. *Advances in Librarianship* 29:73–97.

Mather, Mark, and Kelvin Pollard. 2008. U.S. population projected to hit 400 million in 2039. Population Reference Bureau. www.prb.org/Articles/2008/us400million.aspx.

Matsuda, Mari J., Charles R. Lawrence, Richard Delgado, and Kimberlé W. Crenshaw, eds. 1993. *Words that wound: Critical race theory, assaultive speech, and the First Amendment.* Boulder, CO: Westview.

Mayer, Susan E. 1997. Trends in the economic well-being and life chances of America's children. In *Consequences of growing up poor,* ed. Greg J. Duncan and Jeanne Brooks-Gunn, 46–69. New York: Russell Sage Foundation.

McAllister, Gretchen, and Jacqueline Jordan Irvine. 2000. Cross cultural competency and multicultural teacher education. *Review of Educational Research* 70, no. 1 (Spring): 3–14.

McCaffrey, Meg. 2005. Star power. *School Library Journal* 51, no. 1 (January): 48–49.

McGrath, Anne. 2005. A new read on teen literacy. *U.S. News and World Report,* February 28. www.usnews.com/usnews/culture/articles/050228/28literacy.htm.

McKee, Diane, and Jason Fletcher. 2006. Primary care for urban adolescent girls from ethnically diverse populations: Foregone care and access to confidential care. *Journal of Health Care for the Poor and Underserved* 17, no. 4 (November): 759–774.

McQuillan, Jeff, and Lucy Tse. 1995. Child language brokering in linguistic minority communities: Effects on cultural interaction, cognition, and literacy. *Language and Education* 9 (3): 195–215.

MDC Incorporated. 2008. *Disconnected youth in the Research Triangle region: An ominous problem hidden in plain sight.* www.mdcinc.org/docs/disconnected-youth.pdf.

Mellon, Constance A. 1990. Leisure reading choices of rural teens. *School Library Media Quarterly*, Summer, 223–228.

Meyers, Elaine. 1999. The coolness factor: Ten libraries listen to youth. *American Libraries* 30, no. 10 (November): 42–45.

Michie, Gregory. 1999. *Holler if you hear me: The education of a teacher and his students.* New York: Teachers College Press.

Miller, Sarah Elizabeth, and Lauren A. Jensen. 2007. Connecting and communicating with students on Facebook. *Computers in Libraries* 27, no. 8 (September): 18–22.

Minkel, Walter. 1999. Keeping up appearances. *School Library Journal* 45, no. 12 (December): 27.

Moll, Luis C., Cathy Amanti, Deborah Neff, and Norma González. 1992. Funds of knowledge for teaching: Using a qualitative approach to connect homes and classrooms. *Theory into Research* 31, no. 2 (Spring): 132–141.

Morris, Vanessa J. 2007. Inner city teens *do* read. Paper presented at the Beyond the Book Conference at University of Birmingham, Birmingham, UK.

Morris, Vanessa J., Sandra Hughes-Hassell, Denise E. Agosto, and Darren Cottman. 2006. Street lit: Flying off teen fiction bookshelves in Philadelphia public libraries. *Young Adult Library Services* 5, no. 1 (Fall): 16–24.

National Training Institute for Community Youth Development Work. 2000. Youth development program for Public Libraries as Partners in Youth Development. Washington, D.C.: Academy for Educational Development.

Neuman, Susan B. 1999. Books make a difference: A study of access to literacy. *Reading Research Quarterly* 34, no. 3 (September): 286–311.

Neuman, Susan B., and Donna Celano. 2001. Access to print in low- and middle-income communities: An ecological study of 4 neighborhoods. *Reading Research Quarterly* 36, no. 1 (December): 8–26.

Nielsen Norman Group. 2005. Teenagers on the Web: 61 usability guidelines for creating compelling websites for teens. www.nngroup.com/reports/teens/.

Norton, Bonny. 2003. The motivating power of comic books: Insights from Archie Comic readers. *Reading Teacher* 57, no. 2 (October): 140–147.

OCLC. 2005. *Perceptions of libraries and information resources.* Dublin, OH: OCLC. www.oclc.org/reports/2005perceptions.htm.

OCLC. 2007. *Sharing, privacy and trust in our networked world.* Dublin, OH: OCLC. www.oclc.org/reports/sharing/default.htm.

Ohio Department of Education. 2003. Worthington City School District: [2001–2002] District report card. www.ode.state.oh.us/reportcardfiles/2001-2002/DIST/045138 .pdf.

———. 2008a. Worthington City School District: 2007–2008 School Year Report Card. www.ode.state.oh.us/reportcardfiles/2007-2008/DIST/045138.pdf.

———. 2008b. MR81: Data for free and reduced price meal eligibility. ftp://ftp.ode.state .oh.us/MR81/.

O'Malley, Gavin. 2008. Study: Teens join boomers in searching health issues online. Online Media Daily, October 21. www.mediapost.com/publications/?fa=Articles .showArticle&art_aid=93143.

Orellana, Marjorie Faulstich. 2003. Responsibilities of children in Latino immigrant homes. In *New directions for youth development: Understanding the social world of immigrant youth,* ed. Carola Suarez-Orozco and Irina L. G. Todorova, 25–39. New York: Jossey-Bass-Wiley.

Organista, Kurt C. 2003. Mexican American children and adolescents. In *Children of color: Psychological interventions with minority youth,* 2nd. ed., ed. Jewell T. Gibbs and Larke N. Huang, 344–381. San Francisco: Jossey-Bass.

Osgerby, Bill. 2004. *Youth media.* New York: Routledge.

Ottaviani, Jim, Donna Barr, Marie Severin, and Romana Fradon. 2000. *Dignifying science: Stories about women scientists.* Ann Arbor, MI: G T Labs.

Palfrey, John, and Urs Gasser. 2008. *Born digital: Understanding the first generation of digital natives.* New York: Basic Books.

Phinney, Jean S. 1990. Ethnic identity in adolescents and adults: Review of research. *Psychological Bulletin* 108, no. 3 (November): 499–514.

Pilgreen, Janice L. 2000. *The SSR handbook: How to organize and manage a sustained silent reading program.* Portsmouth, NH: Heinemann.

Pipher, Mary. 1995. *Reviving Ophelia: Saving the selves of adolescent girls.* New York: Ballantine.

PLDS Public Library Data Service. 2007. *Statistical report 2007.* Chicago: American Library Association.

Pollack, William S. 1998. *Real boys: Rescuing our boys from the myth of boyhood.* New York: Henry Holt.

Prothrow-Stith, Deborah, and Howard R. Spivak. 2006. *Sugar and spice and no longer nice: How we can stop girls' violence.* San Francisco: Jossey-Bass.

Quinn, Lois M., and John Pawasarat. 2001. Confronting anti-urban marketing stereotypes: A Milwaukee economic development challenge. www4.uwm.edu/eti/purchasing/markets.htm.

Quiroz, Pamela Anne. 2001. The silencing of Latino student "voice": Puerto Rican and Mexican narratives in eighth grade and high school. *Anthropology and Education Quarterly* 32, no. 3 (September): 326–349.

Rapacki, Sean. 2007. Social networking sites: Why teens need places like MySpace. *Young Adult Library Services* 5, no. 2 (Winter): 28–30.

Reutzel, D. Ray, and Paul M. Hollingsworth. 1991. Investigating topic-related attitude: Effect on reading and remembering text. *Journal of Educational Research* 84, no. 6 (August): 334–44.

Rhoads, Jean E., and Anita B. Davis. 1996. Supportive ties between nonparent adults and urban adolescent girls. In *Urban girls: Resisting stereotypes and creating identities,* ed. Bonnie Ross Leadbeater and Niobe Way, 213–225. New York: New York University Press.

Richardson, Caroline, Paul J. Resnick, Derek L. Hansen, Holly A. Derry, and Victoria Rideout. 2002. Does pornography blocking software block access to health information on the Internet. *Journal of the American Medical Association* 288, no. 22 (December 11): 2887–2894.

Rideout, Victoria. 2001. Generation RX.com: How young people use the Internet for health information. Menlo Park, CA: Henry J. Kaiser Family Foundation, 2001. www.kff.org/entmedia/loader.cfm?url=/commonspot/security/getfile.cfm&PageId=13719.

Rideout, Victoria, Donald F. Roberts, and Ulla G. Foehr. 2005. Generation M: Media in the lives of 8–18 year olds. www.kff.org/entmedia/upload/Generation-M-Media-in-the-Lives-of-8-18-Year-olds-Report.pdf.

Roberts, Sam. 2007. Census: New York region has widest income gap. *New York Times, City Room Blog,* http://cityroom.blogs.nytimes.com/2007/08/28/census-new-york-region-has-widest-income-gap/.

Rosenblatt, Louise. 1996 [1938]. *Literature as exploration.* 5th ed. New York: Modern Language Association.

Rosenthal, Robert. 1995. Critiquing Pygmalion: A 25-year perspective. *Current Directions in Psychological Science* 4, no. 6 (December): 171–172.

Ross, Catherine S. 1995. "If they read Nancy Drew, so what?" Series book readers talk back. *Library and Information Science Research* 17, no. 3 (Summer): 201–236.

Rubin, Richard E. 2004. *Foundations of library and information science.* 3rd ed. New York: Neal-Schuman.

Santos, Fernanda. 2008. Bloomberg expands translations in agencies. *New York Times,* July 23, 2008, B2(L).

Sautter, R. Craig. 1994. Who are today's city kids? Beyond the "deficit model." *CITYSCHOOLS* 1 (1): 6–10.

Savolainen, Reijo. 2008. *Everyday information practices: A social phenomenological perspective.* Lanham, MD: Scarecrow.

Schacter, John. 2003. Preventing summer reading declines in children who are disadvantaged. *Journal of Early Intervention* 26, no. 1 (Fall): 47–58.

Scrogham, Ron E. 2006. The American public library and its fragile future. *New Library World* 107 (1/2): 7–15.

SDP School District of Philadelphia. 2008. *Regional offices and school information.* https://sdp-webprod.phila.k12.pa.us/OnlineDirectory/schools.jsp.

Search Institute. 2007. *40 developmental assets for adolescents.* www.search-institute.org/content/40-developmental-assets-adolescents-ages-12-18.

Shenton, Andrew K., and Dixon, Pat. 2003. Youngsters' use of other people as an information-seeking method. *Journal of Librarianship and Information Science* 35, no. 4 (December): 219–233.

Shklovsky, V. 1966. Art as technique. In *Russian formalist criticism: Four essays*, ed. L. Lemon and M. Reis, 3–24. Lincoln: University of Nebraska Press.

Short, Kathy G., ed. 1995. *Research and professional resources in children's literature: Piecing a patchwork quilt.* Newark, DE: International Reading Association.

Short, Kathy G., and Kathryn M. Pierce, eds. 1990. *Talking about books: Creating literate communities.* Portsmouth, NH: Heinemann.

Sibley, David. 1995. *Geographies of exclusion: Society and difference in the West.* London: Routledge.

Silver, Harvey F., Richard W. Strong, and Matthew J. Perini. 2000. *So each may learn: Integrating learning styles and multiple intelligences.* Alexandria, VA: Association for Supervision and Curriculum Development.

Simmons, Rachel. 2002. *Odd girl out: The hidden culture of aggression in girls.* Orlando, FL: Harcourt.

Skolnick, Andrew A. 1994. Collateral casualties climb in the drug war. *Journal of the American Medical Association* 271, no. 21 (June): 1636–1639. www.marijuanalibrary.org/JAMA_Collateral_Casualties_060194.html.

Slote, Stanley J. 1997. *Weeding library collections: Library weeding methods.* Englewood, CO: Libraries Unlimited.

Smith, Catherine A. 2006. I am not a specialist: Why we need to be worrying about medical information. *Journal of Education for Library and Information Science* 47, no. 2 (Spring): 96–105.

Spielberger, Julie, Carol Horton, and Lisa Michels. 2004. *New on the shelf: Teens in the library.* Chicago: Chapin Hall Center for Children, University of Chicago.

Stanovich, Keith, and Richard West. 1989. Exposure to print and orthographic processing. *Reading Research Quarterly* 24, no. 4 (Autumn): 402–433.

Stephens, Michael. 2005. Do libraries matter: On library and librarian 2.0. ALA TechSource. www.techsource.ala.org/blog/2005/11/do-libraries-matter-on-library-librarian-20.html.

Stewart, David W., and Prem N. Shamdasani. 1990. *Focus groups: Theory and practice.* Newbury Park, CA: Sage.

Strommen, Linda T., and Barbara F. Mates. 2004. Learning to love reading: Interviews with older children and teens. *Journal of Adolescent and Adult Literacy* 48, no. 3 (November): 188–200.

Subrahmanyam, Kaveri, and Patricia Greenfield. 2008. Online communication and adolescent relationships. *Future of Children* 18, no. 1 (Spring): 119–146.

Suellentrop, Tricia. 2007. Step right up. *School Library Journal* 53, no. 12 (December): 24.

Sullivan, Edward. 2001. Some teens prefer the real thing: The case for young adult nonfiction. *English Journal* 90, no. 3 (January): 43–47.

Sullivan, James G. 2007. Decision model for public sector assessment of sustainable buildings in Florida. Ph.D. diss., University of Florida.

Sullivan, Michael. 2003. The fragile future of the public libraries. *Public Libraries* 42, no. 5 (September/October): 303–308.

Suskind, Ron. 1998. *A hope in the unseen: An American odyssey from the inner city to the Ivy League.* New York: Broadway.

Swope, Christopher. 2008. Revolution in the stacks. *Governing* 21 (June): 32–36.

Taney, Kimberly B. 2002. *Teen spaces: The step by step library makeover.* Chicago: American Library Association.

Tate, Greg. 2003. *Everything but the burden: What white people are taking from black culture.* New York: Broadway Books.

Tatum, Alfred. 2005. *Teaching reading to black adolescent males: Closing the achievement gap.* Portland, ME: Stenhouse.

Tatum, Beverly Daniel. 1997. *"Why are all the black kids sitting together in the cafeteria" and other conversations about race.* New York: Basic Books.

Taylor, Ronald L. 1995. Black youth in the United States: An overview. In *African-American youth: Their social and economic status in the United States,* ed. Ronald L. Taylor, 3–27. Westport, CT: Praeger.

Teens and TPPT. 1999. *Teens of Tucson and Pima County: A plan for youth development, June 1999.* Tucson, AZ: Pima County Public Library.

Thelwall, Mike. 2008. Social networks, gender, and friending: An analysis of MySpace member profiles. *Journal of the American Society for Information Science* 59, no. 8 (June): 1321–1330.

Thorndike, Robert L. 1973. *Reading comprehension education in fifteen countries: An empirical study.* New York: Wiley.

Tsikalas, Kallen, and Elisheva F. Gross. 2002. Home computer use among low-income, minority urban adolescents: Fulfillment of basic needs and impact on personal and academic development. Paper Presented at the Annual Meeting of the American Educational Research Association, New Orleans, April 1–5.

Twenge, Jean M. 2006. *Generation me: Why today's young Americans are more confident, assertive, entitled—and more miserable than ever before.* New York: Free Press.

U.S. Census Bureau. 2000. Census 2000 Summary File 1, Matrix P1. http://factfinder.census.gov/servlet/GCTTable?_bm=y&-geo_id=01000US&-_box_head_nbr=GCT-P1&-ds_name=DEC_2000_SF1_U&-format=US-1.

———. 2007a. American Fact Finder. http://factfinder.census.gov/home/saff/main.html?_lang=en.

———. 2007b. Census 2000 urban and rural classification. www.census.gov/geo/www/ua/ua_2k.html.

Valdés, Guadalupe. 1996. Con respect: Bridging the distances between culturally diverse families and schools. New York: Teachers College Press.

Van Slyck, Abigail A. 1995. *Free to all: Carnegie libraries and American culture: 1890–1920.* Chicago: University of Chicago Press.

———. 1996. The lady and the library loafer: Gender and public space in Victorian America, *Winterthur Portfolio* 31, no. 4 (Winter): 221–242.

Vargas, Karen. 2005. Teenagers, health, and the Internet: How information professionals can reach out to teens and their health information needs. *Journal of Consumer Health on the Internet* 9, no. 3 (Fall): 15–23.

Vaughan, Dawn Baumgartner. 2006. Workshops focus on improving teens' prose. *Herald Sun* (Durham, NC), February 13, A1.

Vavrek, Bernard. 2004. Teens: Bullish on public libraries. *Public Library Quarterly* 23 (1): 3–12.

Vélez-Ibáñez, Carlos, and James Greenberg. 2005. Formation and transformation of funds of knowledge. In *Funds of knowledge: Theorizing practices in households, communities, and classrooms,* ed. Norma E. González, Luis C. Moll, and Cathy Amanti, 47–70. Mahwah, NJ: Lawrence Erlbaum.

Versaci, Rocco. 2001. How comic books can change the way our students see literature: One teacher's perspective. *English Journal* 91, no. 2 (November): 61–67.

Voice of Youth Advocates. 2009. Teen rooms in Worthington libraries. Vol. 31, no. 6 (February): 512–515.

von Oech, Roger. 2008. *A whack on the side of the head: How you can be more creative.* New York: Warner Books.

Wallace Foundation. 1999. *Public libraries as partners in youth development.* New York: Wallace Foundation.

Wallace, Raven McCrory, Jeff Kupperman, Joseph Krajcik, and Elliot Soloway. 2000. Science on the Web: Students online in a sixth-grade classroom. *Journal of the Learning Sciences* 9, no. 1 (January): 75–104.

Walter, Virginia, and Elaine Meyers. 2003. *Teens and libraries: Getting it right.* Chicago: American Library Association.

Westerfield, Lindsay U., and Kimberly M. Jones. 2007. Comparing stereotypes and cross-cultural knowledge in Argentine and U.S. university students. Paper presented at the National Conference on Undergraduate Education, April 12–14, Dominican University in San Rafael, CA. www.dominican.edu/query/ncur/display_ncur .php?id=379.

White, Rob. 1990. *No space of their own: Young people and social control in Australia.* New York: Cambridge University Press.

Wilson, Melvin N. 1986. The black extended family: An analytical consideration. *Developmental Psychology* 22, no. 2 (March): 246–258.

Wilson, Paula A. 2004. Technology and literacy. *Public Libraries* 43, no. 1 (January/February): 28–29, 32.

Worthington City Schools. 2009. District profile. www.worthington.k12.oh.us/district .php.

Wright, David. 2006, July 15. Collection development "Urban Fiction": Streetwise urban fiction. Library Journal. www.libraryjournal.com/article/CA6349018.html.

YALSA Young Adult Library Services Association. 2003. Young adults deserve the best: Competencies for librarians serving youth. www.ala.org/ala/yalsa/profdev/ youngadultsdeserve.cfm.

Yohalem, Nicole, and Karen Pittman. 2003. *Public libraries as partners in youth development: Lessons and voices from the field.* Washington, DC: Forum for Youth Investment. Available at http://forumfyi.org/node/133.

Yosso, Taro J. 2006. Whose culture has capital? A critical race theory discussion of community cultural wealth. In *Critical race theory in education: All God's children got a song,* ed. Adrienne D. Dixson and Celia K. Rousseau, 167–190. New York: Routledge.

Zirinsky, Derik, and Shirley A. Rau. 2001. *A classroom of teenaged readers: Nurturing reading processes in senior high school.* New York: Longman.

CONTRIBUTORS

JUNE ABBAS, PH.D., is an associate professor in the School of Library and Information Studies, University of Oklahoma. Her research interests include children and youth's uses of technologies, their information use behaviors, and designing age-appropriate systems for youth.

ANTHONY BERNIER, PH.D., assistant professor at San Jose State University's School of Library and Information Science, developed the first public library space designed exclusively to meet the developmental needs of young adults (the Los Angeles Public Library's Teen'Scape) and inaugurated the YA Services Department for the Oakland Public Library. His primary research interests explore public space equity for young adults and the administration of library services with them.

REBECCA L. BUCK completed her M.L.I.S. at Drexel University in 2009. Prior to working with teens at the Public Library of Charlotte and Mecklenburg County (N.C.), she worked on an adult reference desk and taught computer classes with the Chesterfield County Public Library in Midlothian, Va.

SARAH COFER is a lead librarian at Worthington (Ohio) Libraries and has served as the teen librarian at the Northwest branch since 2000, helping to develop many of the digital services that Worthington Libraries provides teen patrons.

MICHELE GORMAN is the teen services coordinator for the Public Library of Charlotte and Mecklenburg County (N.C.). She is also on the YALSA board of directors, is a freelance writer, and is a renowned national speaker.

ELIZABETH J. GREGG worked as a library technician at Radford Public Library (Va.) for two years, where she created and ran a creative writing workshop for teens. She has worked with young adults in a variety of settings including residential treatment centers, afterschool programs, summer camps, and public libraries and is currently employed at Braswell Memorial Library (N.C.), where she serves as education support services librarian.

DANA HANSON-BALDAUF is a doctoral student in the School of Information and Library Science at the University of North Carolina at Chapel Hill. Previously a special educator, Dana's research interests involve the life information needs and practices of children and young adults, and how school and public libraries can best support these individuals.

LEWIS HASSELL, PH.D., received his M.S. and Ph.D. from the College of Information Science & Technology at Drexel University. Besides his focus on social justice for disadvantaged groups, he is also interested in information systems security and education, particularly with relation to library schools.

ELAINE MEYERS is a consultant and adjunct faculty member at the School of Information Resources and Library Science at the University of Arizona. She has over thirty years of experience working with teens in public libraries and served as national director for the Public Libraries as Partners in Youth Development initiative.

VANESSA J. IRVIN MORRIS is an assistant teaching professor in the College of Information Science & Technology at Drexel University. Her research interests include the sociocultural anthropology of urban and rural libraries; reading interests and social epistemologies of inner-city adolescents; multicultural literature, especially pertaining to picture books and storytelling; and cultural competency practices for urban public service librarians.

ANN PECHACEK is a librarian at Worthington (Ohio) Libraries and has served as the teen librarian at the Old Worthington branch since 2001. She received her M.L.I.S. from the University of Southern Mississippi in 1999.

KARA REUTER, PH.D., is the digital library manager at Worthington (Ohio) Libraries. For more than ten years she has developed and managed digital libraries for young people and adults in school, academic, and public library settings.

MANDY R. SIMON is a librarian at Worthington (Ohio) Libraries and has served as the teen specialist at the Worthington Park branch since 2006. She received her M.S. in library and information science from the University of Illinois at Urbana-Champaign's Online Education (LEEP) program in 2006.

AUTUMN WINTERS is a young adult librarian in Durham, North Carolina. She received her M.L.S. from the University of North Carolina at Chapel Hill in 2001 and a B.A. in English from the University of North Carolina at Greensboro in 1997.

AMY WYCKOFF completed her M.L.S. at Indiana University in 2008 and currently works with teens at ImaginOn (Charlotte, N.C.) as the teen librarian in the Loft.

INDEX

A

academic achievement and racial identity
    development, 16
activity logs as data collection method, 26
administration, support from, 121, 123
adolescent development. *See*
    developmental areas of adolescence
adversity in lives of urban teens, 12
African American culture as urban culture,
    4, 13–14
African American English (AAE), 64
alternatives to reading, 43–44
American Standard English in street lit,
    64–65
anger and resentment and racial identity
    development, 16
aspirational capital, 14
attitudes
    effect of home computer use on, 25
    of staff toward teens, 34–35
audience for digital services, 172–174
audio journals as data collection method,
    26
author interviews on social media sites,
    182–183
authors' websites, 45–46, 75

B

behavioral policies, 34, 37–38, 85
Belmont (N.H.) High School Library, 71
biracial teens, 16
Black (Brown), 64
blogs, 76, 178–180

Blow (50 Cent), 57
B-More Careful (Holmes), 55, 63
book clubs
    blogs as, 178
    and conversations about genre, 60
    at ImaginOn, 149
    and street lit, 53, 61, 65
    and summer reading, 50
    in Tucson-Pima PLPYD program,
        138
book talks, podcasts of, 184
books and libraries, beyond, 98
Boss Lady (Tyree), 56
Brooklyn Public Library, 133

C

camera tours as data collection method, 26
Ceazia Devereaux series (Chunichi), 59
celebrations, 167
celebrities, reading about, 47–48
chairs. *See* seating options for YA space
Charlotte and Mecklenburg County
    (N.C.) Public Library, 46, 110, 134,
    143–151
children's rooms, relation to YA spaces,
    114, 119–120, 126n6
Children's Theatre of Charlotte, 143, 146
civic engagement programs, 149–150
clothing in urban culture, 4, 16
coding of data
    information-seeking study, 27, 28f
    for library use survey, 89–90
cognitive self, development of, 31

The Coldest Winter Ever (Sister
    Souljah), 54, 55, 58, 60–61,
    62–63, 64
collaboration with community
    organizations, 96, 98–99. *See
    also* partnerships
collection development
    culturally relevant information
        resources, 94
    ImaginOn, 146–147
    and leisure reading, 47–49
    teen recommendations for,
        35–37
collection maintenance, 95, 121
comic books for leisure reading,
    47
coming-of-age stories in street lit,
    57–59
community, knowledge of, 33–34.
    See also demographic
    information
community center, library as, 39–
    40
community groups
    partnerships on health
        information, 111
    in space planning, 123
    in Tucson-Pima PLPYD
        program, 137
computers, home, availability of,
    25, 88, 176
computers, library, 37, 146, 176
constant comparative method, 89
control of content for library
    websites, 80
copies of popular books, need for,
    36
covers for literary magazine, 165,
    166f
Crashboomlove (Herrera), 15
creative self, development of, 31
Criminal Minded (Brown), 64–65
critical race theory and cultural
    wealth, 14–15
cross-cultural knowledge, 11
cultural wealth of urban teens,
    13–15, 48, 62, 85
culturally relevant information
    resources, 94
curricular materials, 121
"cut and paste" technique, 89

D

decoration of YA library space,
    118–119, 125
demographic information, 5–6,
    11–12. *See also* community,
    knowledge of
Denver Public Library, 71, 183

developmental areas of
    adolescence, 29–31
    and information seeking, 23–25
    and library services, 93–94
    and social interactions, 95
    space planning for, 115, 119
    tasks of, 27, 29, 30f
    See also youth development
digital divide, 169–170
digital (electronic) services, 169–186
    blogs, 178–180
    case study, 170–171
    as gateway to other library
        services, 175–176
    Internet access, 176–177
    need for, 169–170
    podcasts, 184–185
    principles of effective service,
        171–176
    social media sites, 182–184
    and space planning, 123
    trends, 185
    websites, 177–178
    See also Internet; social
        networking sites
digital media, use of by teens,
    172–173
Dime Piece (Brown), 63, 64
diversity, 5, 11–12, 94
double voicedness and double
    entendres in titles of street
    lit, 63
Durham County (N.C.) Library,
    51, 153, 156
Dutch series (Woods), 59

E

economic diversity. *See* poverty and
    wealth in definition of *urban*
education for social change. *See*
    social activism and critical
    race theory
826 Valencia writing workshop, 154
electronic services. *See* digital
    (electronic) services
Elizabeth (N.J.) Public Library,
    86–87
emotional self, development of, 30–31
employment of youth in Tucson-
    Pima PLPYD program, 138
English as a new language, 10–11
Enoch Pratt Free Library, 134
equipment for digital technologies
    in ImaginOn, 146
    for podcasts, 184–185
evaluation of websites, 110–111
evaluation of writing workshops,
    160–161, 162f
expectations of urban teens, 13–15

F

Facebook. *See* social networking
    sites
failure, responses to, 176
familial capital, 14
Fast Talk on a Slow Track
    (Williams-Garcia), 11
Flake, Sharon, 17
Flyy Girl (Tyree), 36, 49, 55, 56, 59,
    61, 62, 63, 64
For the Love of Money (Tyree), 56
Fort Bend (Texas) County Libraries,
    132, 134
Forum for Youth Investment, 134,
    135–136f
"4dspace" in architecture, 123
"fourth dimensional" YA spaces,
    123
Framework for 21st Century Skills,
    139, 140f
Free Library of Philadelphia,
    50–51, 134
free reading time and leisure
    reading, 46–47
frequency of library use, 87–88
friending by library, 81, 181–182
friends, communications with, and
    social networking, 79, 80
From the Notebooks of Melanin Sun
    (Woodson), 10
funding for Write On! program,
    163
funding for YA spaces, 124
funds of knowledge theory, 14–15
furnishings for YA spaces, 119–122

G

gaming, 37, 149
genre blending in street lit, 62–63
goals of library, 136
Goines, Donald, 53
Google as information source, 24
Gossip Girl series, 44
graffiti art, 145–146
graphic novels for leisure reading,
    47
"green" spatial solutions, 122,
    126n11, 148
group interviews in information-
    seeking study, 27

H

Harry Potter series (Rowling), 44
health information, 101–111
    at ImaginOn, 150
    implications for practice,
        106–110
    on the Internet, 101–104, 109f
    on library websites, 104–106

quality of information on,
108–110
survey of, 104–106, 107–108f
Health on the Net Foundation,
108
Health Summit Working Group,
108
Hennepin County (Minn.) Public
Library, 46
hip-hop music and culture, 5,
33–34, 64
home computers, availability of, 25,
88, 176
homework
homework assistance programs,
130, 177
use of library for, 91
The House on Mango Street
(Cisneros), 11
humans as information sources, 24

I

Iceberg Slim, 53
identity building and social
networking, 70, 71
identity formation, 61, 65
If You Come Softly (Woodson), 13
ImaginOn Program (Charlotte and
Mecklenburg County [N.C.]
Public Library), 143–151
audience and vision, 144–145
collection, 146–147
programming, 148–150
space, 145–146
youth participation, 147–148
immigrant populations
and need for culturally relevant
information resources, 94
uses of library space, 114
individuals, teens as, 18–19, 51–52
information gateway, library as,
90–91, 94–95
information literacy instruction
evaluating health information
websites, 110
using social networking sites,
181
See also literacy support services
information seeking, 23–40
for health information, 103–104
implications for librarians,
31–32, 33f
in library use, 83–85
model of, 27, 29–31
population studied, 25–26
review of literature, 23–25
study methodology, 26–27, 28f
teen recommendations for,
32–39

information technology. *See*
technology
inner city as synonym for *urban*, 6
intergenerational relationships and
space planning, 114
Internet
authors' websites on, 45–46
best practices, 176–177
difficulty in searching, 104
health information on, 101–104,
109f
as leisure reading, 44
See also library websites; social
networking sites
intertextuality in street lit, 60
interviews as research technique,
43

K

"kid" as term repellent to teens,
177–178
King County (Wash.) Library
System, 134

L

latchkey kids, 54, 176
learning styles
in design of study, 26
and space planning, 121, 122
LEED (Leadership in Energy and
Environmental Design)
certification, 126n11, 148
leisure reading, 41–52
effect of reading street lit on,
65
findings and discussion, 43–45
implications for librarians,
45–52
study methodology, 42–43
use of library for, 91
Let That Be the Reason (Stringer),
55
librarians
absence or shortage of YA
librarians, 32–33
characteristics of excellence,
51–52
and leisure reading programs,
45–52
as reason for visiting library, 92
teen perceptions of, 96
as users of social networking,
174–175
See also staff
libraries
appeals to teens by, 8
teen perceptions of, 32–39
use of by teens, 93–98

use of social networking sites,
71, 72, 73–74f, 75–77, 80,
81, 147, 181
See also marketing and
promotion; programming;
public libraries
library as physical place, 92–93,
96–98, 144
library as source of financial
support, 93, 97
Library 2.0, 172
library use by teens
research studies, 23–40, 85–86
in urban areas, 7–8, 93–98
library websites
access to community-based
organizations, 110
best practices, 177–178
community of reading on, 46
health information on, 104–111
at ImaginOn, 147
and information gateway
categories, 94–95
low usage of, 170
marketing of programming on, 164
section for teens on, 177
and social networking sites, 80
use of social networking sites,
71, 72, 73–74f, 75–77, 80,
81, 147, 181
and volunteers, 97
life information, information
seeking for, 24–25
linguistic capital, 14. *See also*
storytelling
linguistic patterns in street lit, 64–65
literacy support services, 94,
149, 156–157. *See also*
information literacy
instruction
literary magazines, sponsorship of,
158–159, 164–167
Loft at ImaginOn. *See* ImaginOn
Program
Love Don't Live Here No More
(Snoop Dogg), 57
low-income youth
need for access to Internet, 170
programs for, 130–131
See also poverty and wealth in
definition of *urban*

M

magazines
as leisure reading, 44–45, 47
shelving of, 115
teen recommendations for, 36
teen-written literary magazines,
158–159, 164–167

manga for leisure reading, 47
marketing and promotion
    on digital media, 175–176
    emphasizing non-book-related
      services, 98
    of leisure reading, 49
    race and ethnicity in, 6
    on social media sites, 183
    in social networking, 74, 82
    stunts, 179
    of writing workshops, 164
mentoring in lives of urban teens, 12
metropolitan areas, definition, 3–4
Mexican immigrants, cultural
    wealth of, 13
Mid-Hudson Library system, 111
Midnight: A Gangster Love Story
    (Sister Souljah), 56
mission of library, 136–137
moderation of blogs, 179–180
moderation of social networking
    and social media, 184
moral inclinations in street lit,
    63–64
movies, teen recommendations
    for, 36
multicultural titles and leisure
    reading, 48
multilingualism, 10–11
music, teen recommendations for,
    36–37
Myers, Walter Dean, 54
MySpace. *See* social networking
    sites

N

navigational capital, 14
negative perceptions of libraries,
    counteracting, 98
nonfiction for leisure reading, 48
nonuse of libraries by teens, 84–85

O

Oakland Public Library, 134
Oklahoma City Metropolitan
    Library system, 76–80
online etiquette, maintenance of, 180
outcomes for youth development,
    132–133
outreach services, 98, 111

P

parents
    and leisure reading, 51
    monitoring of social networking
      sites, 78, 80, 82
    and writing workshops, 164

Partnership for 21st Century Skills,
    139
partnerships
    on health information, 111
    and ImaginOn, 150
    in Tucson-Pima PLPYD
      program, 138
    in Write On! program, 163
    See also collaboration with
      community organizations
pathfinders, 95
peer feedback in writing workshops,
    154–156
permissions for podcasts, 185
personal improvement and
    volunteer programs, 97
personal interests, use of library for,
    91, 95
personal knowledge, library as place
    for, 93
personal narrative in critical race
    theory, 17–18
Philadelphia, Free Library of,
    50–51, 134
Phoenix Public Library "Teen
    Central" space, 126n9, 133
photo galleries on social media
    sites, 183
physical self, development of, 31
Pipe Dream (Jones), 55
PLPYD. *See* Public Libraries
    as Partners in Youth
    Development (PLPYD)
    initiative
podcasts, 184–185
poetry in street lit, 62–63
policies in libraries, 34, 37–38, 85
POP!!! (program, outcomes, and
    participation), 132
popular culture and leisure reading,
    47–48
portal to YA space, 119
poverty and wealth in definition
    of *urban*, 6, 11–12. *See also*
    low-income youth
printer fees, 37
privacy issues, 104, 185
process knowledge, 11
profiles of library on social
    networking sites, 81
programming
    afterschool, 130
    at ImaginOn, 148–150
    partnerships on health
      information, 111
    promotion of, 164, 183
    as reason for use of library, 85
    teen recommendations for, 38
    writing workshop, 153–164
    and youth development, 95–96, 132

promotion. *See* marketing and
    promotion
protagonists in street lit, 57, 65
public libraries, 83–99
    implications of survey, 93–98
    reasons for use of, 88–90
    survey methodology, 86–88
    use of by teens, 84–85
    use of by urban teens, 85–86
    use of in general, 83–84
    See also libraries
*Public Libraries as Partners in Youth
    Development*, 133
Public Libraries as Partners
    in Youth Development
    (PLPYD) initiative
    applications for practice, 8,
      141–142
    evaluation of, 134, 136
    survey of teens, 85–86, 129–132

Q

quality of information on health
    information sites, 108–110
questionnaires. *See* surveys, written

R

race and ethnicity in definition of
    urban, 5–6, 10
racial identity development theory,
    15–17
readers' advisory and street lit, 33
reading levels and leisure reading,
    44–45
reading logs, use of, 43
reflective self, development of, 31
refuge, library as. *See* safe place,
    library as
resiliency in urban teens, 12–13
resistant capital, 14
Ride or Die (Jones), 63
Riding Dirty on I-95 (Turner), 63
role of library for urban teens
    as information gateway, 90–91
    as physical place, 91f, 92–93
    as space for social interaction,
      91–92
RSS feeds, use of, 178, 181, 186n1

S

safe place, library as
    ImaginOn as, 144–145, 150–151
    and library services, 97
    as role of library, 93
    at Tucson-Pima library, 141
safety in social networking, 70–71,
    72, 79, 80, 82

scheduling of programs, 164
school librarians
    absence or shortage of, 32–33
    partnerships on health
        information, 111
school libraries
    difficulties for teens to use, 38
    funding for, 49–50
    teen recommendations for, 39
school-public library relations,
    140–141
schoolwork. *See* homework
seating options for YA space, 120
security guards, 37–38
self-exploration as use of social
    networking, 70
self-publishing by street lit authors,
    64
Sellers Memorial Free Public
    Library (Upper Darby,
    Penn.), 87
series works, 59–61
sexual predators on social
    networking sites, 70
sexual self, development of, 31
Sheisty series (Baker), 59
shelving in YA spaces, 115, 118
signifying in street lit, 60
The Skin I'm In (Flake), 54
Skokie (Ill.) Public Library, 183
social activism and critical race
    theory, 18–19
social capital, 14
social contact with existing friends
    as use of social networking,
    68–70
social experience and design of YA
    spaces, 122
social interaction, library as space
    for, 91–92, 95–96
social media sites, 182–184
social nature of reading, 44, 45–46
social networking, 67–82
    benefits and drawbacks, 70–71
    definition, 67–68
    extent of, 68–69
    implications for service, 80–82
    for low-income teens, 170
    pitfalls, 182
    study findings, 79–80
    study methodology, 76–77
    teen uses of, 69–70
    and urban teens, 77–78
social networking sites
    best practices, 180–182
    use of by libraries, 71, 72, 73–
        74f, 75–77, 80, 81, 147, 181
social self, development of, 30
socialization and social networking,
    70–71

socioeconomic status in definition
    of *urban*, 6
solitary reading, 44
space planning, 113–126
    applicability to practice, 117–
        125
    definition of space, 120
    history of, 113–117
    ImaginOn, 144–146
    need for, 96, 115–117, 126n7
    teen recommendations for, 39,
        137
    and youth development,
        141–142
Spanish-speaking teens and leisure
    reading, 48–49
staff
    space for in YA spaces, 121
    and space planning, 120, 123
    teen recommendations for,
        33–35
    training on digital services,
        173–174
    unfriendliness of, 85
    See also librarians
stereotypes of urban teens, 8, 9,
    15–16
storytelling
    in critical race theory, 17–18
    in information-seeking study, 27
    See also linguistic capital
street culture, reading as alternative
    to, 60–62
street lit (urban fiction), 53–66
    as bridge to mainstream YA
        titles, 49
    characteristics of, 56
    classic novels of, 55–56
    formats, 62–64
    linguistic patterns in, 64–65
    teen recommendations for,
        35–36
    themes, 57–62
stunts in promotion of library, 179
summer reading, 44, 50–51, 178
surveys, written
    as data collection method, 26
    on leisure reading habits, 43
    on public library use, 86–98
    on use of social networking,
        77–80

T
tables. *See* seating options for YA
    space
talking in library, teen
    recommendations for, 37–38
technology
    ImaginOn, 146

library leadership into, 172
    in planning of YA spaces,
        120–121
    staff training on, 173–174
    use of by teens, 79
Teen Central (Phoenix Public
    Library), 126n9, 133
teen events calendar on website,
    177
teen participation in planning,
    39–40, 139
Teen Read Week, 150
Teen Second Life, 149
teen space
    need for, 96
    teen recommendations for, 39
    and youth development,
        141–142
    See also space planning
Teen'Scape project, 115–116,
    126n8
text-messaging and reference
    services, 185
Thuban Phenomenon, 142
time for reading during the day,
    46–47
titles for youth literary magazines,
    164–165
titles of street lit, double meanings
    of, 63
toleration in definition of *urban*, 5
True to the Game (Woods), 55–56,
    61, 62, 63, 64
Tucson-Pima Public Library, 132,
    134, 136–138
Twilight (Meyer), 44

U
updating library sites, 179, 182
urban, definitions, 3–7
    as demographic group, 5–6
    in marketing, 6–7
    in popular culture, 4–5
    as population center, 3–4
urban fiction. *See* street lit (urban
    fiction)

V
video contests on social media sites,
    183
vocabulary in urban culture, 4
voice in critical race theory, 17–18
volunteer programs
    as community service, 93
    at ImaginOn, 148
    and library as refuge, 97
    and social networking sites, 181
    and space planning, 121

W

waiting times for computers, 37
Wallace Foundation
  Challenges and Opportunities,
    130
  *Programs for School-Age Youth in
    Public Libraries*, 129–130
  See also Public Libraries
    as Partners in Youth
    Development (PLPYD)
    initiative
Washoe County (Nevada), 134
weeding of collection, 118–119,
  146
white culture and racial identity
  development, 15, 16–17
White Lines (Brown), 63

widgets, use of, 178
women as disruptive library users,
  113
Woods, Teri, 56
  True to the Game, 36, 49
WorldCat, 167
Worthington (Ohio) Libraries,
  170–171
Write On! 153–164
  background, 153–154
  philosophy, 154–156, 159–160
  planning, 155–158
  publications, 158–159
  results, 161–164
  structure of program, 159
  student response to, 160–161
writing contests, podcasts of, 184

Y

youth development
  core elements of, 132–133
  in ImaginOn services, 147–148
  libraries as setting for, 135–136f
  and space planning, 141–142
  See also developmental areas of
    adolescence
youth participation
  goals for, 133
  in ImaginOn, 144, 145–146,
    147–148
  in literary magazines, 159
  in program planning, 130
  in space planning, 120, 122,
    123–125
youth spaces. *See* space planning

You may also be interested in

Designing Space for Children and Teens in Libraries and Public Places: Providing background, tips, and suggestions on the critical issues that surround designing spaces for children and teens, as well as a full color photo gallery, this how-to book will help you create a space that they will never want to leave.

The Readers' Advisory Guide to Graphic Novels: With energy and commitment born of professional experience and a deep love for graphic novels, Goldsmith provides the first guide to the genre aimed specifically at readers' advisors, while presenting an abundance of resources useful to every librarian.

Multicultural Programs for Tweens and Teens: This one-stop resource encourages tweens and teens to explore different cultures. Dozens of flexible programming ideas allow you to choose a program specific to your scheduling needs, create an event that reflects a specific culture, and recommend further resources to those interested in learning more about diverse cultures.

The Hipster Librarian's Guide to Teen Craft Projects: The recycled no-cost and low-cost projects included address most budget constraints, giving you the freedom to get creative with projects for teens in your library. Brimming with unique ideas and step-by-step instructions, this book is sure to save you both time and money.

CPSIA information can be obtained
at www.ICGtesting.com
Printed in the USA
FSOW04n0854011215
14068FS